Gems From God's Word
That I May Know Him
New Testament Vol. 2
July—December

Gems From God's Word

That I May Know Him

A DAILY QUIET-TIME IN HIS WORD
by Tim Ruthven
New Testament, July—December

GEMS FROM GOD'S WORD, taken from GEMS by Tim Ruthven, copyright 1988 Tim Ruthven; 80,000 published and distributed by the Gems Bible Reading Fellowship.
Originally published in the U.S.A. by GEMS PUBLISHING HOUSE A Ministry of Tim Ruthven Evangelistic Fellowship, Inc.

OTHER BOOKS BY TIM RUTHVEN

Albany
A Man from Down Under
heart to HEART
He Brought Us Out. . . To Bring Us In
Gems from God's Word, Old Testament, Vol. 1, 2
Gems from God's Word, New Testament, Vol. 1
Rediscover Your Baptism

Dedicated to:

My devoted wife Marjorie, whose love for Jesus continually provoked me to want to know Him more.

My children, who gave up their father, made allowances for my absence and, with their mother, prayed for me through the task they knew Jesus had given me to do.

Lastly to the believers in America, to whom I was called. May your hearts yearn to have an intimate relationship with Jesus in His Word.

FOREWORD

This book will drastically and radically change your life! Tim Ruthven, one of God's special servants, has tapped into a heavenly storehouse of riches far more valuable and lasting than gold, silver or precious stones. The "Gems From God's Word" offered here are those which will have an eternal impact upon you in fulfilling God's ultimate purpose for your life.

Occasionally there comes a work penned by man that carries the awesome anointing of God. These pages are filled with the call for His children to come away to a quiet place where He can fellowship intimately with them. He has much to tell us if we will only take time to listen. Never in history has the need been so great for His sheep to hear His voice.

As President of Christian Believers United and Executive Director of the National Leadership Conference, it has been my privilege to direct and host hundreds of conferences on Christian growth for the equipping of the saints of God for service. Some of our speakers over the years have included, along with Tim Ruthven, such distinguished men and women as Jamie Buckingham, Kenneth Copeland, John and Anne Gimenez, Jane Hansen, Bob Mumford, Derek Prince, James Robison, Oral Roberts, Ken Sumrall and Iverna Tompkins. Rev. Ruthven is in that company of speakers used of God to impart His truths to those serious about knowing His agenda for their lives. Rev. Ruthven is an "in demand" special instrument of blessing and encouragement to hundreds attending conferences throughout the world.

Tim Ruthven has been uniquely called and favored of God and anointed by the Holy Spirit to literally teach the nations the principles contained in this book. Personally, I am convinced there is "no truth" for the believer more urgently needed than this one. When practiced, no other activity will produce more results. Few people in ministry today have had, for me, the personal impact of Rev. Tim Ruthven. He is a man of great integrity. His life is reflective of the close and intimate relationship of the Holy Spirit which brings to surface the presence of God. He is both a co-laborer in Christ and, I'm privileged to say, a close friend. I have grown to respect and recognize him as an anointed, effective man of God.

It is, therefore, my distinct honor to humbly recommend this book to you. I know it will prove to be an effective tool God will use to reveal Himself to you in a dimension greater than you could have ever known possible. You will be enriched as you read these Old Testament "Gems From God's Word" and apply to your own life the principles it contains.

Jim Jackson
Pres. Christian Believers United

A DAILY QUIET-TIME
IN HIS WORD

The quiet-time in God's Word is probably the most difficult spiritual practice to maintain; however, it is also the most rewarding. It could be compared with good nutrition and exercise habits. Our spiritual lives function well when we properly feed on the Word of God and learn to listen to and have fellowship with Him.

St. Paul wrote to Timothy, *all scripture is given by inspiration of God, and is profitable* (2 Tim. 3:16). For this reason the Bible-reading plan meditates on "all scripture," from Genesis to Revelation. This way God has the opportunity to speak to us from His entire Word, not just portions of it.

After almost 30 years of reading through the Bible, using the same program, a God-given, inspirational thought has come to mean a lot to me. God appreciates my plan, understands it, and knows where He can find me in His Word every day of my life.

Hebrews 11:6 tells me that God is *the rewarder of those who diligently seek Him.* As we come into His presence with our Bible-reading plan on a regular, daily basis, reading and meditating on God's Word, we will come to know Him who is the author of the Word. It is good to have an understanding of the Scriptures. The scholars in Jesus' day did; yet they didn't know Him as the Word made flesh that dwelt among them. To know about Jesus is good, but to know Him is even better. Go to church, seminars, etc., and learn about His Word, but also build a relationship with God in His Word on a regular basis if you are to know Him whom to know is life eternal.

The quiet-time in His Word is a place for quiet discourse with God, waiting patiently in His presence. It is not a place to bring your prayer petitions before God. Another time should be set aside for that. Setting aside everything else that you could be doing to sit quietly in His presence, for the sole purpose of knowing Him, communicates your seriousness. When you confess your love for the Lord and take time to sit with Him, your confession has meaning. Putting God first by giving Him a special time and scheduling your day around that, instead of scheduling a time for God into your busy day, says more than all your words. This way God is convinced that you have need of Him.

In God's presence your spirit thrives, but the old nature, carnal and fleshly, dies and is maintained in a state of death. You can reckon it dead if you constantly expose it to His presence. As we constantly sit before Him, taking in His Word, our heart-lives are developed, and He develops our spiritual understanding beyond the natural.

Through the quiet-time in His Word experiential Christianity at its best becomes ours. That quality of life—eternal life—is the Word of God manifesting itself in our hearts and finding its way into our experience so we find ourselves walking in the Word. Here are some good reasons why we should read God's Word:

> *My son, attend to my words; incline thine ear unto my sayings. Let them not depart from thine eyes; keep them in the midst of thine heart. For they are life unto those that find them, and health to all their flesh* (Prov. 4:20-22).

> *The entrance of thy words giveth light; it giveth understanding to the simple* (Ps. 119:130).

> *Being born again, not of corruptible seed, but of incorruptible, by the word of God, which liveth and abideth for ever* (1 Pet. 1:23).

> *Man shall not live by bread alone, but by every word that proceedeth out of the mouth of God* (Mt. 4:4).

Helpful Hints

1. Draw aside to a quiet place.

But you, when you pray, go into your inner room, close your door and pray to your Father who is in secret, and your Father who sees what is done in secret will reward you (Mt. 6:6, NASB).

2. Apply the blood of Jesus Christ to your life.

"Father, it is my desire to know You, not just in my intellect, but in my heart. Growth comes from You. Like a little seed planted in the ground, You alone give the increase, and so I offer You my heart today. May the Word that I receive into my heart by meditation and prayer give me a life-changing experience. Teach me to use my time wisely that I might give myself to study to show myself approved and to minister to myself with songs and psalms and to You with praises. Revive me, O Lord, and make thy Word as a lamp unto my feet and a light unto my path. I commit myself to a daily

When the curtain of the tabernacle was lifted the very first piece of furniture encountered in the outer court was the altar of burnt offering where sacrifice was made for the people's sin. Next there was a laver for cleansing. The blood of Jesus Christ is always available, so sit quietly in an attitude of humility and allow the Holy Spirit to remind you of anything that needs repentance. Keep short accounts with God, and this will not be time-consuming.

I want to encourage you that this is the place that initiates change and causes our lives to take on the character of God. If we allow the Spirit of God to convict us of sin each day and fellowship with Him over the areas He uncovers, gradually we will become doers of the Word and have life-changing experiences in the "closet."

3. Pray for God to open His Word and your heart, that you might receive like a small child from your heavenly Father.

The following is a prayer that God gave me specifically for the quiet-time. I believe that as this prayer becomes the cry of your heart each day, God will indeed answer it:

"Father, it is my desire to know You, not just in my intellect, but in my heart. Growth comes from You. Like a little seed planted in the ground, You alone give the increase, and so I offer You my heart today. May the Word that I receive into my heart by meditation and prayer give me a life-changing experience. Teach me to use my time wisely that I might give myself to study to show myself approved and to minister to myself with songs and psalms and to You with praises. Revive me, O Lord, and make thy Word as a lamp unto my feet and a light unto my path. I commit myself to a daily fellowship with You in Jesus' name, Amen.

4. Read the Scripture reading for the day, allowing God to speak to you through His Word.

If one or more verses "leaps" out at you, spend time with it and allow God to give you further revelation through meditation. Wait on God so He can speak to you, and write down the word God gives you. If you don't receive anything, you have another opportunity to receive from something Tim has shared in his journal.

Thy word I have treasured in my heart, that I may not sin against thee (Ps. 119:11).

The law of Your mouth is better to me than thousands of gold and silver pieces (Ps. 119:72, NASB).

Thy word is a lamp to my feet, and a light unto my path (Ps. 119:105).

5. Read what Tim has written. Perhaps God will give you revelation through what he has shared.

And He gave some as apostles, and some as prophets, and some as evangelists, and some as pastors and teachers, for the equipping of the saints for the work of service, to the building up of the body of Christ (Eph. 4:11-12, NASB).

6. Quiet yourself before the Lord.

This will again give God His opportunity to fellowship with you or allow you to remain in His presence to know quiet fellowship and communion. *Be still, and know that I am God* (Ps. 46:10).

7. You can keep your own journal in two ways.

First write down what you want to tell God, and then write down His response. Or you can just wait for Him to speak into your spirit and then write it down. Fellowship with Him about how you are feeling or some area you need to talk over with Him, especially a portion of the day's reading that you want Him to work into your life. Just relax and let that still, small voice within you flow. Write down everything that comes into your mind. Don't distrust it. The time to judge what you've written, whether it is God or self, is later. You will find that most of what you have written is God.

8. Pray through.

Take the inspirations you have received and recorded in your journal to God in prayer until they become your God-given experience.

GEMS GROUP FELLOWSHIPS

Find someone else who is interested in a quiet-time alone with the Lord and is using *Gems From God's Word* for this purpose. Meet with that person or persons on a regular basis. You could even form a small group. The important thing is that each of you has a chance to share with one another what God might be saying to you through His Word.

INTRODUCTION

As a young, married man about to become a father for the fourth time and being so poorly equipped to handle life and get the best out of it, the greatest thing that could have ever happened to me took place. God reached out to my heart to reveal the Lord Jesus Christ crucified for my sin. As a result I was born again, born of the Spirit of the Lord Jesus Christ from above. My human spirit was literally invaded by His Holy Spirit as we became one. Surely it must be the greatest of God's gifts, the most wonderful miracle a person can experience by God's power and grace!

Not long after being born again, with a hunger in my heart to understand what this new, God-given experience was all about and with a great desire to know the person of the Lord Jesus Christ, I was given a Gideon's Daily Bible Reading Calendar. Each morning, before the family had begun to stir, I would get up and read the selected portion of scripture for that day. I would ask the Lord Jesus Christ to teach me, to "grow me up," disciple me and make me useful to Him in the kingdom of God. (In my book entitled, *A Man From Down Under*, you can read about the patient and loving discipleship which ensued from these daily encounters.) Year after year, one day at a time, I read my way through the Bible with an ever-increasing desire to know Him. It was and continues to be life changing!

That was 30 years ago, and the children are now grown with children of their own. I still get up each morning with the same desire in my heart, to know Him, for *the LORD's compassions* [lovingkindness] *are new every morning.* He has been faithful to me, using the Bible-reading plan to help "grow me up." By my following the Bible-reading plan these 30 years God knows where He can find me in His Word any and every day of the year. He can also use the entire counsel of His Word as I go through it each year.

Throughout my walk with God He has been good to me and has granted me many wonderful experiences in Him. When I would have failed, He has been my victory. Oh God, *thy word is a lamp unto my feet, and a light unto my path*! (Ps. 119:105). Truly the following scriptures have been my experience: *And thine ears shall hear a word behind thee, saying, "This is the way, walk ye in it, when ye turn to the right hand, and when ye turn to the left"* (Isa. 30:21). *I will instruct thee and teach thee in the way which thou shalt go: I will guide thee with mine eye* (Ps. 32:8). After all these years my heart knows the truth of Jeremiah's cry, *O Lord, I know that the way of man is not in himself: it is not in man that walketh to direct his steps* (Jer. 10:23).

As I share my quiet-time—my time alone with God in the closet—with you through the pages of these books, my prayer is that you too will be inspired to make a covenant with God to walk with Him as Enoch walked and to know what Paul meant when he wrote: *That I may know him, and the power of his resurrection, and the fellowship of his sufferings, being made comformable unto his death* (Phil. 3:10).

My desire is to encourage you to pursue God in and through His Word. I pray you discover many of His wonderful gems from His Word for yourself, out of your own intimate quiet-time alone with God. I leave you with the whole of God's Word and a wonderful Bible-reading plan that has blessed me. Let this promise from His Word be yours in a very special way, *faithful is he that calleth you, who also will do it* (1 Thess. 5:24).

God be with you as you seek, knock and find. Pursue Him, for *the law and the prophets were until John: since that time the kingdom of God is preached, and every man presseth into it* (Lk. 16:16).

Yours in Christian fellowship and love from my quiet place,

Tim Ruthven
Gems Bible Reading Fellowship

Meditation. *On the morrow, as they went on their journey, and drew nigh unto the city, Peter went up upon the housetop to pray about the sixth hour* (10:9).

Peter was about to enter into a whole new experience with God. He had been boldly proclaiming the gospel to the Jews since the day of Pentecost, but now God was about to change his direction in ministry. Because of Peter's traditionally religious and cultural background, he must have had difficulty with this new direction (the gospel of Jesus Christ to the Gentiles); however, God does not have a communication problem and made all things work together for good. To me, the key to Peter's experience is that he was in the right place for God to speak to him. Peter went to the roof to pray, and God reached out to him through a vision, changing the whole direction of his ministry.

So often in my own experience God has had more to say to me when I have been in a place of quiet and in the state of prayer. I am so grateful to those Christians who shared with me the necessity for a daily quiet-time. I have been a Christian for twenty years, so if the number of days in a year is multiplied by twenty, then I would have a figure of the number of opportunities God has had to speak to me or redirect my ways through His Word. Every prayer time is an opportunity to have an encounter with God. I must say that virtually every major decision, and most of the minor ones which I have made, have had their beginning in my quiet-time. When God speaks to me through the Word, which I have systematically read every day for twenty years, no room is left for guessing or hoping.

Faith moves us to pray, looking and seeking, never disappointed when God seems to have nothing to say. When there is no communication or direction, rejoice. It probably means you are walking in God's way. If God has not chastened you of late, then praise Him that everything is going so well. Didn't you get an answer to your prayer request? When you ask God for something and there is no response, then praise Him; He must be satisfied that you don't need it. Didn't He promise to provide your every need? You say, "Oh God, if I could only feel your presence as I have on some other occasions." However, all is quiet, and there is no exhilarating experience. Then praise God, my dear friend, because you are growing up. God can trust you to walk by faith. Be diligent in keeping your daily appointments with Him. So much can happen when you consistently have a daily time alone with God. In Peter's experience it all happened when he went up on the housetop to pray.

TODAY'S GEM: *Seek the* LORD *and his strength, seek his face continually* (1 Chron. 16:11).

Old Testament Reading Job 21-22

Meditation. *And Cornelius said, Four days ago I was fasting until this hour; and at the ninth hour I prayed in my house, and, behold, a man stood before me in bright clothing* (10:30).

In yesterday's reading Peter, while praying on a rooftop, had a spectacular experience in God. Today we read about another exciting experience that a Gentile man had. While he was praying, an angel visited him. However, in themselves neither of these experiences were of great value unless these men were willing to walk in them. Peter would not have gone down to the Gentile Cornelius' house if God had not first of all prepared him while he was fasting and praying. In turn, Cornelius may not have known who Peter was, nor would he have been bold enough to send for him if God had not sent His angel.

The outpouring of the Holy Spirit upon the Gentiles and the assurance that salvation was for all men (Jew and Gentile), through faith in Jesus Christ, came about by two men maintaining good, daily prayer habits. Perhaps even more important was their willingness to be obedient and walk in what God had said to them during their prayer time.

One occasion I recall praying and reading my Bible, when suddenly the portion of scripture that I was reading came alive. Within me there was a great welling up of excitement because God had spoken to me. It was early in the morning, and I was alone in church when that inner excitement so took hold of me that I found myself running up and down the aisle. Then immediately it dawned on me. What on earth was I doing? What was all the excitement about? God had spoken to me, and that in itself was sufficient to make my day. But what did God say? I was so excited that God should speak to me through the Word that I did not pay enough attention to what He had said. If an angel had appeared, I probably would have gotten so excited that I would have told everybody about the angel, instead of being still and waiting to hear God's instructions and then, by faith, getting on with what the angel had instructed me to do.

Isn't it interesting that all this happened to two men who maintained good prayer habits? These two men were willing to walk by faith in obedience to what God had said. The real excitement in the Christian life is walking in the Spirit in obedience to a God that we get to know personally through our daily prayer life. Faith and adventure begin in the Word and so often come to birth in our hearts in the quiet-time.

TODAY'S GEM: *When you pray, go into your room, close the door and pray to your Father* (Mt. 6:6, NIV).

Old Testament Reading Job 23-25

Meditation. *When he* [Barnabas] *came, and had seen the grace of God, was glad, and exhorted them all, that with purpose of heart they would cleave unto the Lord* (11:23).

This chapter of the book of Acts relates an incident of when God, by His grace, poured out His Holy Spirit upon the Gentiles. This was the birth of the Gentile Church. From this day forward Gentile believers followed Jesus. When Barnabas went to see what this new move of God was all about, he found Gentile believers trusting in the blood of Jesus to cleanse them from all sin. God's grace had been extended to them, and they were trusting in the Lord Jesus Christ for their salvation.

It was not uncommon for a Gentile to believe in God; however, these Gentiles not only believed, but they turned to the Lord Jesus Christ. In his testimony to the brethren Peter said, *"And as I began to speak, the Holy Ghost fell on them, as on us at the beginning. Then remembered I the word of the Lord, how that he said, John indeed baptized with water; but ye shall be baptized with the Holy Ghost"* (vv. 15-16).

When I visited Mel Tari's Presbyterian church in Soe, Timor, to speak at the seventh celebration of the Indonesian revival, I can remember my thoughts. This is the church where the Holy Ghost fell just as it was described in the book of Acts. Water was turned into wine, and all sorts of wonderful miracles were recorded. Indeed, every miracle mentioned in the Gospels also happened in Indonesia. I can recall contemplating what I might preach or teach these people who had experienced so much of God. Much time was spent in fervent prayer, seeking the Lord as to what I might say.

I can't help but wonder if Barnabas felt the same way when he met the Gentile Christians and observed the truth of what Peter had said. The Gentiles did indeed believe, and it was evident that the Holy Ghost had fallen on them as He had on the disciples at the beginning (on the day of Pentecost). What was to happen next? With so much God-given grace, what could Barnabas deliver to them, and what more would God have for these people? He exhorted them all, that with purpose of heart they would cleave unto the Lord, and there, my Christian friend, lies the key to the Christian life—with purpose of heart (to remain true to the Lord with all their hearts).

We also have a responsibility to cleave to the Lord with all our hearts. So you have been a born again and perhaps even baptized in the Holy Spirit, then you should be asking yourself this: after this God-given experience, what is next? Let me tell you again what Barnabas would say to us. With purpose of heart, cleave unto the Lord.

TODAY'S GEM: God's grace is always available for the next step.

Old Testament Reading Job 26-28

Meditation. *And when he had considered the thing, he came to the house of Mary the mother of John, whose surname was Mark; where many were gathered together praying* (12:12).

What an experience Peter had when he was imprisoned by Herod and Jesus sent an angel to release him from his captors. Verse five says that *prayer was made without ceasing of the church unto God for him.* The early Church was a people who gathered together to pray. As I am writing this, multitudes from all over the nation will descend upon Washington, D.C., for prayer. Isn't it exciting to contemplate what might happen when God's people come together to pray!

The highest political authority in the land had thrown Peter into prison, and many gathered in Mary's home for a prayer meeting. The Christians were a threat to the national religion. If they were right and had heard from God, then the whole religious and political system would have to repent and turn to God. All their traditional religious beliefs would need to be examined. The Temple sacrifices would have to cease. God would have access to their lives in a very personal manner. It was comfortable to have God in the Temple, but to have God personally in their hearts, wow!

What changes might take place in our lives if we were to meet together in somebody's home for prayer? What power of God might be exhibited! Why, men might even tremble with fear, being so threatened by the power and presence of God that some would be thrown into prison to please the people. For Peter this was an opportunity to walk in the power of a very personal God.

The presence of God in Israel meant the very death of King Herod. Bad politics were destroyed, and God's rebellious people were chastened. How much of this happened because many were gathered together praying? Where does the power of the Christian Church lie? I believe the power is first of all in the individual believer's personal relationship with the Lord as he meets with Him daily. All sorts of things will happen in the believer's life as a result of this.

Secondly, there is power in gathering together in private homes and then in prayer, setting before the Lord those things He has set before each of us in our own quiet-time experience. The whole nation could undergo a spiritual revolution if we concentrated on these two principles, however, not to the exclusion of church life. Why, church life would enter into a whole new experience in God if we touched God in the prayer closet and in the home.

TODAY'S GEM: *For where two or three are gathered together in my name, there am I in the midst of them* (Mt. 18:20).

Old Testament Reading Job 29-30

JULY 5 Acts 13:1-23

Meditation. *As they ministered to the Lord, and fasted, the Holy Ghost said, Separate me Barnabas and Saul for the work whereunto I have called them* (13:2).

In the early Church there seems to be a difference between ministering to the Lord and fasting and praying. Ministering to the Lord could mean only one thing, that whatever act was performed it was done as unto the Lord. If they were singing praises before the Lord as David had, then their songs must have been dedicated. Every word was yielded to the Lord for His pleasure. Possibly they were songs confessing to His greatness and His pleasure in them.

When the early Church was assembled together in Jesus' name, we can imagine that they saw or discerned the individual needs of each member of Christ's Body and reached out to Jesus for direction. (Perhaps it was just a glass of water given in Jesus' name.) Whatever happened in those meetings, you can be certain that it was performed as unto the Lord. The presence of Jesus motivated it. His need inspired it. It was so important that they did not even bother to stop and eat, as food was laid aside so they could minister to the Lord.

While ministering to God they received direction. I would not like to imply that they were ministering to get direction; however, while ministering they certainly received it. The Holy Ghost told them to separate two of the brethren for the work to which He had called them.

There is that same principle again. While the people of the early Church were occupied in prayer meetings that ministered to the Lord and where Jesus was the center of their activities, things happened. The Holy Ghost directed the affairs of the Church, and two men of God were sanctified for the ministry.

There is a fellowship in the Holy Spirit that leads us into all truth. What would happen in our quiet-time experience if we would encourage the Holy Spirit to teach us and lead us into the experience of this scripture? Why, our meetings would be revolutionized if we learned to minister to the Lord, to say nothing of what would happen in our personal relationship with Jesus.

TODAY'S GEM: *The things of God knoweth no man, but the Spirit of God* (1 Cor. 2:11).

Old Testament Reading Job 31-32

Meditation. *And the disciples were filled with joy, and with the Holy Ghost* (13:52).

The disciples angered the Jews with their profession of faith in Jesus as the messiah. They were even more angry when many of the Jews came under conviction of their failure to recognize Jesus as the prophesied Christ and turned to Him in repentance, believing in Him. The outcome of all this for Paul and Barnabas was persecution and expulsion. Yet Dr. Luke could write that the disciples were filled with joy and the Holy Ghost. The book of Galatians explains why. *But the fruit of the Spirit is love, joy, peace, longsuffering, gentleness, goodness, faith, meekness, temperance: against such there is no law* (Gal. 5:22-23).

In the midst of persecution the Holy Spirit could so manifest Himself in the lives of the believers that they experienced joy. An inner spiritual communication took place. It could be that the indwelling Holy Spirit spoke to the believer of things to come, and the promises contemplated were far greater and so much more meaningful than the present circumstances. Whatever the word was that stimulated a joy that overcame, a joy that produced light in dismal circumstances, the all-important principle was not the joy produced, although this was a miracle of God. The important principle was the believer's relationship with the Holy Spirit. It was the Holy Spirit indwelling the believer that produced the joy. It was a combination of what the believer knew to be true and with whom the believer fellowshipped. If he fellowshipped with the Holy Spirit and kept a sensitive relationship with Him, then the fruits of the Spirit would manifest themselves. A recognition of the manifestation of these fruits would in itself produce a joy.

In the natural it would be very difficult, and in some cases impossible, to manifest joy in the midst of persecution. That joy which the believer experiences while enduring suffering is the joy of the presence of the Holy Spirit and the experience of Him. A fullness of joy seems to go hand in hand with the fullness of the Holy Spirit. Therefore, be filled with the Spirit, and go on being filled. In this there is the corresponding fullness of joy.

TODAY'S GEM: The fullness of the Holy Spirit equals the fullness of joy itself.

Old Testament Reading Job 33-34

Meditation. [Paul and Barnabas returned to Lystra], *strengthening the souls of the disciples, exhorting them to continue in the faith, and saying, "We must through many tribulations enter the kingdom of God"* (14:22, NKJV).

My, what hardships Paul suffered for the privilege of proclaiming the gospel. He was misunderstood, and once he was even thought to be a god whom they desired to worship. I wonder how some of us would have handled that. Spiritual pride and popularity can be just as devastating to the Christian worker as any other sin. However, pride and popularity couldn't get Paul, so the town turned out to stone him. Indeed, they succeeded and left him for dead outside the city. No sooner had Paul gotten over his near escape from death by the hands of the people of Lystra, than he was back in their midst, exhorting them to continue in the faith. Brethren, today let us either be exhorting the Christians to continue in the faith or be exhorted ourselves. One of the most powerful spiritual stimulants I know that will build up your personal faith in a time of tribulation is to exhort others to continue in the faith.

I remember an occasion on one of my many missionary journeys when I visited a Christian army officer. I had gone with a friend of mine to solicit the soldier's help in getting some things through customs, where they had held them for some months hoping to be paid a bribe. The morning we arrived, the officer's teenage son was brought in, having been cruelly tortured until his mind had snapped. He was held for no other reason than for being a Christian. In no time at all, in the midst of his suffering and grief, this army officer was busying himself to leave his grief-stricken family to attend to the needs of other Christians, exhorting them to continue in the faith. What an example!

Is this not one of your better days? Are you hurting or suffering because of some injustice? Then look around, my friend. Find some Christian who is in need of an uplifting word, and exhort him or her in the faith. You will be surprised what it will do for you. It really is more blessed to give than to receive.

TODAY'S GEM: The kingdom of God is better seen when he who suffers exhorts.

Old Testament Reading Job 35-37

Meditation. *But we believe that through the grace of the Lord Jesus Christ we shall be saved, even as they* (15:11).

Can you imagine it, Gentiles have been saved! God, in His mercy and grace, has turned to the Gentile with the gospel of salvation in Jesus. God has poured out His Holy Spirit on them just as He did for the Jewish believers on the day of Pentecost. In Jesus' time this was a mystery not yet revealed. There were certain Jews who were not at all against the Gentiles sharing the kingdom of God with them, but they did try very hard to lead them into the bondage of their antiquated and now useless law. It is always sad when we see Christians in bondage to some religious truth. Oh, they preach freedom and full salvation in Jesus, but then immediately try to bring other Christians into bondage to some religious principle with which they are stuck.

The apostles reminded these Christian Pharisees that the Gentiles were saved by grace even as they were. Why the emphasis on grace? What is so important about confessing salvation by grace and not by works? In his letter to the Ephesians Paul said, *"For by grace are ye saved through faith . . . not of works, lest any man should boast"* (Eph. 2:8-9). In these words we find the key. It is not a good thing for us to take any credit for our own salvation experience. Of course we had to do some things. We had to repent, and surely that was a credit to us, but isn't repentance the work of the Holy Spirit? You say you were saved by an act of your will by making a right decision? Yes, that's right, but even your will was persuaded. Didn't the Holy Spirit so reveal to you the reasonableness of salvation and the unreasonableness of your own heart in its sinful state, thereby influencing your judgment, so that you freely made a proper decision? Why, without the influence of God on your life you would not have known how to make a proper choice.

There is ample evidence to declare salvation by grace through faith, not to make a point or to insist that all believe as we do, but to safeguard ourselves from the wickedness of the heart. Maybe your heart is not like mine. If I were given an opportunity to take some credit for my salvation experience, I would become puffed up. It wouldn't be long before pride would consume me, and I would be confessing how I worked for my salvation, but Paul wrote, *Not of works, lest any man should boast* (Eph. 2:9). I am not ashamed to confess my need for the grace of the Lord Jesus Christ to save me and to go on saving me. If I needed saving yesterday, I certainly need saving today. So continue to save me, Lord Jesus Christ.

TODAY'S GEM: *Therefore we conclude that a man is justified by faith without the deeds of the law* (Rom. 3:28). *Even so faith, if it hath not works, is dead, being alone* (Jas. 2:17).

Old Testament Reading Job 38-39

Meditation. *Forasmuch as we have heard, that certain which went out from us have troubled you with words, subverting your souls, saying, Ye must be circumcised, and keep the law: to whom we gave no such commandment* (15:24).

Today's meditation scripture sets forth one of the most important decisions of the early Church council. Some of those old, converted Pharisees would have done anything to hang on to the covenant God made with Moses. Possibly they distrusted their ability to keep the covenant of Jesus. If so, they were right.

Through Old Testament law God made a covenant with Israel, and Moses was the leader or captain of God's people. It had a built-in contingency that one day a more perfect leader, a messiah, would come and lead them. He would not lead them by the law of works but out of the bondage of the law into the liberty of submission, trusting in and relying on the ability of the messiah, who would be the captain of their faith.

Under Old Testament law, their works of obedience saved them by their ability to fulfill the law, but now we have a better covenant and a better Leader—the Messiah Jesus. Our salvation is in Jesus' willingness and obedience to be our sacrifice for sin. Instead of demanding obedience to the law, which we would have had to struggle and strive to keep, Jesus fulfilled it, and our obedience to God's law is complete in Him.

Having fulfilled the law and having attained righteousness by His sacrifice, Jesus invites us to share and to live in His fulfillment. Instead of trying to lead a people of God to success through their obedience, the Lord Jesus Christ leads us in His already won righteousness. Praise God, the Captain of our salvation leads us, not to success, but in His success. We are not attaining to something, as those who were under the law did. If we are in Christ, trusting in His success and living in His righteousness, we have already attained righteousness.

Any salvation experience that requires more than faith in the Lord Jesus Christ and His ability to save us to the uttermost is just as the scripture says, troubles us with words, subverting our souls. Aren't you glad the apostles said that they gave no such commandment? No, we do not deserve what Jesus did, and we cannot enter in any other way, except by a full salvation experience that is already complete for us in Jesus. Otherwise we do not enter at all. There never will be another sacrifice, and there is no need for any other way.

TODAY'S GEM: *Neither is there salvation in any other; for there is none other name under heaven given among men, whereby we must be saved* (Acts 4:12).

Old Testament Reading Job 40-42

Meditation. *And a certain woman named Lydia, a seller of purple, of the city Thyatira, which worshipped God, heard us: whose heart the Lord opened, that she attended unto the things which were spoken of Paul* (16:14).

I think it is really neat that Dr. Luke recorded this event at the riverside when Lydia, who was probably the first convert in Europe, was converted to faith in Jesus Christ. Let me remind you that Luke was not writing a textbook, and it probably did not enter his mind that his writing would have any historical value; nor was he writing from a theological point of view. He did not have to be theologically correct. This was simply written to his friend Theophilus to inform him of all the wonderful things that were taking place in the lives of the believers by the presence of the Holy Spirit.

This was another one of those exciting experiences for those who walk in the Spirit. Paul attended a place of prayer on a riverbank, since there was probably no synagogue in which the Jews could gather on the Sabbath. Paul attended this place, which was frequented by his fellow Jews. Here he took the opportunity to share the gospel with them. Again the Holy Spirit took the word that was proclaimed and opened Lydia's heart to respond to Paul's message. No wonder Paul had such boldness and confidence in the Holy Spirit. How many men are intellectually convinced? Who but God can open the hearts of men? True religion is of the heart, and it was a heart experience that was necessary if Lydia was to be saved.

Have you been having difficulty witnessing? Does there seem to be something lacking? Let me suggest that you develop your relationship with the Holy Spirit into a partnership. You do the witnessing and encourage the Holy Spirit to do the convicting and convincing. God's best for you is to be a yokefellow or co-laborer with Him, for He speaks to the hearts of men. The real adventure is being part of what God is doing while you are witnessing, watching the Lord open hearts. It is exciting to observe His grace, love, perseverance, and His willingness to take our words and, through them, reveal Christ until there is a melting of the heart and an all-embracing experience of Jesus as Savior. I don't know of a more wonderful Christian experience than being part of what God is doing and observing Him opening the hearts of men.

TODAY'S GEM: *Not by might, nor by power, but by my spirit, saith the Lord of hosts* (Zech. 4:6).
Old Testament Reading Psalms 1-3

Meditation. *And they said, Believe on the Lord Jesus Christ, and thou shalt be saved, and thy house* (16:31).

Back at the riverside where Lydia was converted, in today's reading Paul meets a woman possessed with a spirit of divination. There was nothing untruthful about what the woman was saying, but the author of what was being said was not the Spirit of God. Recognizing this, Paul addresses the spirit and commands it to come out in the name of Jesus. This caused a lot of trouble for Paul and Silas, and the outcome of it all was that these two men were put in stocks deep within the prison.

From their stocks Paul and Silas sang and praised God. I believe they were actually enjoying the opportunity of another adventure with the Holy Spirit. Paul and Silas didn't have long to wait before the whole prison was shaken by an earthquake and they were released from their stocks. This was their opportunity to escape, but Paul was not moved to run but to wait, and it wasn't long before God's purpose in all this was seen. The jailer, fearing that his prisoners had taken the opportunity to escape, sought to take his own life. But Paul cried out to him not to harm himself, because they were all there. After the jailer saw for himself the truth of what Paul had said, Paul took this opportunity (God's opportunity) to testify of God's salvation through Jesus, which resulted in the salvation of the jailer and his household. For this man and his family to be saved, it took an earthquake, an example of joy in the midst of suffering, a willingness to submit to a very uncomfortable situation even though there was an opportunity to escape, and finally it took God's man speaking forth the word of salvation.

What will it take to save our households, imprisonment? I hope not. Will it take an earthquake? Surely God has some easier and quieter ways. We probably have to be the first to believe for our families, and if anybody has to have faith for their complete salvation, then it must be us. It is not enough to believe that God can save them, but let us get hold of God's best and believe that He will save them. If I am saved, then God's best is still to save my whole household. God's promises of salvation are still for us and our seed. Therefore, let's not limit God by unbelief, but by faith we shall look forward to that day when God will be faithful and our households will believe the gospel and be converted.

TODAY'S GEM: *For God sent not his Son into the world to condemn the world; but that the world through him might be saved* (Jn. 3:17).

Old Testament Reading Psalms 4-6

Meditation. *These were more noble than those in Thessalonica, in that they received the word with all readiness of mind, and searched the scriptures daily, whether those things were so* (17:11).

The Jews of Berea were of a better disposition than the Jews of Thessalonica. They were not so prejudiced and obstinate, being at least willing to hear what Paul had to say. And what he said was received with great eagerness, as they examined the Scriptures to see if it was true. In response, God prepared their hearts to receive the gospel. What a difference it makes in our lives when we come to the Scriptures with an open heart, allowing God to communicate life to us by His Holy Spirit.

I can remember a time in my Christian life when my mind was made up about a certain doctrine. When anything contrary to my doctrinal position was rejected, my belief that I was doing the right thing was very strong. In that way I was no better than the Thessalonian Jews. We can learn from these Bereans who kept an open mind by keeping our hearts and minds open, thereby allowing the Word of God to have complete freedom in our lives. With such a freedom the Holy Spirit can take the Word and lead us into all truth. Even more importantly, He can lead us into the experience of the Word itself.

It is possible to receive the Word but reject the experience of it through unbelief. It is also possible to believe the Word and yet refuse to believe that we do not have the experience of it. The answer does not lie in self-examination, refuting, and contending. The answer is found in having a teachable spirit, opening our hearts to the Holy Spirit and remaining open to Him by a permanent dependence upon Him to lead us into all truth. Jesus said that He himself had no doctrine except that which the Father gave Him. Again He said, *"I do nothing of myself; but as my Father hath taught me"* (Jn. 8:28). Always Jesus was dependent upon the Father.

We are going to have many life-changing experiences if we will follow the Bereans' example of daily searching the Scriptures for the truth. Let God make up our minds for us by exposing our hearts each day to His Word.

I once worked with an alcoholic for a year. Twice a day, every day, he listened to the Word. One day he tried to backslide and return to his drinking. He told me that every time he put a glass of liquor to his mouth a scripture would come to his mind. He was full of the Word of God and full of the life of the Word, which is spirit and not law.

TODAY'S GEM: *For the word of God is quick, and powerful, and sharper than any twoedged sword . . . and is a discerner of the thoughts and intents of the heart* (Heb. 4:12).

Old Testament Reading Psalms 7-9

Meditation. *They should seek the Lord, if haply they might feel after him, and find him, though he be not far from every one of us* (17:27).

God's desire is for man to seek and reach out to Him. The Bible tells us that *he is a rewarder of them that diligently seek him* (Heb. 11:6), and it also says that we are to search for God with all our hearts and souls. Man does not just stumble over God or run across Him accidentally. God will be found by us and will not hide Himself from those who seek Him.

Ask, and it shall be given you; seek, and ye shall find; knock, and it shall be opened unto you (Mt. 7:7). According to that scripture God seems to be waiting to hear from us, and I personally know of two practical things that impress upon me the seriousness of my actions. Therefore, they should impress God that we really are seeking and do want that which we are asking. The first thing is to set aside a particular moment in a particular place to be alone with God. It should be where you can open your mouth and speak or even cry out to God in an audible voice. The second thing is to fast. Both of these suggestions are very practical, but they seem to add something to our praying. Every major prayer experience I have had has quickly developed into a vocalization of my requests. I know I can have a heart-to-Heart relationship with God, and I do not doubt that He knows my every thought, but the Word does say that we have what we say. God spoke things into being. There is a time to confess and speak out before the Lord. Surely seeking and knocking speaks of more than nice or good thoughts. I pray when I am driving my motorcar, but God does not have my total attention, at least not if I want to stay on the road.

It is obvious to me that if we are to know the meaning of the Scriptures, we are going to have to make some special effort to get alone with God where we won't be self-conscious and can open our mouths to seek and knock. Today's meditation verse suggests that we "feel after God," that we reach out to Him from our innermost beings. It is more than an intellectual experience, more than just the imaginations of the mind, although they too may respond. It is a reaching out to God of man's soul and spirit. Whenever I have made the effort of going alone to the sanctuary of the church or just stayed an extra day in a motel, the Holy Spirit of Jesus dwelling within me takes the opportunity given to commune with God. The exciting thing is that God is not far off somewhere. He is right here willing and waiting to meet with us. If you have been seeking and knocking ("feeling after God") in your quiet-time, why not extend this to have a day and go off to be alone with Him.

TODAY'S GEM: I will be found by Him.
Old Testament Reading Psalms 10-12

Meditation. Jesus' words to Paul: *For I am with thee, and no man shall set on thee to hurt thee: for I have much people in this city* (18:10).

Nobody is going to get upset with you for going to church. However, if you really believe in the lordship of Jesus Christ, live according to what you believe, and get so excited about this new life in Christ that you preach it to others, somebody is going to get upset with you. In today's reading Paul, upon his arrival in Corinth, meets Aquila and Priscilla and joins forces with them. On the Sabbath he went to the synagogue, and the Word says he persuaded both Jews and Greeks. Why, even the chief ruler of the synagogue and his family were converted. Many of the Corinthians believed and were baptized; so a little church grew up out of their born-again experience. However, this did not happen without opposition. Maybe Paul was tiring from the opposition to his ministry, but whatever it was Paul had a need of encouragement. So the Lord spoke to him in the night through a vision, saying, *"Be not afraid, but speak, and hold not thy peace"* (v. 9).

I am not an angel, but I am a messenger of God. Someone needed to pick up this devotional book today and read these words from the Scriptures: *For I am with thee, and no man shall set on thee to hurt thee.* God is with you, and *if God be for us, who can be against us?* (Rom. 8:31). I feel that someone is in a situation that seems totally unjust and unfair, and that person is hurting. Well, I want you to know that Jesus is touched with the feelings of our infirmities. All that we might be called on to suffer He has already suffered. I remember a dear old saint in my country who was shockingly treated. He went to the Lord to empty his heart. This man told me that the Lord had spoken to him, and these were His words. "Doc, have they spat in your face yet? They spat in mine."

Be encouraged, my friend. The Lord has given us His assurance through His words to Paul, and what a promise for Paul to receive. Not only did he have the assurance that God was with him, but he had the promise of much fruit to come from his ministry. So go on confessing Jesus, my friend. Continue to share with others what good things the Lord is doing. There cannot be fruit from your ministry unless you broadcast the seed. Paul was so encouraged that he went on teaching the word of salvation in that city for another eighteen months.

On those occasions when the opposition is the most fierce and the people are really mean and ugly, I have found that God uses their ugliness to show off the righteousness in which we walk. What seems so negative is often the very thing that God uses to open the doors to the gospel.

TODAY'S GEM: Even a mud puddle can reflect the likeness of Christ if the saint is willing to look.

Old Testament Reading Psalms 13-16

Meditation. *He said unto them, Have ye received the Holy Ghost since ye believed? And they said unto him, We have not so much as heard whether there be any Holy Ghost* (19:2).

I am very grateful to God for the dimension of life which the presence of the Holy Spirit provides. About two and a half years after I was born again, I suddenly became aware that the third party of the Godhead, the Holy Spirit, was Somebody I had heard about every Sunday but knew nothing about. As my Presbyterian minister held up his hands and announced the benediction (in the name of the Father, Son, and he said communion of the Holy Ghost), I knew that I was totally ignorant of who the Holy Spirit was, or for that matter, anything at all about Him. I asked a very dear friend of mine who the Holy Spirit was, and his answer was that I should go and ask Jesus. I prayed about it but had no further understanding, just a persistent gnawing deep down inside. Again there was the realization that I didn't know.

Quite early one morning I was kneeling at a chair in my friend's kitchen when I suddenly became aware of something happening. From where I was kneeling I could see this great, glass, shiny sea that stretched forever and ever. As if I were in a cathedral, I heard my voice echoing, "Thank you, Jesus. Thank you, Jesus." It welled up from deep within, and love was flowing like a river. I could barely contain what was happening and became very sensitive to the presence of God. The smallest suggestion of sin had to be taken care of right away. I had always enjoyed prayer, but now there was a new excitement about it as I seemed to live and walk in the very presence of God. Little scriptures would leap out to me from the pages, and they were accompanied by understanding.

Many people had a variety of opinions as to what had happened to me, but it wasn't long before I realized that this was what Paul was speaking about when he asked, *"Have ye received the Holy Ghost since ye believed?"* Realizing what he was talking about, I set out to develop a relationship with the Holy Spirit, to find out from Him what this relationship could mean. I discovered He would lead me into all truth, and that is what I wanted. He wanted to glorify the Son, so we immediately became co-laborers in our desire to glorify Jesus, and He was a very active partner in all this. The most important thing I learned was to build my Christian life in the closet or quiet-time with the Holy Spirit.

TODAY'S GEM: It is easier to first receive the Holy Spirit than to understand a doctrine about Him.

Old Testament Reading Psalms 17-18

Meditation. *Many of them also which used curious arts brought their books together, and burned them before all men: and they counted the price of them, and found it fifty thousand pieces of silver* (19:19).

I am so grateful to God that I can be a Christian in these days. He has allowed me to experience a move of God's Holy Spirit in New Zealand and in Indonesia. No doubt you have had opportunities to witness similar moves here in the United States. In these moves of God that I have witnessed, the Holy Spirit flowed, converting many. It was obvious that man didn't initiate these moves; therefore, we were very sensitive to the responsibility we had to flow with it. When the Holy Spirit had freedom to move in people's lives and we were willing to give Him the liberty He needed, wonderful things happened. However, if we resisted something the Holy Spirit was doing and took control of it, the flow ceased. We were then quick to repent and give the Holy Spirit liberty in our lives.

The need to burn those things that were of the past and had sinful associations was one of the things I have seen the Holy Spirit do. However, I didn't appreciate the benefit of this until I could look back and see the results in the lives of those who were obedient. In my own experience I felt a real need to burn any books in my house that Jesus couldn't read. Nobody told me to do these things. The church people didn't seem too concerned about it, but we who were young Christians were obviously being motivated by the Holy Spirit. For us it was no big deal to get rid of those things that would not have their place in the kingdom of God.

People removed pictures from their walls, burned clothes, and got rid of jewelry. Anything that was doubtful was disposed of. In those days there was no one to teach these things; it was all part of what the Holy Spirit was doing in the lives of the young believers. The reason I felt the need to draw your attention to today's meditation verse is that there is a certain liberty, a real release that comes when we, like those early Christians in Ephesus, dispose of those things from the past. After disposing of them we discover what a real hindrance they were. When we hang on to something of the past that was associated with sin or some hurt, it seems as though the Holy Spirit can't release to us the liberty which we desire. A word of caution, don't try to personally profit when disposing of these things. Destroy them, or let some Christian organization dispose of them so that the proceeds can be used for the kingdom of God. Of course, if they will be a source of sin to anyone else, destroy them.

TODAY'S GEM: True revival separates us from the doubtful and sinful past.

Old Testament Reading Psalms 19-21

Meditation. *And upon the first day of the week, when the disciples came together to break bread, Paul preached unto them, ready to depart on the morrow; and continued his speech until midnight* (20:7).

In practically every move of the Holy Spirit in which I have participated, it seems the Holy Spirit has a total disregard for time, tradition, and schedules. First of all we read in the Book of Acts that the disciples were gathered together to break bread. They had established regular meetings each Sunday for this purpose, and on this particular occasion Paul was available to speak to them. Except for Paul's presence, the Sunday meeting was much the same as any other. Perhaps Paul stopped speaking to have a little break, and at that point there were those who probably went home. When a meeting has extended beyond what you anticipated and there has been an obvious opportunity to leave, how often have other considerations of your time caused you to go? There was nothing unreasonable about your leaving at that particular time, but the next day maybe you heard of some wonderful experience that happened after you left, but you missed it. Imagine having been at that meeting with Paul, leaving before the others, and then hearing the next day how God had literally raised a young man from the dead.

That miracle was not the only thing that happened. For those disciples who had an ear to hear and a spirit to receive, the obvious presence of the Holy Spirit so invaded their lives that many would remember the presence of the Holy Spirit there that evening. It would not only be remembered because of the obvious miracle, but also remembered as an evening when God spoke to them. It was a time when God led them into some new revelation of truth. When the Holy Spirit is in a meeting to perform miracles, you can be assured that He is there to communicate to all who will listen. Unfortunately in one sense, He is sensitive to our desires. If we want to go He will not hinder us, but we could miss out on some good thing in God.

Let me encourage you to train yourself by adopting a different attitude toward meetings, whether they be public or your quiet-time. Whenever you have an opportunity to hear the Word, develop an expectancy to hear from the Lord. Believe in God's ability to communicate life by the presence of the Holy Spirit. Try to remain patient and open to the possibility of God doing something in your life, and don't leave until you are sure God has finished with the meeting (public or private).

TODAY'S GEM: God may keep the best until last.
Old Testament Reading Psalms 22-24

Meditation. *I have shewed you all things, how that so labouring ye ought to support the weak, and to remember the words of the Lord Jesus, how he said, It is more blessed to give than to receive* (20:35).

Let me remind you that as you read the Book of Acts you are reading about Holy Spirit revival. You are having an opportunity to see the effect of God's Holy Spirit on people's lives. You cannot copy or imitate revival. God must initiate it; however, you can do certain things with your environment that are conducive to the Holy Spirit. It is almost like a great big invitation, "Holy Spirit, come and live in my life." Sometimes we are guilty of praying the prayer but not willing to make the necessary changes that would enable the Holy Spirit to actually come.

When Paul said that he had shown them all things, he was reminding them of their need to give to the poor. Let me repeat myself so that you will understand. Paul was drawing attention, not to the needs of the poor, but to each Christian's need to give. That is why he could quote Jesus as saying that it is more blessed to give than to receive. The real reward for giving is for the one who gives, because giving cultivates a generous heart, generous toward God and man. The Spirit-filled life thrives in a generous heart. This is an area where the believer can establish a very sensitive relationship with the Holy Spirit, but remember that the Holy Spirit flees from selfishness or self-centeredness. He cannot fellowship or abide in the heart that is selfish.

It would have been very easy to pass over today's meditation verse in our reading. The really important things that create an environment conducive to the residence of the Holy Spirit in our hearts are not necessarily the big things. The only way of which I know to cultivate a generous heart is to give. Give expecting nothing in return from the person to whom you are giving. Even if that person doesn't do what you think he or she should with the gift, don't be judgmental. To be so means that you have not given as unto the Lord and haven't let go of the gift. Give, not just to please the person, but to please the Lord.

After a while you will find the Holy Spirit will fellowship with you in this area of your life and give direction to your giving. This, in turn, will present you with another challenge. It is one thing to give out of the desire of your heart and quite another to do so as the Holy Spirit wills and determines. My, what a revival you could experience in this area of your life. Then you will know what Paul meant when he said, *"It is more blessed to give than to receive."*

TODAY'S GEM: Don't pass up the little things, for it is the little things lived that become the big things.
Old Testament Reading Psalms 25-27

Meditation. *And finding disciples, we tarried there seven days: who said to Paul through the Spirit, that he should not go up to Jerusalem* (21:4).

There is something in today's scripture verse that can help us learn what the walk in the Spirit is all about. Sometimes our doctrine can get in the way. Preconceived thoughts on a certain scripture can really interfere with what the Holy Spirit wants to say to us at a particular time. A legalistic approach to the Word can rob us of a simple communication by the Holy Spirit. When something comes up that doesn't appear to fit in with where we are at the time, we discard it as being not of God because of what we believe to be God's will.

Allow me to use my experience of the Holy Spirit's ways to try to interpret the verse for today so that it can be a real blessing to you. Paul had no doubt that it was God's will for him to go to Jerusalem, but I do not think it was God's will for Paul to suffer. However, there are times that in order to do God's will, we are faced with suffering. The Holy Spirit was making it very plain to Paul that he now had a choice. It had been pointed out to him that should he go to Jerusalem he would face suffering. God himself could not promise Paul that he would not face suffering should he choose to do God's will. We still have a free will, and God's desires are best accomplished when, by choice of our own free will, we lay our desires down to take up the will of the Father. We are responsible for our choices and our actions. Should we suffer in the execution of God's will, we cannot hold Him responsible.

Just before I was to sail to America a very dear brother and elder of our church came to me in distress. In his spirit he had felt that I would suffer many things if I were to sail away from New Zealand. All night he had wept and prayed. We submitted his experience to our pastor, who simply reminded me that they believed it was God's will for me to go. The decision was then left to me.

The Holy Spirit will help us understand the Father's will but will not make our decision. He will even warn us of sufferings we might face should we decide to do God's will, but the decision is ours to make. That way we are amply prepared for whatever we must face in order to do God's will. When we take up the Father's will, we must be willing to trust in His grace to enable us to carry it out. *Not by might, nor by power, but by my spirit, saith the LORD of hosts* (Zech. 4:6).

TODAY'S GEM: The will of God will not lead us where the grace of God cannot keep us.

Old Testament Reading Psalms 28-30

Meditation. *And when he had saluted them, he declared particularly what things God had wrought among the Gentiles by his ministry. And when they heard it, they glorified the Lord* (21:19-20).

Testimony is powerful. We are not all expected to be Bible teachers or teachers of doctrine, but we are expected to be able to share what good things God has done in our lives. Testimony communicates, encourages, and even provokes.

I can remember being asked to speak at a convention to give my first public testimony as a young Christian. Looking back, I can hardly believe my reaction to this request. As fear overwhelmed me, I was like a drowning man. My past suddenly leapt before me, and my only desire was to forget that it had ever existed so I could enjoy this whole new life in Christ. One thing I certainly didn't want to do publicly was make known the past, so I turned down the invitation. Worse even than declining to speak, I told God that if He provided for me I would go. He did provide, but I still didn't go. Feeling guilty, I later confessed my sin in this matter and regretted my inability to respond to their request. It stayed with me all year, so when time came around the following year for this annual convention, I just went without being asked.

No sooner had I stopped my motorcar than the sponsors of the convention greeted me and took me to the speaker's room. A dear, old saint (one of those great men in God) greeted me, and I was introduced to him as the man who could not give his testimony. "Son," he said to me. "Do you love the Lord Jesus?" I replied, "Yes, Mr. England." He said, "Then go to where you are staying, get down on your knees, and make notes of the way Jesus found you, where He found you, and what took place in your life at that time. Then come back here ready to glorify Jesus."

Well, God was with me in a very special way. After my testimony the people rejoiced and praised God so that Jesus was indeed glorified. What opportunities do we pass up when we neglect to share with others what Jesus has done in our lives? If you want an uplifting experience, then find somebody who will listen, and share exactly what Jesus has done in your life. Share it in such a way that Jesus will be glorified. See that you give Him the credit and the glory. It will fan a spark back into your own Christian experience.

TODAY'S GEM: Our testimony not only glorifies Christ but is like a tonic to our own Christian experience.

Old Testament Reading Psalms 31-33

Meditation. *Then he said, "The God of our fathers has chosen you that you should know His will, and see the Just One, and hear the voice of His mouth"* (22:14, NKJV).

God told me to go to America and strengthen the hands of the brethren. Today let me say to you, as surely as Ananias said it to Paul, "The God of our fathers has chosen you"—*for many be called, but few chosen* (Mt. 20:16).

Are you born again? Has God's Spirit descended on you from above so that your spirit and God's Spirit are one? Then let me again say to you that *the God of our fathers has chosen you.* You are not just a happening. God has reached out to you, laid hold of your life and chosen you. Yes, very deliberately He has chosen you *that you should know His will.* God has plans for your life and desires you to walk in them; therefore, take time and give God ample opportunity to communicate His will to you.

What is God's will for our lives? What is the first and most obvious thing that God intends to do in our lives? I believe the answer is in our text. We are to see that *Just One* and *hear the voice of His mouth.* Praise God! Get hold of this text. Meditate on it for the remainder of the day. It is God's intention for you to see the Lord Jesus Christ in all His glory and to hear His voice. Let a desire for Jesus be stimulated in you, then let it grow and remain with me. According to this text, what greater plan could your life have? In what better way could your time be spent? Dedicate a little time to the Father each day for the duration of your life and see if He won't reveal Christ to you.

Yes, I have had visions and revelations of Christ, and they have remained with me. However, the most powerful but barely discernible invasion of my life by the Lord Jesus Christ has come from my daily quiet-time. My friend, if you are to know the fullness of this text in your own life, then believe and receive these words: God has chosen you. Make this your boast in Him. Share this truth with other people whom you know are chosen of God. Remind them that long before they made their decision for Christ, God had selected them. He had a choice, perhaps a variety of choices, but He selected you. Go to sleep tonight reminding yourself that you are chosen of God and rejoice in this truth. Dear Father God, today write this truth on my readers' hearts that they might have great joy in the knowledge that they are chosen of God.

TODAY'S GEM: *He hath chosen us in him before the foundation of the world* (Eph. 1:4).

Old Testament Reading Psalms 34-35

Meditation. *And the night following the Lord stood by him, and said, Be of good cheer, Paul: for as thou hast testified of me in Jerusalem, so must thou bear witness also at Rome* (23:11).

If he went to Jerusalem Paul knew he would suffer many things, even imprisonment. It is heartbreaking to have to suffer misunderstanding when you are trying to share life and truth. Paul's testimony of his experience with Jesus Christ on the road to Damascus was rejected. To the Jews it must have seemed that this learned and devout Jew was discarding his whole God-given heritage to become a Christian. There was tremendous opposition to his proclamation that Jesus Christ, whom they had hung as a common thief, was their Messiah. The Sadducees didn't even believe in the resurrection of the dead. Paul was not only proclaiming salvation by faith in Jesus' sacrifice, but faith in Jesus' resurrection from the dead as an example to all believers that they also would be resurrected to eternal life with Him.

What an uproar! Soldiers had to step in and literally save Paul's life. Paul, alone at the castle where the soldiers had taken him after his rescue, was visited by the Lord Jesus Christ the following night. Jesus encouraged Paul and told him to be of good cheer. To me the exciting thing about this text is that when the Lord says something, that which He speaks forth happens. I can imagine the good cheer and joy that welled up from within Paul as Jesus said, *"Be of good cheer."*

An occasion comes to mind of a very difficult time in my life. Hurting and not knowing which way to turn, I found my eyes would not even focus on the Scriptures. However, I persevered until they did, but I really had no understanding of the words. Then I kept right on reading until understanding came. Eventually the Word penetrated my spirit, and life came. Had Jesus not said, *"Lo, I am with you always?"*

Though Jesus didn't stand beside my bed, nor did I hear an audible voice, but His Word had the same effect on my spirit. Where darkness had been there was now joy. Good cheer was mine, for His Word spoke it into my very heart and soul. It was not long before the outer man, the man of flesh, began responding to the Spirit within and looked forward to pressing on with what Jesus had given me to do. Believer, the Holy Spirit can take the written words of Jesus and speak them into our experience to produce the same results that Paul experienced.

TODAY'S GEM: *The entrance of thy words giveth light* (Ps. 119:130).
Old Testament Reading Psalms 36-37

Meditation. *And when Paul's sister's son heard of their lying in wait, he went and entered into the castle, and told Paul* (23:16).

If he went to Jerusalem Paul knew he would suffer because God had already warned him. Paul also knew that it was God's intention for him to bring a witness of the gospel to Rome, and it had been made plain to him by God that his calling was to the Gentile world. By a personal visit of the Lord Jesus Christ to Paul, Jesus had said, *"So must thou bear witness also at Rome"* (v. 11).

During Paul's captivity in Jerusalem some fanatical Jews pledged to fast until they had taken his life. Somehow Paul's nephew had overheard the plans of these men and was able to warn his uncle of the danger to his life. Paul did not tell his nephew that everything was all right because God had told him to preach in Rome. To the contrary, we all have a part to play in the providence of God. Paul had a purpose of God to fulfill and to save himself from this danger. His nephew also had to play his part.

Today's meditation scripture really spoke to me. See how important it was for Paul's nephew to do the right thing. I am not saying that God would have allowed the whole operation to fail and Paul to suffer death at the hands of these fanatics if his nephew had failed; however, it must be obvious to us all that Paul's nephew was God's choice and provision to save his uncle. All he had to do was deliver a message to the right person at the right time.

How often does God give us an opportunity to be the very providence of God to one of His servants? Can you imagine the blessing this boy must have received from helping Paul? I'm sure a strong bond of love was established between them. Every ministry of God is established by someone's faithfulness. It won't always be a life-saving experience, but most of the time it's that steadfast faithfulness that keeps ministries going.

Let's be sensitive to God when we see some situation that could develop into a disaster. We can be judgmental and critical, reading failure into the circumstances and ignoring the possibility that if God has given us the opportunity to see the danger, then it could well be that we are the ones whom God has chosen to divert the danger and save the situation. It can be a wonderful opportunity to serve, so be very careful what you do when you see a need. Be open to the possibility that you might be God's answer.

TODAY'S GEM: Being judgmental or critical can cause us to miss the possibility of being God's answer.

Old Testament Reading Psalms 38-40

Meditation. *But this I confess unto thee, that after the way which they call heresy, so worship I the God of my fathers, believing all things which are written in the law and in the prophets* (24:14).

Here we see a man on trial for his very life. It is more than a dispute concerning his doctrine. For several years Paul has successfully evangelized the Gentile world, going first to the Jews with the good news that Jesus Christ is the much awaited and promised messiah. Paul is one of the most carefully called, chosen and prepared men of God, and he is to take the gospel to the Gentile world. He arrives in Jerusalem carrying large sums of money for the support of those Jews who were suffering in Israel. No sooner had he arrived, discharged the customary greetings to the brethren, and given his report of what God was doing in the Gentile world, than a fanatical conflict erupted which threatened his very life.

The violence of that conflict and threat on his life gives us an opportunity to see the stature of this man Paul. He faces months, possibly years, of imprisonment; yet, instead of pleading for his life or seeking his release by a bribe, we find him taking the opportunity to fearlessly proclaim the gospel of Jesus Christ. At no time does he deny his Jewish inheritance as a son of Abraham, Isaac, and Jacob. That is not in question. The conflict is with those Jews who refuse to believe in Jesus as their messiah and with the Jews who refuse to believe in the resurrection of man—the just or the unjust—let alone the resurrection of Jesus Christ.

Paul is not defending his convictions. I'm sure his accusers also had strong convictions about what they were doing. Their convictions were strong enough for them to want to take his life, but Paul, standing in court before judge and council, simply proclaimed the truth, which was full of life and spirit. It glorified the Lord Jesus Christ. He demonstrated his faith, not in convictions, but in truth. *But this I confess unto thee . . . so worship I the God of my fathers . . . And have hope toward God . . . that there shall be a resurrection of the dead, both of the just and unjust* (vv. 14-15).

This confession was made before a court that had the power to pass the sentence of death upon Paul. Facing death over and over again, he still proclaimed the truth of the resurrection. Facing death just seemed to make the resurrection all the more real to Paul, and you can rest assured that he believed what he preached. Death offered him the opportunity to live what he preached. Is this your confession: *For to me to live is Christ, and to die is gain* (Phil. 1:21)?

TODAY'S GEM: Polycarp (a martyr for his faith) said something like this as they burned him at the stake: A fool dies for his convictions but a man will give his life for the truth.

Old Testament Reading Psalms 41-43

Meditation. *For if I be an offender, or have committed any thing worthy of death, I refuse not to die: but if there be none of these things whereof these accuse me, no man may deliver me unto them. I appeal unto Caesar* (25:11).

There was a new plot underway by the Jews to kill Paul. All this time spent in prison had not silenced him. The arrival of Festus in Jerusalem gave the Jews another opportunity, so they requested that Paul be brought to Jerusalem for another trial. Just as before, they planned to lie in wait and kill Paul on the way to Jerusalem. God took a hand in the situation, and Festus refused their request but invited them to accompany him to Caesarea where Paul was being held.

As Paul again faced his accusers, it was obvious to Festus and Agrippa that there was very little substance to the Jews' accusations. No doubt Paul's Roman citizenship kept his judges from being overly influenced by the Jews, because they dared not sentence him to death over some religious scandal. Paul's courage and persistence really impressed me. He showed no fear of death and even confessed a willingness to die if his accusers were correct in their judgment. On the other hand, it is also obvious that Paul was not about to throw his life away. Paul had something for which to live. Jesus had visited Paul and told him that he would go to Rome. God's will was set before him, and he was determined to live to perform it.

In Paul's life there was a quality, a richness that triumphed over adversities. I want to suggest to you that even though Paul looked forward to the resurrection of his body in Christ, he had good reason to live. Paul understood that with the resurrection of the body there can be no fear of death or dying (Richard Baxter called it the saint's everlasting rest). To die simply meant to be present with the Lord. There were times when Paul was torn between the two, and he decided on living because he had something for which to live. He had such a vision, such a concept of his life in Christ, that he insisted on living even if it meant years of imprisonment. The circumstances could not rob Paul of his life in Christ or his Christian experience, which Paul had found to be quite adventuresome. It was worth living, and he wanted to explore it to the fullest.

TODAY'S GEM: *For to me to live is Christ, and to die is gain* (Phil. 1:21).

Old Testament Reading Psalms 44-46

Meditation. *And Paul said, I would to God, that not only thou, but also all that hear me this day, were both almost, and altogether such as I am, except these bonds* (26:29).

Brought before King Agrippa by Festus and given an opportunity to speak, Paul immediately begins to give his testimony. He tells Agrippa of his zeal for the law and his intellectual attainments. Paul confesses that he persecuted the Christians until his encounter with the Lord Jesus Christ. He speaks of the way God has led him and appeals to King Agrippa's understanding of the prophets and their predictions of the messiah. Very carefully Paul presents his testimony before the court, and King Agrippa is so moved that he says, *"Almost thou persuadest me to be a Christian"* (v. 28).

By my own experience and understanding of such things, let me attempt to interpret what I believe was going on in Paul's heart. He was not just trying to bring those listening from a place of unbelief to believing that Jesus was the Messiah according to the prophets. Their Jewish religion was already the victim of beliefs that continually led to contention. It was not enough to believe. Agrippa was almost persuaded but persuaded to what and why? To change his mind? It is possible to change your mind about what you believe and about who Jesus is without entering into the experience of the life in Christ about which Paul was speaking. When King Agrippa confessed that Paul had almost persuaded him, Paul responded that it was his prayer that King Agrippa and all who were listening would become what he was. Paul was not speaking about his bonds but about his life. He was not just talking about what he believed concerning the things the prophets wrote about the Messiah but what he was living and experiencing right before their eyes.

Paul's zealousness for living, his faith and excitement, were motivated by his personal experience and relationship with Jesus. They were only highlighted and given substance by his knowledge of who the prophets said the messiah was. Paul's enthusiasm for living the Christian life was stimulated by the hope within him that he might experience the promises yet to come (those outside of his immediate experience). He could confess his obedience to the heavenly vision that had filled the imagination of his mind with greater attainments in Christ. This was a vision of receiving more of the life of Christ, not knowledge or beliefs about it, but the life Jesus had set before them.

TODAY'S GEM: *But as many as received him, to them gave he power to become the sons of God* (Jn. 1:12).

Old Testament Reading Psalms 47-49

Meditation. *Wherefore, sirs, be of good cheer: for I believe God, that it shall be even as it was told me* (27:25).

Wouldn't it be nice to have a Paul around when we have to face what appear to be disastrous circumstances? However, during the storm and impending shipwreck, no one listened to Paul's warnings. They chose to receive the captain's counsel rather than a man of God. But Paul had a visitor during the night. It was an angel who said, *"Fear not, Paul; thou must be brought before Caesar: and, God hath given thee all them that sail with thee"* (v. 24). Therefore, Paul again spoke to those aboard, telling them that they should have taken his advice. Paul then went on to encourage them. *And now I exhort you to be of good cheer: for there shall be no loss of any man's life among you, but of the ship. For there stood by me this night the angel of God, whose I am, and whom I serve* (vv. 22-23).

When God speaks to us we can afford to be bold. Whether an angel visits us or God chooses to speak through the Word, circumstances, or a still small Voice, the all-important thing is that God speaks to us, and we have that inner witness of the Spirit that He has indeed spoken. Paul's confidence was in God's word. Still, in the midst of a raging storm and the sea threatening to demolish the ship, his circumstances hadn't changed. Everything that could be had been thrown overboard to save them, so in the natural the situation couldn't have looked worse. Can you imagine these seasick men, who were facing shipwreck and possible drowning, listening to Paul say, *"Wherefore, sirs, be of good cheer: for I believe God, that it shall be even as it was told me"*? (So we can afford to be cheerful if we have God's Word, because we have what He has promised.)

The secret to the life in Christ that Paul lived with boldness and faith is not the result of an angelic visitation but because of what the angel had said. Who could take away what God had given or what God had promised? Paul's security was no longer in a hope but by faith in what God had promised. There was not a man on that ship or a wave big enough to rob Paul of God's promise. His faith was in what God had said, not in what Paul himself was able to do, but what God said He would do.

TODAY'S GEM: *As for God, his way is perfect; the word of the LORD is tried: he is a buckler to all them that trust in him* (2 Sam. 22:31).

Old Testament Reading Psalms 50-52

Meditation. *And so it came to pass, that they escaped all safe to land* (27:44).

God's rescue of Paul and the others from the shipwreck probably did not happen just the way Paul thought it would. Has that also been your experience? When God has told you He would do something, maybe you had it all figured out how He would do it and when. Surely, at least according to our way of thinking, the way for God to fulfill His promise to Paul was to simply speak to the storm, commanding it to cease. After all, that's what Jesus did. If I had been Paul, when that lifesaving boat went over the side, I would have wanted to be certain that was what God had intended to do. Certainly with the lifesaving boat gone, God would still the sea, but it didn't happen that way. They had to go on trusting God's word in that storm, even when their soundings told them they were running out of water and there was a chance they would break up on a reef. The promised rescue by God did not come immediately but came after many testings and in the face of great trials.

During a break in the weather they saw an opportunity to run to the shelter of the mouth of a creek. A little sail was turned out to the mercy of the wind, and they again trusted God. As soon as the anchor was up, the ship headed for that creek mouth where two currents met. The sea had built up a sandbar, and the ship plowed right into it. Stuck fast, they again had to trust God. It was bad enough being in a situation where they could lose their lives because of the sea since some of them could not swim. If they lost their prisoners they could face death anyway, so when it was decided not to kill the prisoners they again had to trust God. Their faith was rewarded as they were driven safely to shore by the storm.

When God speaks to me, I still get just as excited as I did when I was a baby Christian. The only difference between then and now is I have learned that it is one thing to hear from God and another thing to trust Him in carrying out His word. If God hasn't said how He is going to carry out His word in my experience, then I have to trust Him in the circumstances in which I find myself, even if they are contradictory to what He has said. God is capable of making all things work together, and His word cannot fail Him or return to Him void. Patience is usually rewarded by this promise, and so it came to pass.

TODAY'S GEM: God is able to save me to the uttermost.
Old Testament Reading Psalms 53-55

Meditation. *And when they were escaped, then they knew that the island was called Melita* (28:1).

If you have been reading the last three days about Paul's shipwreck experience on the high seas, then you can't help but be impressed by Paul's ability to believe God's word, to walk trustingly in it, and also to exhort others to do the same.

As you will recall, God sent an angel to tell Paul not to fear. On the basis of everything the angel had said was God's word for him, Paul trusted in that word over and over again, and it was not just a one-time thing. He had to trust that word when the lifeboat was gone and when the ship ran aground. He had to continue to trust when the suggestion was made that the prisoners be killed, when he faced the angry waves, and when he was thrown upon the beach.

What joy there must have been in Paul's heart as he saw God's word working over and over again for their good. How he must have rejoiced when every man was found. They gathered wood to light a fire and dry their clothes because it was winter. But in spite of the cold weather and shock of being in the water, I am sure Paul was the happiest man there. If he wasn't praising God out loud for his deliverance from the raging seas, I am sure he was praising Him in his heart and almost dancing for joy. I can imagine Paul still hitting a high note of praise in his heart when a viper fastened itself to his hand. There must have been a moment of silence as all were stunned by this new threat to Paul's life. Suggestions were made in ignorance, but Paul just went on trusting the word of the Lord as he shook the viper off into the fire. All were amazed at his deliverance, and God even used him to heal the father of the island's chief official. Paul had some pretty fast-changing circumstances, but the word of the Lord remained stable and faithful. His word was equal to Paul's every need.

TODAY'S GEM: In faith they overcame.
Old Testament Reading Psalms 56-58

Meditation. *Be it known therefore unto you, that the salvation of God is sent unto the Gentiles, and that they will hear it* (28:28).

One Sunday evening in our church we had the rare privilege of hearing an Israeli government official give his testimony of how he had come into the understanding of Jesus as his Messiah. It was obvious that he had had a real experience and had received the Spirit of Jesus into his heart. It was a very precious moment as this man of Israel intimately shared with us. I know every person in that church was really moved.

After the service I talked with a Jewish businessman, who, as far as I know, had never been in a Christian church before. This man was very moved by what he had heard. He did not believe in Jesus as the Christ or Messiah, but with a lot of passion he did say to the brother who gave his testimony, "Go back to Israel and tell the people these Christians have our God." That is exactly what Paul said he himself would do, and, upon Israel's rejection of Jesus as the Messiah, God turned Paul's attention to the Gentiles with the gospel of salvation. (I am careful to say Israel, because many Jews believed and suffered for the Lord Jesus Christ because of that rejection.)

The only Gentile writer we have in the New Testament is Dr. Luke, who wrote his Gospel and this book of the Acts of the Apostles. All the rest of the authors were Israelites, so we virtually owe everything we have to the Jewish writers and evangelists. Israel's rejection of Jesus was the open door to salvation for the Gentiles. I want to praise God today for what took place, not for the rejection of Jesus by the Jews, but that God would have such grace and compassion for us that He would send the Jewish believers to the Gentile world with the gospel. The cultural and religious shock must have been terrible. No wonder they had difficulties as to what the Gentile believers in Jesus should do with some aspects of the Jewish heritage. Oh, praise God, they did not give way to their lifetime of religious experience but paid a great price for the Gentiles' salvation. What a wonderful, life-changing experience they must have had to be able to forsake so much to follow Jesus and then to be led by Him into the Gentile world.

Let us be appreciative of the people who brought the gospel to us and remind ourselves that Israel's rejection was our gain. Let's be certain that we, as a people of God and as a nation, don't make the same mistake as Israel, who, as a nation, rejected Jesus. Praise God for our Christian nation!

TODAY'S GEM: We are one nation under God. Pray that the government might be upon His shoulders.
Old Testament Reading Psalms 59-61

Meditation. *Among whom are ye also the called of Jesus Christ* (1:6).

You and I did not stumble into the kingdom of God by coincidence, nor can we impress God with good works and earn salvation. Each and every one of us came into the kingdom by God's grace. Since the day Jesus stood on the shores of Galilee, He has been calling men and women into a reconciled relationship with the Father. The pauper is called the same way as the king, for God is no respecter of persons (Eph. 6:9). Rich and poor come into the kingdom of God exactly the same way.

In this chapter of Paul's letter to the Roman Christians he reminds them that they are called to be saints. You and I are also called. Whatever you think your calling in God is there is one thing of which you can be certain: Jesus Christ has called you out of this world, its power and temptation, and into the kingdom of God to share His righteousness with you. Today you are the righteousness of God in Christ (2 Cor. 5:21).

He has called us to no longer walk in darkness but in His glorious light so we can be saints. I don't know what sort of image you have of yourself, but why not let the Word of God change that. You cannot afford to live in less than what God says you are. His Word calls you a saint, but is it because of your works or religious habits? Certainly not! You are a saint because Jesus has called you and made you the righteousness of God, and you are just that if you live in His righteousness. Don't try to accumulate any righteousness of your own because the Bible considers it as filthy rags (Isa. 64:6). God's righteousness makes you righteous. Look in the mirror, my friend. Unseen by you is what God sees, which is the righteousness of God (Christlikeness). You don't have to try to be saints because in the Scriptures Paul has called you to be one according to the work that Jesus has already done for you. Hallelujah!

Now you can live according to what the Word of God says for saints. Keep a sensitive, daily relationship with the Holy Spirit. Do nothing to grieve Him. Let the blood of Jesus flow for the cleansing of your sin. Meet with Him in His Word on a regular, daily basis by maintaining a quiet-time. Then you will be what Jesus has called you to be.

Beloved, now are we the sons of God, and it doth not yet appear what we shall be: but we know that, when he shall appear, we shall be like him (1 Jn. 3:2). We shall be saints with His mind, His love, and His righteousness, reflecting His glory, for we are His handiwork. Praise God, do you know who you are today, my friend?

TODAY'S GEM: I am a saint of God today, and I will live according to what the Word says I am.

Old Testament Reading Psalms 62-64

AUGUST 1 Romans 2

Meditation. *But he is a Jew, which is one inwardly; and circumcision is that of the heart, in the spirit, and not in the letter; whose praise is not of men, but of God* (2:29).

This must have been a heavy word for those Roman Christians to receive. I can imagine how offensive it must have been to those Jews who were trusting in their traditions and the faith of their fathers for salvation. In this scripture it is very clear that they were not Jews merely because of circumcision. The circumcision which made a Jew was that of the heart—their hearts had to undergo a radical change. A Jew was one who trusted in the covenant that God had made with Abraham. It was also one whose heart was open to God, willing to walk in obedience before Him.

We Christians can learn a lot from this letter of Paul's to the Roman Christians. First we must examine our hearts. Is there an inner witness of the Spirit that we are born again? Has our faith in God's perfect plan of salvation been firmly established in Christ's blood sacrifice for our sin? Is our fellowship with God based upon His covenant, His new covenant? True Christian experience is an experience that changes our hearts. Since it is the heart that must be developed, we would be wise to cultivate our heart lives so that our desires are turned toward God.

Educational systems have taught us to develop our intellects so that a great portion of our lives, and in many cases our fortunes, are spent in the development of our minds. As a young Christian my heart experience with God was developed way beyond my intellectual understanding of Him, but very soon I learned to listen to the still, small voice of God within. When He spoke to my heart, a love developed for what Jesus had accomplished in delivering me from the bondage of sin. Though my poorly developed intellect tried to rationalize and cast doubts about the word God was speaking to my heart, Jesus was able to communicate it, and my heart-changing experience grew as a result. Given liberty to develop the experience of God within our hearts, the Holy Spirit will also establish the fruits of the Spirit within us.

It is not God's intention to set before us a code of conduct, standards or principles to be legalistically applied to our lives. Rather, it is God's intention for us to know an inner dependence upon the Holy Spirit. As a result, out of the depths of a circumcised heart will come the desire and motivation to make all that we are available to that still, small Voice. Our obedience will come from love. This month may the Scriptures be used by God to develop the life of the heart so our understanding of Him will be more than just intellectual.

TODAY'S GEM: True Christianity is a heart-changing experience.

Old Testament Reading Psalms 65-67

Meditation.   *For all have sinned, and come short of the glory of God* (3:23).

My earliest introduction to this scripture was as a baby Christian. It was to be used constantly in my witnessing to the non-Christian, for I understood that it was the non-Christian who was the sinner and came short of God's glory. However, one day I received quite a shock when the Holy Spirit reminded me that the apostle Paul wrote this scripture to Christians in Rome. If we are to keep our hearts pure before God, then it is necessary to appreciate that even after we have been born again, born of the Spirit from above, it is possible to sin. But, praise God, He has made provision. *If we confess our sins, he is faithful and just to forgive us our sins, and to cleanse us from all unrighteousness* (1 Jn. 1:9).

Adam, the first man, came short of the image of God by sinning. From henceforth all men were born less than God had originally intended, for he came short of God's glory. Man did not need to learn to sin because the sin principle or sin nature was inherent within him. Transgression of the law (sin) was merely an outward expression of the inner sin nature or sin principle. It is the Holy Spirit's ministry to convict us of sin so we can trust in the blood of Jesus Christ to cleanse us. If you are desiring a heart cleansing in your Christian walk, then expect to experience conviction. Only sin confessed is sin forgiven, and for that reason the Holy Spirit will convict you of wrongdoing.

Jesus, the second Adam, is God's glory. He is God's best for us, and the very image of God is seen in the Son. We are to have the mind of Christ, and our actions, intentions, and everything we do is to glorify Jesus. Since our righteousness is in Him, the Holy Spirit can't help but glorify Christ because His character, nature, and all that He is in the Godhead are dedicated to glorifying Jesus. When the Holy Spirit gets His own way in our hearts He will convict and convince us of sin. He will always be working in our hearts so that we might turn to the Blood for continual cleansing, thereby glorifying the Son. As the Holy Spirit purges and cleanses, our minds and bodies will learn to respond. Then the outward man will also respond and glorify Jesus. Until that happens we all come short of the glory of God.

TODAY'S GEM: *For out of the abundance of the heart the mouth speaketh* (Mt. 12:34).
Old Testament Reading Psalms 68-69

Meditation. *And being fully persuaded that, what he had promised, he was able also to perform* (4:21).

Faith becomes alive in the heart that is fully persuaded. Doubt cannot survive in the heart that is fully persuaded. Fear disappears and timidity flees in the presence of the fully convinced believer. *"For I am persuaded,* Paul said, *"that neither death, nor life, nor angels, nor principalities, nor powers, nor things present, nor things to come, Nor height, nor depth, nor any other creature, shall be able to separate us from the love of God, which is in Christ Jesus our Lord* (Rom. 8:38-39). Would you say Paul was fully persuaded? In his letter to Timothy he wrote, *I . . . am persuaded that he* [Christ] *is able to keep that which I have committed unto him against that day* (2 Tim. 1:12). Paul was convinced that nothing could destroy God's word of promise, and nothing could void it or make it of no effect. There was no person or power on earth that could rob Paul of the complete salvation that was in Christ Jesus. He was not assured of his own ability to keep himself from falling, nor was his confidence in his own strength, works, or even religious experience. Paul was convinced that his eternal salvation experience would be completed by the working of the Spirit of God in his life according to God's grace and promise.

If it is your wish to be fully persuaded and to be an overcomer, then be assured that the One to whom you have committed your life—the Lord Jesus Christ—will never ever give up on you. Be fully persuaded this day that He will keep whatever promise or whatever word He has spoken into your heart because *God is not a man, that he should lie* (Num. 23:19).

Let the Word of God so fill your heart that you, like Paul, are fully persuaded. Through some form of media or person, the spirit of the world will try to convince you otherwise. That same spirit will work very hard to persuade you that you have reason to fear, reason to doubt, and that you will fail; so feed your heart on God's Word. Get His promises into your heart by meditating upon Him. Take today's scripture and make it your own. Meditate upon it all day, being fully convinced that God is able to perform the promise He has made to you through His Word. Then lift up your head and walk with assurance that *greater is he that is in you, than he that is in the world* (1 Jn. 4:4). Let me convince you today to be a fully persuaded Christian.

TODAY'S GEM: *Being confident of this very thing, that he which hath begun a good work in you will perform it* (Phil. 1:6).

OLD TESTAMENT READING Psalms 70-72

Meditation. *But we also joy in God through our Lord Jesus Christ, by whom we have now received the atonement* (5:11).

I like the way today's text is paraphrased in the Living Bible. *Now we rejoice in our wonderful new relationship with God—all because of what our Lord Jesus Christ has done in dying for our sins—making us friends of God.* What a wonderful experience is ours in Christ to know that our sins are forgiven! There is no condemnation because our hearts are made clean by the blood of Jesus Christ. When this truth and the experience of it becomes ours, we can hardly live with the excitement of it; however, today's text offers us even more, much more. Meditate on this today, and see for yourself what happens to your faith.

We are to rejoice in our wonderful new relationship with God. The purpose of Jesus' death and resurrection was not only to save us from the wrath of God's judgment on sin but also to introduce us into a new relationship with Him. Each day gives us an opportunity to develop that relationship which Jesus established for us by His blood sacrifice. We are to be a people who know God and are known by Him.

If we are to develop this relationship with the Lord, we will need to read about His dealings with man, who Jesus is, and how He relates to us. However, reading about God is not enough either. As well as learning all we can about God, we must take the time to get to know Him and to talk with Him so we can respond to His promises of love and life from His Word. We can then receive them as His word to us.

Jesus has not only saved us from the consequence of our sin, which is eternal damnation, but He has done more than this. He has made it possible for you and me to establish and possess a wonderful new relationship with God. We will not be strangers to Him when we meet Him face to face. We will know His voice, be sensitive to His ways, and possess a holy desire for Him. The Word says that Jesus' sacrifice makes us friends with God. To be a friend does not imply just a religious experience or encounter, although both of these are necessary. To be friends certainly must mean an extraordinary relationship. By faith I know that He knows and loves me as a friend. Friends fellowship with one another and rejoice in that fellowship. Jesus has made us friends of God; so how is your relationship with Him developing?

TODAY'S GEM: Jesus has given me a relationship with God that is to be developed into a friendship.

Old Testament Reading Psalms 73-74

Meditation. *For the wages of sin is death; but the gift of God is eternal life through Jesus Christ our Lord* (6:23).

Rejoice with me today for we are no longer on Satan's payroll. Nor will we share or participate in the outpouring of God's wrath on all sin, which is eternal damnation. There was a time when we were helplessly bound by sin, walking in spiritual ignorance and darkness. Instead of living we were spiritually dead. It took the light and life of the gospel of Jesus Christ, which is a look at eternal life, to make us realize that we were dead in our sin. Now the cross of Jesus Christ has changed all this for those who believe in Him. To us God has extended the gift of eternal life.

I appreciate the definition of eternal life as one that continues forever. One aspect of it that means so much to me is the substance of that life. Eternal life is not only unending, but it is God's quality of life to which the natural man could never have attained. It is ours only by grace, a free gift of God that we can't work for or purchase. It can only be received as the gift of God through Jesus Christ our Lord.

The more we allow the Holy Spirit to live the life of Christ in and through us, the more we experience eternal life. The more we receive the Word of God into our lives, the more material the Holy Spirit has to work with to produce a Christlike nature in us. With this He can produce the mind of Christ so that God's quality of life, which is eternal, can flow.

If you are born again by the Spirit of God from above, then by God's grace His free gift of eternal life is yours. So let it flow. Jesus has successfully planted the seed of eternal life in our hearts; so feed and water it with the Word. Tend that new seed like you would tend a garden; then God will give the increase.

What will your life yield, and what will be the increase? Will it be thirtyfold, fiftyfold, or a hundredfold? God will give the seed of eternal life, and the yield will be determined by what you do with what God gives you.

TODAY'S GEM: Eternal life is a quality of life to be lived right now. The size of the yield depends upon you.

Old Testament Reading Psalms 75-77

Meditation. *Wherefore, my brethren, ye also are become dead to the law by the body of Christ; that ye should be married to another, even to him who is raised from the dead, that we should bring forth fruit unto God* (7:4).

The Bible calls us the redeemed, born-again people, the bride of Christ. How can this be? Jesus told Nicodemus that we must be born again, that is, born of the Spirit from above (Jn. 3:5-6). At this time God's Spirit and our spirit become one as a union takes place between the spirit of man and the Spirit of God. We then become part of the Body of Christ, His Church. Now it is God's purpose for us to develop a tender, loving relationship with His Son.

Imagine what would happen if you bought a handbook on marriage and became so engrossed in reading it that you didn't bother to apply any of its principles. That is what seems to happen to many Christians. After becoming born again they do not neglect to read their Handbook (the Bible) and, as a matter of fact, enjoy reading, meditating, and even memorizing scripture about their spiritual marriage. However, they totally neglect the relationship responsibilities this new, spiritual marriage brings. Soon they stop reading and wonder why their spiritual lives are so empty. It is because they have neglected to give time to knowing the Person to whom they are spiritually wed. They read the Handbook but never apply its principle, which is to intimately know their God.

Jesus is to be like a husband to us. There are to be times of intimate sharing, confessions of love, and no secrets. Our hearts are to be wide open to this relationship without fear of being hurt. We should have complete faith and trust in Jesus' faithfulness. The fruit of our relationship with Him is not to be just the result of a great deal of learning but the fruit of a personal relationship. How much of your life and time do you give to the development of your spiritual marriage?

TODAY'S GEM: To be the bride of Christ is to have an intimate knowledge of *him who is raised from the dead.*
Old Testament Reading Psalm 78

Meditation. *Ye have received the Spirit of adoption, whereby we cry, Abba, Father* (8:15).

Some very special girls who lived and worked in an inner-city ministry used to sing a song that was called, "Do You Know Who You Are?" Why not let your thoughts dwell on this today. Meditate on the fact that you have received the Spirit of adoption, and by that same Spirit you are a child of God. (Spirit of adoption is translated Spirit of sonship in the New International Bible.) God is your Father. I think that should be said again. God is your Father!

You are not just something that happened. By giving your life to Christ you did not join a club or even a local church. It was more than being involved in an intellectual discussion. Certainly you had to make some right decisions, but by the Spirit of God much, much more has happened in your life. You have been adopted into a family with roots going back to the very beginning of time. By that same Spirit of adoption, God, who creates and controls and is the biggest thing this old world has ever known and will ever know, has become your Father. Our Father is so great and so beyond the ability of our minds to comprehend that there is not a man, nation, or kingdom that can boast of such resources or standard of prosperity and security that the kingdom of your Father has. Before the world existed He was. When all things have passed away, when kingdoms have fallen and perished, when nations have disappeared, the sonship to which you have been adopted will still stand. If you are the poorest or weakest member of this family into which you have been adopted, you will still be greater and wealthier than any prince or king of this world!

How did all this happen to you? The Spirit of adoption brought you into an intimate Father-and-son relationship with the Godhead. Now you can intimately, affectionately, lovingly, and fearlessly call Him God, Abba ("father" in Aramaic).

The life that the Spirit of adoption sets before you as a son or daughter is eternal. What God has in mind for you can scarcely be compared with what you have or what you are right now in Christ. God has plans for you in His eternal kingdom. The honors and riches are a quality of life to which this world will never attain. So cry "Abba, Father," and get to know the One who has called you and adopted you as His son or daughter. Look up. Look to the eternal future of knowing and enjoying who you are in Christ.

TODAY'S GEM: *The Spirit himself testifies with our spirit that we are God's children* (Rom. 8:16, NIV.)
Old Testament Reading Psalms 79-81

Meditation. *And we know that all things work together for good to them that love God, to them who are the called according to his purpose* (8:28).

One day in the company of some fine Christian businessmen I quoted the above scripture in the following manner, *all things work together for good to them that love God, to them who are the called according to his purpose.* No sooner had I quoted the scripture than this dear old saint leaned over to me and said, "Tim, you misquoted that scripture." I asked him what I had said wrong. He replied, "You left out the most important part, *and we know."* Suddenly I realized what he was saying. It is one thing to understand the meaning of the scripture but quite another to know that the scripture really works in our experience.

Do we actually **know** that all things work together for good? It really is difficult to confess that we know this promise to be true when we are in the midst of some difficult situation. It is a simple confession to make when everything is going smoothly, but what about when everything around us is in conflict and we find ourselves in difficult circumstances? Do we know at those times that God, by His providential grace, can take the most adverse circumstances and made them work together for our good?

Our Christian life can take on a whole new meaning if we let this scripture manifest itself in our hearts, really getting hold of us. To do this means that each day is a new opportunity for God to make the circumstances of the day work for our benefit. Meditate on this scripture, reminding yourself of some of the circumstances of the day that you have faced which appear negative, some situation that just is not working out for you. If you really know the truth of this scripture, then you have the opportunity to experience a real faith adventure. Instead of being overcome by the negative, let this scripture stimulate faith in your heart. As a result you will only have eyes for how and what God will do with your present circumstances. Our problem is that we don't always want to see what God wants us to see and experience. It seems that we need adverse situations to enable us to face up to some problem that we have been overlooking. In any case, it certainly takes the sting and bitterness out of a problem when you know that all things really do work together for good.

TODAY'S GEM: Welcome each day as a new opportunity for God to work your circumstances out for your good.
Old Testament Reading Psalms 82-84

Meditation. *Whosoever believeth on him shall not be ashamed* (9:33).

Can you imagine an occasion when you might be disappointed in or ashamed of Christ? How could He ever leave you comfortless when He has sent a Comforter to you? Jesus can never leave you because He has promised to *never leave thee, nor forsake thee* (Heb. 13:5), so that *whosoever believeth on him shall not be ashamed* (Rom. 9:33). Has He not said, *"And I give unto them* [my sheep] *eternal life; and they shall never perish, neither shall any man pluck them out of my hand* (Jn. 10:28)?

I defy principalities, powers, or men with persuasive words to make of no account Jesus' words. My believing friend, hang on to every word that proceeds from the mouth of God. Put your absolute faith in what Jesus has said and in what He has done. If Jesus promises eternal life, then it is yours by faith. If He assures you that none shall perish or be plucked out of His hand, then He is as good as His word. Rest in what Jesus has said, and you will never have cause to be ashamed.

I remember being in the hospital with a Christian who was dying of cancer. I watched this man, who was only two years old in the Lord, trusting Jesus. He used his last hours wisely, gathering his family around him so that a harmonious, Christlike separation could take place as he committed his family to the Lord. This man passed on talking to Jesus. There was no fear, no fuss, just complete trust in the One who could save him to the uttermost. He had no cause to be ashamed or doubt that Jesus would not be as good as His word.

One of my favorite texts is, *faithful is he that calleth you, who also will do it* (1 Thess. 5:24). I know there will never be a time to give way to doubt or be ashamed because *whosoever believeth on him shall not be ashamed.*

TODAY'S GEM: *God is not a man, that he should lie . . . or hath he spoken, and shall he not make it good?* (Num. 23:19).

Old Testament Reading Psalms 85-87

Meditation. *For with the heart man believeth unto righteousness; and with the mouth confession is made unto salvation* (10:10).

The law was to be our schoolmaster, informing us of our righteousness (or unrighteousness) and our need. However, it could not deliver or save us from the consequences of sin, nor are we capable of fulfilling and walking in obedience to it. Verse four says, *for Christ is the end of the law.* No longer do we have to struggle to keep the law in our own strength.

All that we could not accomplish according to the law to satisfy God, Christ has accomplished for us. We now have an opportunity to live before God in righteousness, not on the basis of keeping the law, but based on Christ's perfect sacrifice and fulfillment of it on our behalf. Cultivate your heart, believing unto righteousness and establishing a complete faith in the Lord Jesus Christ.

Luke 12:34 says, *For where your treasure is, there will your heart be also.* So build your life around and set your affections on those things that are above. Get the Word into your heart, *for with the heart man believeth unto righteousness.* Having Christ is possessing righteousness, His righteousness. We are the righteousness of God in Christ (2 Cor. 5:21). Discipline your heart life. Address your heart; speak to it for its coldness or hardness toward the Lord Jesus Christ. Chasten yourself when you show indifference to the things of God. Constantly feed on the Word of God, and before very long words confessing Christ and life will flow forth from your heart.

When a man speaks with or from the heart it is certainly convincing and leaves no doubt that he believes what he says. We believe the life of the Spirit is in our hearts so that the words that come forth from our hearts are words of salvation and life. Take time to meditate on the Word, constantly reminding yourself that true religion is of the heart. Develop your heart life in the closet, believing in the righteousness that is yours in Christ Jesus. With your mouth confess words of life, words that are salvation, your salvation experience.

TODAY'S GEM: *For out of the abundance of the heart the mouth speaketh* (Mt. 12:34).

Old Testament Reading Psalms 88-89

Meditation. *God hath not cast away his people which he foreknew* (11:2).

In verse one Paul reminds the Christians in Rome that it is not God who is unfaithful. God has not cast His people away. His covenant made with Abraham still stands, for Jesus himself is a Jew. They are reminded of the days of Elijah when all Israel went after Baal and worshiped him. In his loneliness and in his thinking, Elijah was the only one left who had remained faithful to God and His word, so he cried out to God. However, God told Elijah about a remnant of 7,000 who, by His grace, remained faithful.

This great nation of America was founded by men with vision, men who lived in a world where faithfulness to God's word was very difficult. They knew that not all that cried, "Lord, Lord," would enter the kingdom of heaven. Like the days of Elijah this was a time when a state religion, a state form, and a place of worship were set before the people. That remnant, faithful to God, came to America to establish a place where man could be free to worship. With them they brought true religion that changed men's hearts and set their minds and affections on things above. History may have repeated itself by the people going after Baal or mammon, but God still had a remnant, for *God hath not cast away his people which he foreknew.*

Today's scripture reading tells us that the salvation of the Gentiles will ultimately provoke the Jews to jealousy. It will cause them to turn to Jesus as their messiah to deliver them from the judgments of God. If there is one country or one people in the world that could provoke the Jews to jealousy and hasten their turning to Jesus as their messiah, it is America. In a Christian meeting one night in Atlanta, Georgia, I heard a Jewish businessman, who was not a follower of Jesus, confess that, "These Christians have got our God."

My dear American friend, God has raised you up as a people. By His grace God has given you this prosperity. All that you have He wanted to give to Israel. For a very short time in the reign of Solomon God was able to give Israel the prosperity of His heart, but now it belongs to America. It belongs to a remnant of people within this nation, but God's best is yet to come. He awaits a people who will not make their God-given prosperity their God but turn to Him with all their hearts and souls so that when the Jew looks at an American Christian he will see his God and be provoked to jealousy.

TODAY'S GEM: Let Christ so shine in you that the Jew will recognize his God and jealously seek until he finds.

Old Testament Reading Psalms 90-92

Meditation. *For I would not, brethren, that ye should be ignorant of this mystery, lest ye should be wise in your own conceits; that blindness in part is happened to Israel, until the fulness of the Gentiles be come in* (11:25).

Living today and being able to see the prophetic scriptures coming to pass in Israel is so exciting. When I was a boy the nation of Israel did not even exist. Millions of Jews had lost their lives and were without a leader, a lost people. They had been scattered throughout the earth, but since 1948 God has changed all that. The people of promise, the apple of God's eye, have awakened. It is as if God has opened their eyes that they might see.

Today Israel is a fast-growing nation. For generations they have been like a blind people, but the mighty hand of God is changing all this. It is so exciting to go to Israel and sense the Spirit of God in this Promised Land. Simultaneously with Israel's awakening there has been a very real visitation of God in the Gentile world. Everywhere you turn people are coming to Jesus, repenting of sin and turning to God. God's Holy Spirit is being poured out on the Gentile world, and multitudes of people are having life-changing experiences. Could it be that we are living in what the Scriptures refer to as the fullness of the Gentiles, a time when Israel will be provoked to jealousy? Can you imagine what God might do in our personal lives, spiritually and materially, to provoke the Jews to jealousy that they might turn to God?

We live in a day when we could be part of the greatest revival of true Christianity that the world has ever seen. It will be a day greater than the day of Solomon; therefore, pray that God might give us the wisdom of Solomon. Pray that He might give us this wisdom to prepare our hearts before Him and convince Him of our desire for such a visitation. God will spiritually raise us up, lavish His truth upon us, and make the wealth of this nation so commonplace and prosperity such an everyday experience of the Christian that it will provoke the Jew to jealousy.

Friends, that day will come when our motives are right and when we desire this prosperity for the purpose of glorifying Jesus and ushering in the end of the age. Whatever God gives us here is temporal. Our real wealth awaits us in the Kingdom. So hold it lightly and equate its true value in what or how it can glorify Jesus and fulfill the purposes of God.

TODAY'S GEM: In a people of power and spiritual stature the Jew will see and recognize his God.

Old Testament Reading Psalms 93-95

Meditation. *I beseech you therefore, brethren, by the mercies of God, that ye present your bodies a living sacrifice, holy, acceptable unto God, which is your reasonable service* (12:1).

The Jew understood what a sacrifice was. The sacrificial animal given to God never returned, never again lived unto itself. His life was given in the service of God. Now Paul is telling the Jews that they should take their lives, their bodies, all that they are, and give them up to God. They are not to revert to their old way of doing things or their old way of thinking, but are to die to every desire that is not a desire to do God's will. This is how the Living Bible describes it: *And so, dear brothers, I plead with you to give your bodies to God. Let them be a living sacrifice, holy—the kind he can accept. When you think of what he has done for you, is this too much to ask? Don't copy the behavior and customs of this world, but be a new and different person with a fresh newness in all you do and think. Then you will learn from your own experience how his ways will really satisfy you* (12:1-2).

I love this last line: *Then you will learn from your own experience how his ways will really satisfy you.* The other day a dear brother rang me in my office and asked me to go to Indonesia. It was one of those occasions when I didn't have to tell him I would pray about it. As a matter of fact, he had asked me before, but due to other responsibilities I had said no. However, when he rang on this occasion I instantly knew down in my spirit that yes was the only answer. Without questioning from where the money would come or how I would handle my other commitments, I was free in my spirit to say I would go. The very next day there was a check in the mail that would take care of my expenses. Because I presented myself in obedience with God's will He provided for my need. *Then you will learn from your own experience how his ways will really satisfy you.*

Let me encourage you. Having presented your body and life, which is your reasonable service, do not take them back. A God-given opportunity is an opportunity to learn and experience faith. Then the responsibility to work it out in your experience is God's, if you are willing to walk in His ways and not revert to your own. I can promise you that God's ways will be entirely satisfying, and you will rejoice for exchanging your ways for His. I beseech you, brethren, present your bodies.

TODAY'S GEM: I can't, but He can, for *I can do all things through Christ which strengtheneth me* (Phil. 4:13).
Old Testament Reading Psalms 96-98

Meditation. *And that, knowing the time, that now it is high time to awake out of sleep: for now is our salvation nearer than when we believed* (13:11).

Although God is not bound by some chronological order, we are and must observe time. Even though God is not bound by time He is on the move. Therefore, if we are to live a full Christian life we must know what time it is spiritually. Ecclesiastes 3:1 tells us: *To every thing there is a season, and a time to every purpose under the heaven.*

In your life and mine there is a time to move into whatever God has in mind for us. We are to remain sensitive to living in a changing situation and be available and pliable enough to proceed with God. When God wants to work in a certain area of our lives, He will provide the special grace necessary to enable us to progress with Him. If, in our lethargy or laziness, we neglect the opportunity, we are like someone sleeping. We awake to the truth, hearing what God has to say and what He has said through the experience of others, but the same measure of grace may not still be available to us to experience the fullness of this truth. We have slept away a great opportunity, and since God is unique it is possible that He may never again act in that same manner. So the opportunity to experience some wonderful move in God could easily be lost.

Just as there are four seasons, which we observe and use for our physical wellbeing, there are spiritual seasons. These are times of opportunity in God, and the key is in doing the right things and proceeding with God by faith. It is seldom, if ever, that you can have an experience in God without a measure of faith. In His love and generosity God gives us the grace and the faith necessary but expects us to take hold of this grace and faith, do something with them and accomplish it in His time.

It is time to awake, put off our slumber, be sensitive to the direction of the Holy Spirit and proceed with God. If He is telling you to repent, there never will be more grace available for you to do this than there is right now. Whatever the still, small Voice is telling you to do, do it with all your might. Your salvation experience depends upon it. Every day we are nearer to the fullness of our salvation experience, so in God's time let's move with Him. To know a truth and refuse to move with God in it is to deny ourselves the grace and power to enter in, appropriate it, and make it our own.

TODAY'S GEM: In your season God's grace will be sufficient for you.
Old Testament Reading Psalms 99-102

Meditation. *Receive one who is weak in the faith, but not to disputes over doubtful things* (14:1, NKJV).

Although Paul wrote these words to the Christians in Rome, you can sense the compassion and sensitive understanding of the author, which is the Holy Spirit of Jesus. Paul directs the brethren to be patient and tolerant of those weaker brethren who have strong convictions about eating meat sold in the marketplace, which have perhaps been used in some religious ceremony. Paul calls them the weaker brethren because, at this point in their Christian experience, if their convictions were shattered their faith would be undermined. Paul is saying that when you see a brother who is weak in faith and leaning upon some principle of conduct or practice in which you have total liberty, do nothing to undermine his beliefs. Receive him in love, and avoid any arguments concerning this belief that is so important to him.

You who feel your weakness of faith in certain areas of your life should rejoice that the Holy Spirit so loves you that He exhorts the brethren to be sensitive to your weakness and make provision for you. The weak but wise in the faith are quick to see what the Word is saying and look to the Lord Jesus Christ to be their strength in any area of weakness. In verse fifteen Paul explains that it is possible to destroy a Christian brother's faith through judgment of his weakness. If this be so, then it is even more important to seek the Lord Jesus for fellowship in this area of your faith. You can be certain of His charitableness because He will do nothing to weaken or destroy the little you have.

The beginning of wisdom is in knowing your weakness and allowing the Lord Jesus Christ to be your strength. Even if you never become strong in this area of weakness you will still make it. As long as this weakness is confessed and Jesus is allowed to be your strength, you will know no failure. The victory is in the cleansing blood of Christ. There certainly is plenty of room in the Body of Christ for weak people, especially weak people who know their strength in Jesus.

TODAY'S GEM: *My grace is sufficient for thee: for my strength is made perfect in weakness. Most gladly therefore will I rather glory in my infirmities, that the power of Christ may rest upon me* (2 Cor. 12:9).

Old Testament Reading Psalms 103-104

Meditation. *We then that are strong ought to bear the infirmities of the weak, and not to please ourselves* (15:1).

In today's reading we receive the same word as in yesterday's. God makes provision for the weak in the Body of Christ and expects those who are strong to be the very strength of Christ to them.

I recall an incident many years ago when my two eldest boys were very small. We were holidaying on a campsite that was used for summer conventions, and no one else was on the property at the time. I was studying while the boys were playing and was very deeply engrossed when the two boys came running in to tell me about a lost lamb which they had found. My first thought was to tell them to leave me to my studies and that I would get with them later, but they were persistent. As I looked down at my paper two numbers clearly formed before my eyes. Everywhere I looked I clearly saw nine and ninety-nine. Instantly it came to my understanding that Jesus left the ninety-nine and went after the one that was lost. The lost lamb did not seem important to me at the time, but obviously it was important to the boys. Looking back, I can see how important it was for me to respond to the Holy Spirit who knew the boys would never have understood being ignored.

There comes a time when our own priorities are not as important as we think. At these times the Lord requires us to leave what we are doing, to leave the ninety-nine and bear the burden of the brethren that are lost and weak. When the Holy Spirit bids us to go, we are not to please ourselves. In God's economy the weak are cared for, and the strong have the opportunity to enter into a special experience of grace where their faith is strengthened and a God-initiated adventure is enjoyed.

TODAY'S GEM: *Bear ye one another's burdens, and so fulfil the law of Christ* (Gal. 6:2).

Old Testament Reading Psalms 105-106

Meditation. *And I am sure that, when I come unto you, I shall come in the fulness of the blessing of the gospel of Christ* (15:29).

In coming to you through these daily devotional readings, I feel moved to pray that God would use me to come to you in the fullness of the blessing of the gospel of Christ. The fullness of the gospel is the fullness of the Holy Spirit, which is the fullness of life. As a result, out of your innermost being will flow rivers of living water, and this completeness is to be a day-by-day experience.

This completeness surely implies the possession of spiritual gifts and a manifestation of the Spirit within the believer in such a manner that will edify him, exhort the brethren, and glorify the Lord Jesus Christ. At this moment there is a peculiar certainty in my heart that as you read these words, Paul's prayer for the Christians he was going to visit will be your experience also. My desire, as I write to the brethren, has always been for God to impart to my readers the gifts and experiences about which I write. Certainly it has always been my intention that in entering your closet with what I write, you would experience the fullness of the blessing of the gospel of Christ.

"Father, as this dear Christian friend with whom I fellowship meditates upon the Word and is motivated by faith to believe it, reach out to this precious believer by Your grace. Enrich this life with the blessing, yes, the fullness, the overflowing blessing of the gospel. Let it flow from him like rivers of living water. Today glorify Your Son Jesus in a very special way in the life of this believer. Let the fullness of Jesus Christ be so manifested within him or her that these words and meditations will clearly be their experience. In Jesus' name we pray. Amen."

Oh my dear Christian reader, heaven itself flowed through me to you as I penned these words of prayer. I am satisfied a transaction took place.

TODAY'S GEM: *And ye are complete in him, which is the head of all principality and power* (Col. 2:10).
Old Testament Reading Psalms 107-108

Meditation. *I commend unto you Phoebe our sister, which is a servant of the church* (16:1).

Paul, like Jesus, knew and appreciated the value of the many special ministry gifts that the women in the church possessed. Phoebe was probably a deaconess and possibly watched over the female converts, cared for the sick, and visited those who were suffering in prison, bringing them food and news that would encourage and comfort them.

As I write these words there is a particular anointing on me. Within me is a compassion and sense of gratitude for the Phoebes of the church who usually go unnoticed and unrewarded, requiring and receiving little encouragement. But in spite of this they perform a wonderful work of God in serving the Church of Jesus Christ. For those ladies who feel a little unnoticed I want to draw your attention to the fact that Paul did not overlook your ministry. Given the opportunity, he commended you to the brethren, exhorting them to pray for you.

For those Christian ladies who have a desire to serve and wonder if there is a place for them, look to Jesus. He loves you in a very special way, and I am sure He would be delighted to visit with you and open a door of service. However, do not despise small beginnings, being faithful in the little things. Live to give rather than to receive. Who knows, before long the Holy Spirit will have fashioned you into a place of service.

Friends, we who are not like Phoebe should look around us and recognize those who are. Pray for them, thanking God for their compassion, love, and good works in the church. Let us pray that God will raise up the less mature by the example of people like Phoebe who have a service of love. Today let us praise God together in a very special way for the women of our church, commending them unto the Lord.

Ladies, receive a very special blessing and know that you are not overlooked. You are not forgotten, for there is One who intercedes for and loves you with an everlasting love. Treasuring your labors of love, Jesus is waiting for the day when He can bestow His rewards upon you in heaven.

TODAY'S GEM: *Thou good and faithful servant: thou hast been faithful over a few things, I will make thee ruler over many things: enter thou into the joy of thy lord* (Mt. 25:21).

Old Testament Reading Psalms 109-111

Meditation. *So that ye come behind in no gift; waiting for the coming of our Lord Jesus Christ* (1:7).

By this text it is obvious that there was an expectancy by the early Church for Christ's imminent return. The church of Corinth lived in a city where every conceivable and revolting sin surrounded them. Much of this sin was carried out in the name of religion and had a place in their temple worship. Some of it infiltrated the Church. There were those who put their faith in the worldly wisdom of men, while others became contentious and took their eyes off the Lord Jesus Christ. They were looking at man and forming parties within the Church around these men.

Paul saw an opportunity for Christ to be glorified in this dark place and sought to strengthen the brethren by building them up in the faith. He reminded them that they lacked none of the graces or gifts of God who had been generous to them. He also reminded them that they had the responsibility to appropriate and operate these gifts, walking in God's grace so that Jesus might be seen in them. There was to be a great contrast between whatever a person was in the world and what he now was in Jesus Christ. The world was to see that God can take *the foolish things of the world to confound the wise; and God hath chosen the weak things of the world to confound the things which are mighty* (1 Cor. 1:27). Paul also reminded them that God had taken Jesus—not Paul, not Apollos or Cephas—and made Him power and wisdom, righteousness and holiness. Just as their redemption was in Christ Jesus so too was all their power, wisdom, righteousness, and holiness.

The world seeks to impart skills and gifts to its followers, which are those who believe in its system. However, God's kingdom imparts its greatest Prince, its King. God releases His Son into the hearts of the believers, and he who has the Son has life. Every good gift is invested in the Son. He becomes our righteousness, wisdom and power, and it is the Father's will that the Son be seen in us.

Believers, today do you feel like a weak Christian? The answer is in the Son. Are you lacking wisdom? Then cast aside the wisdom of this world for it is foolishness in the kingdom of heaven. Turn to the Son and discover the wisdom of God in Him. If you lack power in your life His Spirit indwelling you will be your power. If you desire righteousness then He will be your righteousness. Every good gift is yours; therefore, make use of them, and glorify Jesus as you await His coming.

TODAY'S GEM: Sin seeks out the weak and foolish, but Christ becomes their strength and wisdom.

Old Testament Reading Psalms 112-115

Meditation. *For I determined not to know any thing among you, save Jesus Christ, and him crucified* (2:2).

What might happen in our lives if we determined to know nothing among the brethren that was not of Christ, nothing in our relationships in the world that was not of Him? Think of what could happen if we dared to make Jesus the source of our wisdom and knowledge in all things, leaving the wisdom and knowledge of this world behind.

What would be the outcome if all the negative emotions to which we have been conditioned to respond were suddenly confronted with Jesus? Just let your imagination contemplate the outcome if we took all our hurts, fears, disappointments, and offences to Him, refusing to accept them as our personal burden but instead giving them to the Healer. We could discover what the Holy Spirit of Jesus now dwelling within us might do given the opportunity.

By your own experience how will you ever know or discover for yourself the meaning of this text unless you determine in your heart to release yourself to the Holy Spirit who has taken up residence within you? If faith is lacking, ask God for it so He can prove this text in your area of need. Then determine that His faith will be sufficient for you.

As I write to you, in my spirit I see a large, heavy door swinging slowly open. It swings sluggishly because of its great weight and would take a mighty strong man to shut it. This text is that door that has been opened to you, so step out in faith. Enter that door and find a Hand waiting for yours. A nail-scarred hand is waiting to lead you into a great adventure of faith if you will determine to know nothing among you except Jesus Christ and Him crucified.

TODAY'S GEM: *I have set before thee an open door, and no man can shut it: for thou hast a little strength, and hast kept my word, and hast not denied my name* (Rev. 3:8).

Old Testament Reading Psalms 116-118

Meditation. *So then neither is he that planteth any thing, neither he that watereth; but God that giveth the increase . . . For we are labourers together with God: ye are God's husbandry, ye are God's building* (3:7, 9).

The other day my wife and I put some tomato plants in the garden. We tilled the soil, fertilized, watered, and very carefully set the plants in place. Each day we have been watching over and carefully watering them. There is no doubt that they will grow better because of our tender loving care, but who gives the life to the plant? Who gives the increase and has provided the elements in the soil and the oxygen for the plant that it might grow? God, of course, but we are co-laborers when we work with what He has given us. The increase is the Lord's to give.

If I plant my tomatoes, heap fertilizer around them, but neglect to water or hoe, I cannot expect them to produce good fruit. Regular daily care must be given if I wish to receive God's best from my plants. In writing to these Christians in Corinth, Paul tells them to get their eyes off the ones who planted the seed of the gospel in their hearts. Even though man accepted the responsibility for that seed, nourished, and cared for it so that God could bless it, they were to keep their eyes on the One who was really responsible for their salvation. There are no shortcuts to becoming a spiritual man. Once the seed of the gospel has been planted in our hearts a foundation to build upon must be laid. This foundation must be a total surrender to the workings and dealings of the Lord Jesus Christ in our hearts. He becomes and is our foundation. We are to follow Him who is the seed of life, not the one who plants and waters.

We must understand that the seed of the Spirit, which is the life of Christ planted in our hearts, requires fertilizing, watering, and daily care. You yourself are responsible for tending your spiritual garden by constantly nourishing it on the Word of life. Nobody else will come to remove the weeds that threaten to choke the very life out of this baby plant, for you are God's gardener, a co-laborer with Him. Tend your garden conscientiously, subjecting it to the right environment, and you can expect God to give the increase. You can't see, feel or touch the God-given growth, but you can see the results of God's husbandry.

TODAY'S GEM: *I am the vine, ye are the branches: He that abideth in me, and I in him, the same bringeth forth much fruit: for without me ye can do nothing* (Jn. 15:5).
Old Testament Reading Psalm 119:1-48

Meditation. *Moreover it is required in stewards, that a man be found faithful* (4:2).

Here is a word that could present us with a great adventure in faith. We all know what it means and what is required of us when we sit down and discuss the meaning of this verse, but somehow we suddenly become blind when it is applied to our own circumstances. Or we feel justified in our disloyalty in certain instances because of our conscientiousness in other areas.

How many married people have been unfaithful in their marital relationships but have felt justified because of their circumstances? When confronted with their circumstances and unfaithfulness, the Word itself simply becomes an adjective to use in the right place, but never becomes their own experience.

How many people make ministry commitments until they are confronted with something that irritates them? Perhaps more is required than they had anticipated. Even so they are called to be loyal to their original commitment; however, a change in circumstances or some other reason seems to justify their unfaithfulness. It is obvious by these examples that God has surrounded us with real, live opportunities to learn what it means to be steadfast.

If we, as individuals and serious-minded Christians, are to advance in the kingdom of God, and if the world is to see the gospel of Jesus Christ by our Christlike lives, then it must see the servants of Jesus Christ as men and women who know how to be loyal to their marriage vows and partners and faithful in their service to the church. To be like Christ we must be faithful in our loyalties to one another. How can we talk about loyalty to Jesus when we are disloyal to His Body, that is, the Church? Let me encourage you to seek this virtue in Christ. Be forewarned that if you desire to know faithfulness in your relationship to Jesus, God will set before you a multitude of opportunities in the Body of Christ to develop that faithfulness.

You will discover the still, small Voice correcting you in your attitudes toward others. In you He will develop an inner hesitancy that you will recognize when tempted to judge or talk about others. You will be more sensitive, more guarded about the words that come out of your mouth. There will be an inner desire for Jesus to find you loyal in some adverse circumstances rather than seeking your own way. If God has set this word before you, be encouraged because He is about to make you one of His faithful servants.

TODAY'S GEM: *Be thou faithful unto death, and I will give thee a crown of life* (Rev. 2:10).

Old Testament Reading Psalm 119:49-104

Meditation. *Therefore let us keep the feast . . . with the unleavened bread of sincerity and truth* (5:8).

To be sincere is not necessarily a virtue. It is possible to be sincerely wrong. There is no doubt in my mind that the Communists are genuine in their beliefs and desire for world domination. If we are to respond to today's word and truly know the meaning of it, then we must go to the Holy Spirit, asking Him to lead us into all truth. As with all of God's Word this is another opportunity for an adventure in faith.

After your mind has exhausted the wisdom which has been crammed into it by this world, an encounter with the Holy Spirit concerning today's scripture will be necessary before it can become part of your experience. The world would like you to understand and experience sincerity because the prince of this world is wholehearted in his pursuit of you. He wants you to be zealous in your pursuit of the things of this world, and if you are sincere enough in worldly pursuits he has a hold on you and is able to control and manipulate you.

It is important to have and experience sincerity but to be genuine and zealous over the right things. Therefore, allow the Holy Spirit to develop in you a genuine zealousness for the truth of the gospel of the Lord Jesus Christ.

Paul desired those in the Corinthian church to be sincere in their desire for a pure heart so the church could be a witness to others of the cleansing power of the blood of Jesus. However, there was sin in the church because some of these Christians continued to live in worldly practices, some of which were not even practiced by many people in the world. If they were to be sincere in their pursuit of the truth, then they had to be willing to put those who were practicing gross sin out of the church, separating themselves from them. Their sincerity was now being tested and tried.

As Jesus' Church we are to come to His table after dealing with our sins, which could permeate the whole Body making it ineffective. *Purge out therefore the old leaven, that ye may be a new lump, as ye are unleavened* (1 Cor. 5:7). It requires faith to be sincere and truthful, and we must be very careful that our sincerity is in the right place and for the right cause, which is the glorious gospel of our Lord Jesus Christ.

TODAY'S GEM: *Ye are the salt of the earth: but if the salt have lost his savour, wherewith shall it be salted?* (Mt. 5:13).

Old Testament Reading Psalm 119:105-176

Meditation. *And such were some of you: but ye are washed, but ye are sanctified, but ye are justified in the name of the Lord Jesus, and by the Spirit of our God* (6:11).

I think we all like to be told something encouraging. When somebody very special expresses love for us, it is quite uplifting. Jesus knows our frailties and our need to be constantly encouraged. From time to time we need to be reminded of truths that have become ours through past experience. Our faith in Christ must continually be renewed and so must the basic truths of the Church. By partaking of the bread and the wine at the communion table we remind others and are ourselves reminded of Jesus' blood sacrifice for our sin.

Our hearts need constant exposure to the truth. They seem to be like sponges, capable of soaking up large amounts of truth, but when left sitting around idle they quickly dry out. One way to revive your heart and bring your feelings into line with the Word is to take a scripture like the one for today and meditate upon it. Let your mind dwell on it all day. Constantly remind yourself of this word until you respond to it and find it coming alive in your heart. David called this meditating on the word day and night.

It must do something for you to know that you are washed by the Blood. Jesus explained to His disciples that there was a need to wash one another's feet, only the feet because that part of their bodies was in touch with the world. In our day there is a real need to wash one another's minds because more than anything else our minds are exposed to the world. Through these writings allow me to humble myself by figuratively taking the towel and washing your minds with the Word of God that tells us *ye are washed, but ye are sanctified.* God has reached out to us and set us aside for a special purpose. If that is not enough He has entered into a legal, irrevocable covenant with us. It is a covenant that offers continual cleansing by the washing of the Word. I don't know what that personally does for you, but I certainly like feeling clean in the presence of God, and if His Word says I am washed then I am.

TODAY'S GEM: *This is my blood of the covenant, which is poured out for many for the forgiveness of sins* (Mt. 26:28, NIV).

Old Testament Reading Psalms 120-123

Meditation. *But as God hath distributed to every man, as the Lord hath called everyone, so let him walk. And so ordain I in all churches* (7:17).

I think the explanation of this scripture is clearer in the Living Bible. *But be sure in deciding these matters that you are living as God intended, marrying or not marrying in accordance with God's direction and help, and accepting whatever situation God has put you into. This is my rule for all the churches.* It is my prayer that each day as you read and meditate on these chosen texts your life will become even more devoted to Christ and seeking His direction in your life.

In writing this verse in Corinthians Paul's desire was that God's people should live as God intended. It was never God's desire for His people to take Paul's words legalistically or to force others to strictly adhere to the letter of the Word. God's intention is for us to press on into the spirit of the Word. If we will devote our time and lives to getting close to God and living in the Word daily, we can really get to know our Lord. Then the task of hearing and knowing His direction will not be so mammoth.

Spiritual harmony will never flow in the believer's life until he sets his heart upon knowing the mind of Christ and carrying out His will. First get yourself in tune with God's Spirit, suppressing the desires of your heart until you are convinced that they are God's desires. The next thing to do is rest. Do not try to make anything happen until you have come to a place of contentment and can accept your situation.

We are usually very slow to walk boldly and with faith in the circumstances into which God has put us. So press on in your fellowship with Jesus. Don't let your mind be continually searching the Word for answers. First of all seek fellowship with the Lord Jesus Christ, for the answer is in Him. Spend more time with the Lord than with counselors. Counselors enlighten us as to what our problem is, but Jesus imparts life and changes circumstances. He also fellowships with us and loves us in our deepest need. Trust Him in whatever circumstance in which God has called you to walk. Be encouraged and lifted up by Him.

TODAY'S GEM: The acceptance of God's circumstances can be like a buoy to a drowning man, for He shall bear you up.

Old Testament Reading Psalms 124-127

Meditation. *But this I say, brethren, the time is short* (7:29).

How difficult it must have been for Paul to answer their questions concerning marriage. He had some insight into what would soon befall the Christians and anticipated their pending persecution. Therefore, he cautioned the young men that if they married it might be more difficult for them to face the trials of their faith, which in this case was persecution. However, at the center of all Paul's cautioning about marriage was the fact that the time was short and the days would be difficult. Also, could they give themselves to one another in marriage and still remain devoted and faithful to the propagation of the gospel of Jesus Christ? They might become so involved with marriage that their fervor and devotion to the Lord Jesus would diminish. Paul was not saying this would always happen; however, as a single person they had more opportunity to devote their lives entirely to Jesus and preaching the gospel.

With the freedom to go or stay, live or die for the gospel's sake, their lives would be less complicated. Paul made it clear that it was not a matter of right or wrong, but in the circumstances that were to face them it might be better not to be married.

Now what about us, we who are married? We also live in a day when time is growing short. The days of our own lifespan are not very long in the light of eternity. How much serious thought have we given to serving Christ versus our marriage? In many marriages it is just that, marriage versus serving Christ. On the other hand, I can't think of anything more important in this life or more God-honoring than a sanctified marriage. However, it was never God's intention that we become so taken up with marriage, family, and home that we neglect the propagation of the gospel of Jesus Christ. Some of us would find a new exciting spirit in our lives if our marriages were more devoted to serving Jesus, especially if we were more available and willing to go when God says go and give when directed to give. The time is short; therefore, let your marriage so serve Christ that it will not keep you from His best for both of you.

TODAY'S GEM: The fullness of Christ can be found in a sanctified marriage.
Old Testament Reading Psalms 128-131

Meditation. *But if any man love God, the same is known of him* (8:3).

Paul faces another question from the Corinthian church. This time it is concerning the eating of meat that has been sacrificed to idols. By his response it sounds as though he was faced with having to answer the "know-it-all" type of Christian, the person who always has an answer and finds it very difficult to say he doesn't know. Knowledge that does not originate in the spirit and is not imparted by the Spirit of God is known today as head knowledge. This kind of knowledge can cause us to become puffed up, and pride is just one of the temptations the Christian must face.

Before Paul tackled the question of eating meat he dealt with the probable cause for the question itself, which was a lack of love. If we really love God then we will be sensitive to our brother's problem. We might enjoy a certain liberty in the Spirit that our brother cannot because of a sensitive conscience, but out of love for that brother, a love which has grown out of our love for God, we should refrain or constrain ourselves from in any way trying his conscience.

Let me give a more modern-day example. If a brother felt strongly about abstaining from liquor because it is such a tremendous social problem, we who know and love that brother should be sensitive to his conscience in this area. Out of love for him and our love for God, we should not exercise a liberty we might enjoy in fellowship with others lest we offend his good conscience and cause our brother to stumble.

Let not our knowledge of the law or the letter of the Word dictate our actions. Rather we should be guided by the love of God. Our hearts should be so sensitive to the heartbeat of God that we respond to the circumstances in His love and not just by protocol or the knowledge of what we should do. It is better to be known for our love, which comes from the love of God shed abroad in our hearts, than to be known as a man of letters or knowledge. Love does not puff up. We do not suffer the temptations of pride when the love of God motivates us. It is the result of God's grace when we solve our problems, not because we have all the answers, not because we can spell out the letter of the Word, but because our love for God overcomes the problem. *But if any man love God, the same is known of him.*

TODAY'S GEM: *For, brethren, ye have been called unto liberty; only use not liberty for an occasion to the flesh, but by love serve one another* (Gal. 5:13).

Old Testament Reading Psalms 132-135

Meditation. *Have I not seen Jesus Christ our Lord?* (9:1).

It seems as though some of the Christians in Corinth were questioning Paul's credentials, his claim to being an apostle. Perhaps they argued that only those men who had seen Christ could be apostles. If this was the reason, Paul's answer put their questions to rest as he said, *"Am I not an apostle? . . . have I not seen Jesus Christ our Lord?"*

What a wonderful testimony Paul had, for he had seen Jesus. It was a beautiful experience and one to be desired. However seeing Jesus doesn't make a man an apostle, but it certainly should inspire a person to pursue Him and should stimulate a greater desire to know Him. In my travels I meet a lot of people who have seen Christ in a great variety of ways—in visions, dreams, formed in the clouds. I have even seen a photo of His appearance in the sky over a volcano in Bali, Indonesia. Every experience of seeing Christ that a person has is special to him. I have noticed the tenderness and joy of individuals as they share the intimacy of their God-given experience. However, there is another way in which Jesus can be seen, that is by revelation. God delights to reveal the Son.

Earlier this year in Israel I was praising the Lord in fellowship with other Christians. While waiting for the moment I would be called on to speak, I had a vision of a great beam of light descending on the old city of Jerusalem. As I watched this light God explained to me what I was seeing. Through His still, small Voice, God told me that to Israel, "the apple of His eye," He would reveal by revelation the Lord Jesus Christ as messiah.

I became so excited that I wanted to be in Jerusalem when all this happened. However, after returning to the States I had an inner assurance that God would also do that very thing here. To our spirits He would reveal the Lord Jesus Christ. Our spiritual man can expect to have a revelation of Jesus of such dimension that our hearts will be so full of Christ that we will never again be the same. Our lives will be turned upside down at the fullness of Jesus dwelling within us! Every scripture will appear to speak to us of Jesus. We will see Him in everything we do. Others who have known us will be staggered at the change in our lives, and our testimony will be: "Have I not seen Jesus Christ our Lord?"

TODAY'S GEM: Run, press on that you might *know the love of Christ, which passeth knowledge, that ye might be filled with all the fulness of God* (Eph. 3:19).

Old Testament Reading Psalms 136-138

Meditation. *There hath no temptation taken you but such as is common to man: but God is faithful, who will not suffer you to be tempted above that ye are able; but will with the temptation also make a way to escape, that ye may be able to bear it* (10:13).

At times have you felt that you were the only one plagued with temptations and that nobody else had to face the persistent temptations that you have had to face? Well, I sympathize with the way you must feel; however, the Word says that such temptations are common and that others have to face the same problems.

Temptations can lead us into adventures in faith if we will commit them to the Lord Jesus Christ and trust Him. It is when we hide them from Jesus or pretend they are not there that we face the probability of failure. A very dangerous attitude is to consider yourself above such temptations, thinking you can handle them by your own strength. The moment you think you can handle temptations and are equal to them without the help of the Lord Jesus, you are ready for a fall.

There is no temptation so great that it cannot be overcome. God promises us in His Word that He is faithful to us and will not suffer us to be tempted above that which we are able to bear. So we are left without an excuse before God for our failures. Failure in temptations is failure to trust in the Lord Jesus Christ and His Word. He has promised to lead us and to show us a way out of our temptations. Fellowship with Jesus in the midst of our temptations assures us of forbearance and ultimate deliverance. He cannot deny Himself or make void His Word. Take the Lord as a partner into your temptations; make room for the Holy Spirit to move, and you will see the power of God working in your life as He gives you victory after victory. Temptation does not need to lead to sin. On the contrary, it can give you a wonderful experience of grace, enabling you even more to understand the mighty workings of the grace of God.

Today's word can be full of experience and victory for you. Memorize and meditate upon it, but above all use it.

TODAY'S GEM: *The Lord knoweth how to deliver the godly out of temptations* (2 Pet. 2:9).
Old Testament Reading Psalms 139-141

Meditation. *Whether therefore ye eat, or drink, or whatsoever ye do, do all to the glory of God* (10:31).

Some years ago my wife and I had ample opportunity to walk in this scripture. We left a secure ministry position with a salary to move into an old, Catholic seminary with about twenty souls, or should I say about twenty mouths to feed. Six of them were members of our own family. We had two dollars and some silver and a lot of faith but no guaranteed support or provision. Most of the people were not able to work at that particular time and had a lot of special needs. Hurting and confused, they needed an opportunity to establish a relationship of faith and trust with Jesus before going out to face the world that had almost destroyed them.

We lacked the financial resources to feed this very large family; however, in chapter eleven of Luke we found that God was even interested in providing fish, eggs, and bread for His children. So from then on we made our eating habits an earnest matter of prayer. We had a little saying, "If you can't pray you can't eat." Space does not permit me to share all the endless miracles of God's provision during this period of our lives. Our daily needs were written on a blackboard. It looked like a shopping list. Each person in the community would pray for those items. As they appeared in the community, they were stacked on the "blessings table" where everybody could see and praise God for His provision. Usually some visitor would bring them, never knowing that God was making them an answer to prayer.

Can you appreciate what every mealtime was like? Every item on the table represented a miracle. Nobody complained about the food. Grace was sung, and it was a time of praise. Every mouthful was eaten to the glory of God. God had allowed me to take a social need and minister to the street scene of prostitutes, junkies, and alcoholics. All of these people who were members of our community were born again and convinced that God provided every mouthful they ate (which He did). As they went to Him with a variety of requests, they eventually saw the answer sitting on the blessings table. They gave thanks to God knowing they were living in a miracle and that God was being glorified. How empty our Christian life becomes when we lack the motivation or the means to glorify God. Faith glorifies Him, so *whatsoever ye do, do all to the glory of God.*

TODAY'S GEM: *Now faith is the substance of things hoped for, the evidence of things not seen* (Heb. 11:1).
Old Testament Reading Psalms 142-144

AUGUST **31**   1 Corinthians 11:1-15

Meditation. *But I would have you know, that the head of every man is Christ; and the head of the woman is the man; and the head of Christ is God* (11:3).

Well, men, how do you feel about this verse? Paul reminds us that God made man and woman in His image, and He made woman for man as a helpmate. He made us men responsible for the physical and spiritual wellbeing of our women. He even likened our responsibility to the relationship that the Son has with the Father. A perfectly healthy body responds to the instructions of the head in a harmonious manner. The hand doesn't refuse directions from the head and say, "Give them to the foot." Can you imagine the foot trying to scratch the ear? From the day the body is formed its members function in harmony with the head.

I think we can follow this example through a little further and say that from the day we are born again we are to flow in harmony with the Head, which is Christ. We should be available to respond to every desire, every direction the Head gives us. If we are to know how to love our wives, then we must open our lives to the love of Christ and imitate or emulate Him. His generous, long-suffering dealings with us should be our example of the way to treat our wives.

We are the head of our wives but not to lord some authority over them. Our duty is to direct their actions. They are to be able to respond to us like the hand does to the head. If they can't and the whole relationship is awkward, it could be that our relationship with the Head—Christ—is awkward and we have not learned to flow with Him.

What a wonderful, exciting faith experience we have right here in the Scriptures. The same relationship and fellowship that the Son has with the Father we are meant to have with the Son. Can you get hold of that? With Jesus we are to enjoy the quality of life He has with the Father. Then when the life in the Son is flowing, we, in turn, are to take that life that is like a generator. That heavenly life is generated to flow from the Father to the Son, from the Son to man and from man to woman. This does not mean that women are totally dependent on the male for their life in Christ. Oh no, this life is a mystery, and I write of only one aspect of it, but it is a dimension of life where we need each other if it is to be developed to its fullest.

TODAY'S GEM: There is security and safety for the believer in divine authority and order. It is in this order that the Life flows.

Old Testament Reading Psalms 145-147

Meditation. *For I have received of the Lord that which also I delivered unto you* (11:23).

Paul found it necessary to correct the Corinthian Christians about the way in which they were coming to the Lord's table. Although Paul could not claim to have been with Jesus in that upper room the evening the Passover was celebrated, he could say that he had received from the Lord that which he had also passed on to these Christians.

As a young Christian I can remember the variety of feelings I had concerning the communion service. There were times when I saw the terrible price Jesus had paid, and, trembling, I would fight back the tears of sorrow when I took the cup. On other occasions I was overwhelmed with joy at the deliverance and cleansing that was mine as a result of the shed Blood and was inwardly excited, wanting to shout out hallelujah!

After the traditional Passover meal Jesus took the cup of redemption from the table, broke bread, looked at His disciples, and made a commitment to them. This commitment was that Jesus himself would be the perfect sacrifice for their sin. For many generations the Jews had been practicing the traditional Passover feast in remembrance of the blood of the lamb that had delivered them from the bitterness and bondage they had endured. However, now the Lamb of God stood in their midst and committed Himself—His body and blood—to be a sacrifice **once for all**. Then from generation to generation those who believed could gather around a table as often as they liked and be reminded of Jesus' commitment (His perfect sacrifice) and could put their faith in the shed blood of the Lord Jesus Christ. In that upper room Jesus made a commitment to offer His blood as their deliverance from the bondage of sin, to redeem them from its consequences and its pollution, and to reconcile them to the Father so they could be acceptable in the Beloved.

When Jesus left that upper room He set His course for the cross, as He immediately began walking in the commitment which He had made. Jesus then went to the garden, praying His way to victory that He could walk in what He had promised. The strength Jesus received from that prayer meeting in the garden took Him all the way to the cross to fulfill that commitment. Today be lifted up in your spirit, my Christian friend, because Jesus has totally committed Himself to your need and fulfilled His promise. So rejoice and live in that which you cannot change but can receive as your own.

TODAY'S GEM: The final sacrifice has been offered. We are sanctified through the offering of the body of Jesus Christ once for all (Heb. 10:10).

Old Testament Reading Psalms 148-150

Meditation. *But the manifestation of the Spirit is given to every man to profit withal* (12:7).

When Jesus was with His disciples the life of the Holy Spirit dwelling within Him was manifested. This fullness of the Spirit was received at the time of His baptism when John the Baptist saw God's Holy Spirit descend upon Jesus in the form of a dove. From that day on He began to manifest the indwelling life of the Spirit. Those signs of turning water into wine, healing the sick, raising the dead, walking on the water, and miraculously feeding a multitude of 5,000 were supernatural in nature.

Jesus displayed great wisdom that He claimed was not His and also disclaimed the miracles He performed as being initiated by Him. Jesus openly confessed that of himself He could do nothing, and when others showed fear He remained calm. Jesus forgave His persecutors, loved His enemies, wept over those who rejected Him, and was faithful to the call of God upon His life, even to the point of presenting His body as a perfect sacrifice for our sin. All of these were manifestations of the Spirit so that all might profit.

When Jesus finally ascended to be with the Father and sit at His right hand, He assured the disciples that the promised Holy Spirit would come to lead them into all truth, to reveal the things of Christ to them, and to glorify Jesus through the many manifestations of the Spirit.

In this chapter Paul was writing to the Corinthian church so they might not be ignorant of the many spiritual gifts and would know the variety of ways the Holy Spirit was to make himself known in their midst. *Now there are diversities of gifts, but the same Spirit. And there are differences of administrations, but the same Lord* (vv. 4-5). All of these are manifestations of the one Holy Spirit: the word of wisdom, word of knowledge, gifts of healing, working of miracles, prophecy, discerning of spirits, divers kinds of tongues, and interpretation of tongues. The Holy Spirit empowers us to flow together as one Body in harmony and love so that each member and every gift is so beautifully displayed in the Body that the life of Christ and the fullness of that life in all its glory will be seen. We will perform miracles and experience wisdom, knowledge, and power in the Holy Spirit. This should all result in the glorification of Jesus. So let the manifestation of the Holy Spirit flow through each of us today to profit every man.

TODAY'S GEM: Lord, make me a willing vessel so the Body of Christ can be made whole. *For the body is not one member, but many* (1 Cor. 12:14).

Old Testament Reading Proverbs 1-2

SEPTEMBER 3   1 Corinthians 13

Meditation. *Charity* [love] *never faileth* (13:8).

The thing that never fails to excite me about my pursuit of God is that there is always more. Meeting God daily in the closet is very satisfying; however, on some particular occasions God also blesses me in some special way and illuminates my understanding. After living on that for days, the realization that there is always more will slip into my mind and down into my heart, whetting my appetite for more of God. I am sure this must also be your experience.

In today's reading Paul reminded the Corinthians of the wonderful manifestations of the Holy Spirit in the Body of Christ. He urged them to earnestly covet these gifts, which are so exciting, edifying, and satisfy our desire to glorify Jesus. Paul then went on with his letter, saying there's more, much more of God. After these wonderful manifestations of the indwelling Holy Spirit, Paul said there is still more!

What could there be that is greater than these signs and wonders? "Love," Paul said. Even if you have successfully given yourself to the Holy Spirit, enabling Him to manifest Himself in and through you, if love does not abound, these gifts will seem so empty. Life in the Spirit can be of no profit to the Body of Christ without love. If these gifts are to glorify Jesus and if you desire to enter into a more excellent way, then the answer is to love one another as Jesus has loved you. If you covet the gift of speaking in tongues, then you must also covet the ability, by grace, to speak in love.

Do you desire the gifts of wisdom or knowledge? Then earnestly desire the gift of love so your wisdom and knowledge will be tempered with love and compassion. What will it profit a man if he gives his life for the gospel's sake if he does not know or manifest love? It certainly will not benefit the Body of Christ. If you are desperately in need of an answer, but wisdom and knowledge seem to fail and you don't know which way to turn, there might be the feeling that the gifts of the Spirit have let you down. However, love does not fail us, so allow the love of God that passeth all understanding to manifest itself in your heart. When a miracle can't change the life of a sinner and the convicting power of the Holy Spirit seems to be of no effect, love will not fail. Earnestly covet the spiritual gifts, but temper them with the greatest of gifts, which is love.

TODAY'S GEM: *Though I speak with the tongues of men and of angels, and have not charity, I am become as sounding brass, or a tinkling cymbal* (1 Cor. 13:1).

Old Testament Reading Proverbs 3-4

Meditation. *Follow after charity, and desire spiritual gifts* (14:1).

Let me present you with the rendering of this text from the Amplified Bible (AMPC). *Eagerly pursue and seek to acquire [this] love [make it your aim, your great quest]; and earnestly desire and cultivate the spiritual endowments (gifts).* As a baby Christian I can remember reading words such as these and wondering how to eagerly pursue what God wanted. To whom do we go? Who has the words of eternal life? The Lord Jesus Christ of course.

In my early days as a Christian there was no one to direct me to someone's teaching or book about love. I read the Word of God, and in my heart knew there was a depth of understanding and an experience that the Word was directing me to obtain, but I couldn't really relate to it. For that reason I took my requests to the prayer closet. Scriptures such as these that have a clear command became my basis for fellowship with the Holy Spirit in and out of the closet as I sought to understand and experience them. As this scripture pressed itself upon my heart I spent hours in fellowship with Jesus through the Holy Spirit, asking God what it meant to eagerly pursue, seek, or acquire this gift. How was I to lay hold of that love which is shed abroad in our hearts by the Holy Ghost? How was I to manifest that love? The more earnest and intense my pursuit, the further I seemed to be from the truth.

One day, while counseling a young married lady with my senior pastor, I became aware of a change in my voice. It was as though I was listening to someone else speaking. There was a change of heart on my part as I experienced fatherly compassion for this baby Christian. The presence of a supernatural love was overwhelming as I learned how important it is in our pursuit of love to be able to give it. As we open our hearts to the Holy Spirit, making ourselves available to the unlovely, overcoming our fears, and are willing to extend ourselves in uncomfortable areas of our lives, the Holy Spirit can teach us. We learn to recognize love as it flows from the very heart of the Father through us to the one to be loved.

Love is at its best when given to others. The love can flow after we have exhausted our ability to show tenderness and have turned to the Lord, confessing our own inability, reaching out to Him to become a channel of His blessing. Let it be the pursuit of a lifetime to acquire the love of Jesus, that it might be shed abroad in our hearts by the Holy Spirit.

TODAY'S GEM: *This is my commandment, That ye love one another, as I have loved you* (Jn. 15:12).

Old Testament Reading Proverbs 5-6

Meditation. *And thus are the secrets of his heart made manifest; and so falling down on his face he will worship God, and report that God is in you of a truth* (14:25).

God's best for us is that we fellowship with one another and allow the Holy Spirit to speak through individual members of His Body. One may exercise the gift of wisdom and another the gift of knowledge, but all should learn to discern the voice of God so that there is an inner witness to the truth being professed. Some groups, you may call them churches or fellowships, have developed this type of meeting about which Paul is writing to the Corinthians. It was a type of worship where there was absolute liberty for people to speak. The praise came forth from the people. Someone would lead out in reading a word or singing a song. A variety of things happened; however, there was order and usually the discipline of an eldership. When the Spirit flows even the unbeliever can recognize the presence of God. The result can be some pretty deep and real searching of the heart.

This type of gathering together of believers can be your experience when you meet with some like-minded Christians who also want to experience the presence of the Holy Spirit and enjoy the manifestation of the Spirit of God in their midst. Every Christian should have the opportunity to participate in this type of gathering because it can add a great deal to our spiritual growth. The word that touched my heart and can best be developed in this sort of fellowship is that God was truly seen in them. My fondest desire is that God be seen in me. Isn't that your wish also? What glorifies Jesus more to the unbeliever than the obvious presence of God in our meetings and in the life of the individual Christian?

The desire of God's heart is to manifest His presence in and through you. He wants and is willing to use you. It may take a little patience and perseverance on your part. You may have to seek to acquire this experience and earnestly want it, but I can assure you that God desires to be real in your life. He wants you to develop a fellowship with the Holy Spirit. The more open you are and the more willing to participate in a manifestation of the Spirit, the more likely it is that you will experience and know the inner joy of God's presence in you, speaking through you and glorifying the Lord Jesus Christ in your life.

TODAY'S GEM: Be adventuresome and release your faith that God might be seen in you. *Quench not the Spirit* (1 Thess. 5:19).

Old Testament Reading Proverbs 7-8

Meditation. *But now is Christ risen from the dead, and become the firstfruits of them that slept* (15:20).

To have the Holy Spirit convict you of sin is a tremendous experience, especially when you discover for the first time the provision that has been made for the convicted sinner—the blood of Jesus Christ that cleanses us from all sin. We probably feel there will never be a greater experience in our lives or that we will never participate in a greater miracle than to be born again. We really were lost, hopelessly lost. There was no way to come to the Father except to repent of our sin and be born again. As we seek understanding through the Word of God, it dawns on us that it will take eternity to understand the magnitude of this miracle of grace. The angels in heaven will never understand what bondage to sin means, but we do.

As our lives change and a relationship with the Lord Jesus Christ is developed, the magnitude of this truth becomes the center of our lives. Everything revolves around the cross of Jesus Christ because it affects every aspect of our lives. The lifespan of our mortal bodies is not long enough for us to fully appreciate or take in all this. Just when we think we are coming to some understanding and fulfillment, the Holy Spirit introduces another truth to us. If the blood of Jesus Christ cleanses believers from all sin and reconciles us to the Father, then His triumph over death and the grave by resurrection puts us right into the presence of God, into the very Holy of Holies. There is nothing hidden. We are to put the cross behind and enter into a whole new experience with God.

This was first of all made possible by the blood of Jesus and secondly by Jesus going before the believer to take His place on the right hand of the Father. Christ has risen from the dead, and we were resurrected with Him. He was our prototype, the firstfruit. The position that is Jesus' because of His resurrection is also ours. The wall between God and us (the curtain separating us from the Holy of Holies) has been torn down. Jesus has saved, cleansed and reconciled all believers so we can enter into a glorious, eternal relationship with the Father that physical death cannot interrupt. The Captain of our faith leads each Christian into an experience of resurrection power that triumphs right now.

Discover for yourself not only what Jesus has saved you from but also what He has saved you to. Now is Christ risen from the dead to live and to live in heavenly power and authority so that where He is we might be also.

TODAY'S GEM: Our redemption is more than freedom from the bondage of sin. We can now enter into the Holy of Holies, which is the presence of God Himself, and are joint heirs with the Son of God.

Old Testament Reading Proverbs 9-10

SEPTEMBER 7   1 Corinthians 15:33-58

Meditation. *But thanks be to God, which giveth us the victory through our Lord Jesus Christ* (15:57).

To keep this particular scripture in context, let me remind you that Paul was assuring the Corinthian Christians that complete victory over death comes through our Lord Jesus Christ. To be a Christian at that particular time in the history of the Church meant that many would be called on to face imprisonment, torture, and death for their faith. Persecution lay ahead of them, and dying for Christ must have been as much a reality as living for Him. Their gospel embraced more than forgiveness for sin; therefore, Paul exhorted them to live the life now. They were called to live with a concept of immortality; eternity was to be real to them. Their fellowship with God and with one another, the work of propagating the gospel, every decision and act had some bearing on eternity. Therefore, they were to live and think beyond what their lives could be in their mortal bodies. Paul's words, however, are not just for those early Christians. We too should live with this same realization that we do not live as the unsaved man whose life has no bearing on eternity. Our lives have meaning and purpose because each action and decision has meaning and fulfillment in the kingdom of God.

To the Corinthians Paul made it plain that they were to give their mortal bodies for Christ's sake. Should they face death trusting in the resurrection power of the Lord Jesus Christ, they would have victory. This would not just be a victory over the fear of death or its suffering, but over death itself when they would put on bodies of immortality. There is no power on earth or in principalities that can hold us in the grave. Our assurance is more than a promise; it is a fact. Has not the Lord Jesus Christ himself triumphed over the grave? Death or hell itself could not hold Him. Paul wasn't talking about victory we might have. He was spelling out a victory that is already ours as we too live our lives knowing they have eternal significance.

It is not as if we have to follow Jesus into death by dying, going to hell, being resurrected, and ascending into heaven, for He has already accomplished this. He died, was buried, entered into hell, and overcame death, breaking the hold that Satan had on us. We will never experience death as it was up until the day of Christ's victory. For us who are in Christ He has overcome on our behalf, and we enter into all the benefits of having the Lord Jesus Christ as our Lord and Savior. Eternal life is ours right now! We have eternal life, which is to be lived right now with power and victory! If Jesus is our savior now, He will be our savior at death, which then will be just a simple entering into the presence of the Lord.

TODAY'S GEM: Death cannot hold the Christian, not in this life nor in the grave. *Who is he that overcometh the world, but he that believeth that Jesus is the Son of God?* (1 Jn. 5:5).

Old Testament Reading Proverbs 11-12

SEPTEMBER **8**   Corinthians 16

Meditation. *Be on your guard; stand firm in the faith; be men of courage; be strong. Do everything in love* (16:13-14, NIV).

Paul was cautioning the believers to keep their eyes open for spiritual danger. It is good for us to be reminded to watch and pray. Since the day of Adam, Satan has sought to rob man of eternal fellowship with God. Since the day you defected from his kingdom into the kingdom of God, Satan has tried to get you right back into bondage to sin every opportunity you have given him.

Until you were born again, your lifestyle was soul dominated. The spirit of this world and the old carnal nature had their own way. The Holy Spirit of God, who has now come to take up residence in our hearts, is an intruder and a conqueror of that old nature. He desires to set up a government within our hearts; however, it is a government that will never violate our free will. The Holy Spirit appeals to our spiritual understanding and helps us to come to a place of maturity where our desire is to do the Father's will and seek His indwelling Spirit for help. Of course the old nature will be resentful, and, given the least opportunity by us, will do everything in its power to again bring us into bondage to sin. But do not let Satan lie to you. He doesn't have that power. Oh, he is crafty and subtle and will try to convince you that he does, but he only has the power in your life that you give him.

Paul's warning is that we are to be watchful for spiritual dangers, standing true to the Lord. If you seek the Holy Spirit to help you walk in the Word so you can be faithful, you are not likely to fall. Let godly loyalty motivate you. Be strong in the face of temptation and demonstrate the supernatural strength of the Holy Spirit that indwells you and is willing to give you the victory. All that needs to be done is to communicate your honest heart desires to Him. Temper every victory with love. You can afford to be generous to those who misuse you *because greater is he that is in you, than he that is in the world* (1 Jn. 4:4).

How sad it is when immaturity strikes out at us, but we can afford to respond with love. When we are despised, defamed, and our reputation destroyed, whatever we do it is to be done with kindness and love. What a wonderful adventure! Only by the grace of God and by faith can we walk in this way. So overcome, for the victory is yours! The power dwelling within you is awaiting your good pleasure to glorify Jesus; therefore, watch and pray. Stand fast in the faith.

TODAY'S GEM: Now that you have defected from the slavery of the world, your passport to heaven is Jesus Christ.

OLD TEST AMENT READING Proverbs 13-14

Meditation. *For our rejoicing is this, the testimony of our conscience, that in simplicity and godly sincerity, not with fleshly wisdom but by the grace of God, we have had our conversation in the world, and more abundantly to you-ward* (1:12).

In today's reading Paul touched upon some deep gospel truths. Jesus himself leaves our minds reeling at the depth and profoundness of the gospel. It is quite beyond the natural mind to fathom, but in the everyday living of these truths it is meant to be simple. Simplicity and godly sincerity are the keys to the Christian life. How do we come into simplicity without complicating everything with our ifs and buts and without having everything figured out for us? Jesus spoke of the answer when He said that we should receive the kingdom of God as a little child. Our faith is to be childlike, not childish, simply trusting Jesus in every area of our lives, trusting Him to supply the answers when we need them, and being willing to live quietly at the pace He sets for us.

To be taught or to learn does not mean just storing knowledge into a computer-like mind. If we approached a motorcar in the same manner in which some people approach the Bible, our lives would be empty, and we would do a lot of walking on our own. Imagine going to classes and being so knowledgeable about a motorcar that thousands of people desire your teaching. Wouldn't it be ridiculous if you had never even learned to drive? That may not be a very good illustration; however, many Christians fill their minds with knowledge about the Christian life but fail to walk in the simplicity of it, making very little effort to put their knowledge into practice. They testify to others about what they know but rarely testify about what Jesus is working out between them and Him in their everyday experience. They are reluctant to give the best time of the day, which for most people is the early morning hour, to getting to know God. Every member of the Godhead—Father, Son and Holy Ghost—is patiently waiting to know you and live out their lives in and through you.

TODAY'S GEM: The greatest asset to living the Christian life is simple, childlike faith.

Old Testament Reading Proverbs 15-16

Meditation. *Now thanks be to God who always leads us in triumph in Christ, and through us diffuses the fragrance of His knowledge in every place* (2:14, NKJV).

Jesus has performed a miracle in our lives. From the day of Adam to the coming of the Lord Jesus Christ, Satan, who has set up his spiritual kingdom on earth, has reigned and ruled men. He has held them in bondage to all sorts of things, but now in your life and mine Jesus has triumphed. He has overcome the authority of the prince of this world and has set us free. This is our testimony and the gospel which we have to preach. Each one of us has a story, a good report that we can bring of once being bound to sin and death, but now we are free.

In returning to some of the places I frequented when I was in the world and part of it, I can actually smell death. It's a sordid, dry, empty smell. Everything looks unreal. The relationships are phony and the conversations meaningless. The people appear happy but empty, ignorant of what the prince of this world has in store for them. It is like watching a fish nibbling at a delicious bait. The hook is still hidden in the bait, but it won't be long before that fish, who is blissfully nibbling away to satisfy its appetite, will be on that hidden hook, struggling for its very life. It nibbles away ignorant of the death that stalks it, insensitive to its smell until it is too late.

Now that Christ has the victory we have a testimony that Jesus has triumphed over sin that held us in bondage. He has triumphed over death and introduced us to eternal life. Now there is the fragrance of freedom in our lives. There is the sweet savor of the presence of the indwelling Christ.

The perfect work of grace that has been performed in our lives has the very aroma of heaven about it. When we testify to others, even those who are ignorant of the prince of this world and to the sentence of death on their lives, they are not insensitive to the fragrance of the life of Christ dwelling within us. They are not blind to the freedom we enjoy. A little of the aroma of heaven can be experienced by them if we will share the gospel, our salvation experience and day-by-day fellowship with the indwelling Christ, who, as the Word says, causes us to triumph.

Power is what you have to share with others. Your experience of the gospel and your deliverance through Christ is the most powerful message in the world. All must submit so that Christ might triumph and spread the fragrance of the knowledge of Himself through us.

TODAY'S GEM: Christians are God's answer to pollution. We are to be a breath of fresh air as we spread the aroma of Christ, which is the fragrance of life.

Old Testament Reading Proverbs 17-18

Meditation. *Now the Lord is the Spirit: and where the Spirit of the Lord is, there is liberty* (3:17).

In verse six of this chapter Paul claimed that God made him a minister of the New Covenant, *not of the letter, but of the spirit: for the letter killeth, but the spirit giveth life.* Of all people Paul understood the emptiness and lifelessness of the letter of the law. It breeds a form of godliness, an outwardly religious appearance of the right things done at the right time and saying all the right things, but there is no manifestation of the life of the Spirit. This appearance of godliness surrounds itself with contention for protection. It fears being exposed and becomes bondage to the believer. However, Paul said that *where the Spirit of the Lord is, there is liberty.*

The Scriptures tell us that the ministry of the law brought death, but the ministry of the Spirit brings righteousness. Paul desired that the believer receive the Spirit of the Word. We are to be letters from Christ with His Word written on the tables of our hearts. The amount of freedom we have in God is measured by how much we allow His Spirit to manifest Himself in and through us each day. Sad to say, there are Christians who receive the Word into their heads but close their hearts and lives to it. Instead of allowing God the freedom to make it alive and real in their everyday experience they get a fixation about some truth and present it in all its legalities until it brings the unwary into bondage.

Paul grew up in bondage to the law. He knew how empty and futile it could be. Even when the law was given to Moses, the glory of it, which was the presence of the Lawgiver himself (God), did not remain. It faded simply because the law became the letter and not life. Now Paul was proclaiming a New Covenant truth and experience where God gives himself, and the Messiah and the Word become one. Paul is saying that we should receive the Word and the Lord of the Word, letting the written word and its Author fill our lives and be Lord. He will not bring you into legalistic bondage to Himself or to His Word. Where Jesus reigns in our hearts there is complete liberty. *If the Son therefore shall make you free, ye shall be free indeed* (Jn. 8:36).

The Word nourishes and becomes our joy and adventure to experience being led by the Spirit of God, which is the Spirit of the Word. To be a living expression of the Word should be our greatest desire. Surely there is a greater glory than Moses experienced under the letter of the law. We should seek that glory so the Lord of the Spirit of the Word would be seen in us, and we would be living letters from Christ.

TODAY'S GEM: Let me be a living, breathing epistle of the Word of God, read of men as an expression of Christ, liberated from the letter of the law.

Old Testament Reading Proverbs 19-20

Meditation. *But we have this treasure in earthen vessels, that the excellency of the power may be of God, and not of us* (4:7).

Paul said that the truth is hidden from those that are lost because the god of this world has blinded the eyes of the unbeliever who will not receive the Lord Jesus Christ as their messiah. Rejection of Christ has hidden the light of the gospel so that the unbeliever lives in spiritual darkness. However, the eyes of those who receive Him are opened to the truth. Christ invades their lives, dwelling within them in all His fullness, until the light of the gospel is seen in them. *For God, who commanded the light to shine out of darkness, hath shined in our hearts, to give the light of the knowledge of the glory of God in the face of Jesus Christ* (4:6).

We are like an earthen vessel which of itself has no great strength but is strong enough to contain the water or wine for which it was made. The vessel was not desired for itself or its beauty. Whatever the earthen vessel held, its real value was in its contents. Paul said that we are like earthen vessels, but we have in us the excellency of the power of God. Of ourselves we can do nothing, but we can do all things through Christ who strengthens us (Phil. 4:13). It is this excellency, the indwelling presence of Christ, that is to be seen by others to open their eyes and remove spiritual blindness.

We are vessels of honor to present the glorious light of Christ to a world of darkness. We are to be full and remain full of the glorious presence of Jesus, overflowing to the hungry and thirsty. We are to fill our vessels daily from the well of salvation. These vessels are to serve our fellowman by living the gospel of Jesus Christ. We have little or no ornamental value in the kingdom of God. The contents of our earthen vessels are what bring light in the midst of darkness and life in the midst of death. We can fill the emptiness of this world with the treasure from God, which is His all-surpassing power.

TODAY'S GEM: The lamp can only shine forth with as much power or light as it contains, so fill your earthen vessel with the excellency of His power.

Old Testament Reading Proverbs 21-22

SEPTEMBER **13** 2 Corinthians 5

Meditation. *Therefore if any man be in Christ, he is a new creature: old things are passed away; behold, all things are become new* (5:17).

Bondages, old habits and those things inconsistent with the kingdom of God cannot survive in the man that is in Christ. When the Holy Spirit calls us by faith to put those things aside, there will be conflict and spiritual opposition. We cannot have them and fellowship with the Holy Spirit in Christ. *If any man be in Christ, he is a new creature: old things are passed away.*

The Bible does not say man is slowly becoming a new creature but that he is already new in Christ. He may be just an infant needing to grow and mature and may even try to function as in the past, doing the things he did before, but now they will seem strange and foreign to his new nature. He may even refuse to lay aside the old nature and encourage it to take over his life again, and if this happens the growth of the new baby creation will be stunted. However, he still has to live with the memory and presence of that new creature. One day he must stand before the brethren and the Lord Jesus Christ to be examined and judged for what he did with that new, God-given nature.

Do not let this cause you to worry, my friend, but be assured that the new creature that you have become when your place in Christ was found is not easily overcome and has great stamina. The words "give up" are not even in its vocabulary, and it has endurance that will take you to eternity. Feed on the Word and walk in obedience to it, then watch your new nature overcome every bondage, habit, and inconsistency with the kingdom of God. All those old things will pass away, and all things will become new. Have faith in your new indwelling creature, and be confident *that he which hath begun a good work in you will perform it until the day of Jesus Christ* (Phil. 1:6). Know that no man, principality or power can put down what God has brought to life and hidden in Christ. Submit yourself to this new nature, no longer living in bondage to what you once were.

The lifeline has been severed; the old self is dead. You are now free to develop a whole new life in Christ Jesus.

TODAY'S GEM: Put on your wedding garment, which is the Lord Jesus Christ, for *as Christ was raised up from the dead by the glory of the Father, even so we also should walk in newness of life* (Rom. 6:4).

Old Testament Reading Proverbs 23-24

Meditation. *For ye are the temple of the living God; as God hath said, I will dwell in them, and walk in them; and I will be their God, and they shall be my people* (6:16).

Our bodies are actually temples of the living God! Jesus left us in no doubt as to where the kingdom of God is when He said that it is within us. *Ye also, as lively stones, are built up a spiritual house* (1 Pet. 2:5).

I am certain there have been times in your experience when God seemed to be so far away. At a time like that the presence of God is sometimes remote and completely out of our reach. Heaven is still far away, but it's a place, even though it is beyond our experience while we remain in these mortal bodies. Heaven is an actual place God reigns and rules and where angels come and go between heaven and earth. It is full of the glory of the Son, where endless praise and worship is practiced by the redeemed. In heaven love abounds, and there are no tears or pain.

Jesus taught His disciples to pray that God's kingdom would come on earth as it is in heaven, and He brought that Kingdom to earth, planting it in the hearts of men. The very Spirit of God that moved across the waters and brought the earth into being as we know it has come to dwell in the hearts of men and women. That same Spirit that knows the very heart of the Father lives in our hearts today.

Paul reminded the Corinthian Christians that the Holy Spirit's dwelling place was within them and that their bodies were holy. They were temples in which the very Spirit of God resided. Now the kingdom of God dwells within each of us, and we are caretakers or guardians of God's temple, which is now on earth as it is in heaven, just as Jesus told His disciples to pray.

By taking seriously this scripture of God's promise to dwell within us, walk with us and be our God so we can be His people, a beautiful opportunity is opened for a wonderful faith adventure without even going beyond the doors of our homes. Just imagine how you could change and develop as God is given more and more liberty in your life. As much as you invite God to take that liberty, that's how much He resides in and walks with you. Just think what use God could make of your life if you continually presented it to Him and encouraged Him to use it. I imagine that you would have to be very careful what you did with His temple and to what you exposed it so that in no way would He who resides in you be offended. However, what is the value of this teaching if you don't step out in faith and explore the possibilities of this text?

TODAY'S GEM: God walks the earth in each one of us. *Him that overcometh will I make a pillar in the temple of my God* (Rev. 3:12).

Old Testament Reading Proverbs 25-27

Meditation. *Having therefore these promises, dearly beloved, let us cleanse ourselves from all filthiness of the flesh and spirit, perfecting holiness in the fear of God* (7:1).

In the previous three verses Paul, writing under the inspiration of the Holy Spirit, reminds his followers of God's promise to dwell in and walk with them, to be their God and make them His people. God tells us to come out from those things that are unclean, and He will receive us. He promises to be a Father to us and that we will be His sons and daughters.

The text we are to meditate upon today is a reminder of these promises. A whole new world, which this world does not know, beckons as God reaches out to us by His Holy Spirit. Through His Word God assures His followers of a dimension of life, a relationship with Him that is not just an experience for the moment but a Father-and-son (daughter) relationship that is eternal. It is full of security and promise because God does not know how to withhold any good thing from those He calls sons and daughters.

There are things in this world, things in our flesh and spirits, from which we need to be removed. They have no place in God. If we are to enter into all that God promises, these things are to be left in the world where they belong, and we are to come out from among them. How can such overtures from the Holy Spirit be resisted? His calling is always with us.

What we are dealing with is not the language of an ideology or a set of beliefs. God is not reaching out to us because He counts converts or has some special need for man to believe in Him. This is the language of the One who loves us even when we had turned away from Him, even when we ignored His calling and when we were still in our trespasses and sin. He loved us when, according to our standards, He should have given up on us.

Through the apostle Paul God has said that our nature is holiness and that we are to cleanse and separate ourselves. God said, "Turn away from all uncleanness and enter into what I am." Friends, we don't become holy without getting God. We are only holy when we enter into what He is. The promise of holiness is set before you, so come out from uncleanness and enter into the spirit and nature of your heavenly Father. Put on the Family character. Enter into the Family name, and let its life-cleansing Blood flow. Enjoy that characteristic by which we are known, that is, His holiness.

TODAY'S GEM: *Ye shall be holy: for I the LORD your God am holy* (Lev. 19:2).

Old Testament Reading Proverbs 28-29

Meditation. *For ye know the grace of our Lord Jesus Christ, that, though he was rich, yet for your sakes he became poor, that ye through his poverty might be rich* (8:9).

This is a scripture to meditate on until God adds to your understanding of it. There is no limit to the degree or depth of understanding and the wealth that is ours in Christ Jesus. In the light of this eternal wealth that we inherit in Christ we cease to think about what we might have given up to be a Christian. The natural man fails to see or understand this wealth. He sees a stable but has no spirit or feeling for the joy that broke forth in heaven. He is insensitive to the plans and preparation of centuries that brought about this event and has no ear for the heavenly choir of angelic beings that heralded this birth. No prince or king on earth has ever been born in the midst of such luxury and wealth as Jesus possesses. This birth affected the world more than any other single event since the day of Adam. As His presence made the stable a heavenly palace, kings bowed before Him with eyes only for the God who had become flesh.

Think for a moment of the baptisms you have attended. Did you ever hear a voice from heaven speaking directly of this event, or did you see the Holy Spirit descend like a dove? After Jesus' baptism, which was heralded by God, Satan soon appeared on the scene. He offered to set Jesus up as a prince over the whole earth, and he had the power to do this; however, his offer conflicted with God's purpose and plans for His Son. Since Jesus' Father owns the cattle on a thousand hills, He was going to set His Son up in His own good time anyway. Every time Jesus spoke with His Father, the wealth of heaven, which is His inheritance, just came tumbling out. It could not be hidden and was supernatural. Sickness had to bow before His wealth. Death could not even separate Him from His inheritance. Everywhere Jesus went or spoke a quality of life that was eternal was manifested and given away freely to all who would believe.

Yes, Jesus left the luxuries of heaven, and for our sakes He suffered rejection, humiliation, cowardly abuse, and finally the most vile of deaths imaginable. However, Jesus could afford to suffer all of this because in His rejection, suffering and death He released to the heirs of the Kingdom all the quality of life He himself displayed. This world's wealth did nothing for Jesus because He had a wealth to share with us that this world cannot give. Christian, there is no natural poverty in this world that can separate us, the heirs of the Kingdom, from the wealth that is ours in Christ Jesus.

TODAY'S GEM: Because Jesus was made poor, we are rich, and because He died we live to inherit the Kingdom.

Old Testament Reading Proverbs 30-31

Meditation. *Every man according as he purposeth in his heart, so let him give; not grudgingly, or of necessity: for God loveth a cheerful giver* (9:7).

When the natural man gives from his resources in the world or when the Christian gives out of his worldly resources, he is limited in his giving, and his worldly or natural resources decrease. When we give that which the Father has given us there is no limit to our heavenly resources, nor do they diminish. When the Word tells us that it is more blessed to give than to receive it implies a necessity on our part to give if we are to build into our lives the more blessed experience.

We can afford to be generous with the wealth of the kingdom of heaven. Only those things we build or establish in the kingdom of God will remain. God has put tremendous resources at our disposal, and He likes us to use them. Giving is to be a heart experience. We are to have such a love for God that we cannot withhold anything from Him. There should be an inner joy at being asked. When God instructed David to obtain a certain field it was offered to him for free, but he insisted on paying for it so the field could be his offering to God. He would not give to God that which cost him nothing.

Most of us need to learn to give. This area of our spiritual life remains undeveloped because we are unable to be adventuresome and trust God. We rationalize our giving and only give to those causes that appeal to us. However, God is waiting for us to give out of our love for Him and His kingdom. If we would all give by looking to the Lord to provide so we could give even more, finding a cause to give to would be difficult. Ministries would not be begging but giving. God raises up men and women He can trust and gives them a ministry of giving. He has never personally granted me a great excess or more than I needed at a time, but He does from time to time require me to do things for Him that need much faith. To do God's will, many times I have had to trust Him for the resources. Even at times like these God gives me the gift of faith. When I have had a real ministry need it has been very common for God to have me give to some other ministry. Giving out of love for Him seems to release a flow. That kind of giving produces a joy that is contagious.

This certainly is an area of our Christian lives that needs to be opened up to the Holy Spirit in order to allow Him to develop in our hearts that heavenly attitude. *Freely ye have received, freely give* (Mt. 10:8), *for God loveth a cheerful giver.*

TODAY'S GEM: *Give, and it shall be given unto you; good measure, pressed down, and shaken together, and running over* (Lk. 6:38).
Old Testament Reading Ecclesiastes 1-3

Meditation. *Casting down imaginations, and every high thing that exalteth itself against the knowledge of God, and bringing into captivity every thought to the obedience of Christ* (10:5).

Man has developed and extended his intellect to the point that a mechanical mind, the computer, had to be built to store the vast amounts of knowledge he needs in today's world. Great ideologies, philosophies and even theologies have been born in the minds of men, but all must submit themselves to the gospel of Jesus Christ. There have been schools of philosophy, schools of higher thought and learning, but the truth of the gospel staggers them all. Paul said that any school of thought that exalts itself against the knowledge of God must be brought into captivity to the obedience of Christ. Our minds are battlefields bombarded with all sorts of ideas, but it's what we do with those thoughts that really matters. Does a thought that you have exalt itself or God? If it is self-exaltation then it needs to be cast down and brought into captivity to the obedience of Christ. We do not have to yield to our thought lives. We are the ones who have authority to cast down those imaginations. Some of us are more imaginative than others, so we have a greater opportunity to practice this scripture.

Our minds are like computers, and in the past some of us have allowed them to be filled with all sorts of things that are not at all edifying. All these thought patterns have to be modified, but they will not change unless we make some effort to bring about that change and possess the mind of Christ. Think about these things; feed and cleanse your minds with the Word of God.

All sins of pride, envy, jealousy, and vanity originate in the mind. It is not a sin to initially have these thoughts of the past that have long since been forgiven and are no more. These produce guilt and condemnation, so bring them into captivity to the gospel of Jesus Christ. We can't blame Satan for all those thought patterns if we just refuse to let go of them. Have you met the person who loses himself in a thought pattern of self-pity every time he is faced with defeat? Paul would not have recommended putting down imaginations if God was not willing to give us the victory.

Today's scripture is another opportunity to prove the effectiveness of God's Word. Prepare by arming yourself with the Word and face that thought pattern that usually robs you of your joy or leaves you feeling condemned. Face it with the assurance that the victory is yours because you have the answer. Cast down those imaginations. Bring those thoughts into captivity to the gospel of Jesus Christ.

TODAY'S GEM: *The LORD searcheth all hearts, and understandeth all imaginations of the thoughts: if thou seek him, he will be found of thee; but if thou forsake him, he will cast thee off for ever* (1 Chron. 28:9).

Old Testament Reading Ecclesiastes 4-6

Meditation. *For I have espoused you to one husband, that I may present you as a chaste virgin to Christ* (11:2).

Paul said that he was jealous for his converts who were won from the world. He had preached the gospel to them with such power that they had been loosed from the bondage of the spirit of this world and cleansed by the blood of Jesus. Into their hearts they had received the Spirit from above that Jesus had spoken of in His conversation with Nicodemus when He had said we must be born again and receive the Spirit from above.

What actually happens is that His Spirit and ours become one in a spiritual marriage. Our spirit was dead in trespass and sin, but the marriage of God's Holy Spirit and our spirit brings about the birth of the Spirit of God in our hearts (the new birth). We are wed from the inception of this new birth. The moment this wonderful, miraculous experience occurs we are spoken for because from birth we are destined to be a bride, the bride of Christ. Whatever we were before, whatever our sin, the cleansing of the blood of Jesus is sufficient and continues to be sufficient until the day we will see Him face to face.

I counseled a nineteen-year-old girl some time ago. Having been immorally used since the age of nine, she was one of the most pitiful creatures I have ever met in my ministry. Because of her uncontrollable desires she was institutionalized and restrained by drugs. Everything possible had been done, and still she could not control herself. As I talked about God's love for her and how practical it was, her eyes lit up and questions tumbled out. She asked if God would forgive her. As I told her she could be cleansed and that the past would be totally wiped out, you should have seen her face. I explained that God had made provision for a perfect cleansing, that she would be like a virgin to Him as He cleansed and prepared her to become a bride for His Son. To be cleansed and have a new life was something she had once dreamed about, but it never would have become a reality except in Christ. Therefore she totally embraced the gospel.

Paul was jealous for his baby converts, his purified ones. The cleansing had been so complete that he saw them as virgins waiting, keeping themselves faithfully for their Bridegroom as they looked for the hour of His coming. One desire was in their hearts, which was to yield themselves to Jesus, the husband and lover of their souls. Jesus is looking for that same quality of love in us, that virgin love of a bride. As we wait it will grow to maturity.

TODAY'S GEM: God's cleansing is complete; *though your sins be as scarlet, they shall be as white as snow* (Isa. 1:18).

Old Testament Reading Ecclesiastes 7-9

Meditation. *If I must boast, I will boast in the things which concern my infirmity* (11:30, NKJV).

Paul did not despise weakness or infirmities but saw them as an opportunity to glorify Jesus. In Philippians 4:13 Paul wrote, *I can do all things through Christ which strengtheneth me.*

It has been my privilege to minister in other countries with great men of God whose bodies have suffered over the years and who do not have the ability to physically function as in their younger days. However, in spite of their physical limitations they looked to and trusted Jesus with their weakness, pressing on to fulfill the call of God on their lives. To them their weakness opened up an area of constantly (day by day) trusting Jesus. It became a very sensitive faith experience of finding a strength in Jesus that surpassed the strength which might have been theirs in the natural. They were quick to give all the credit to Jesus—not gritting their teeth and overcoming through sheer willpower—as they purposefully looked to Him in an attitude of "I can't, but He can."

I thank God for every miraculous healing with which He has blessed the Body of Christ. I am sure that every Christian has either had a personal healing experience or has heard of some who have. I myself can testify to miraculous healings in my body and in my family, but I must confess I still do not understand healing. According to His Word I know that Jesus, by His grace, heals us through faith, but I do not understand why one is healed and another is not. Nor do I understand why a brother can be healed of one affliction and not another. I will leave that for the more knowledgeable to explain. However, I do know that where I am weak Jesus is strong. In my life I do not know of any suffering, affliction, or weakness to which the Lord Jesus Christ has not been equal. There have been times of praying my way through, and the victory and strength came about only after persistent prayer. Then there have been other times when the Lord instantly released His strength and through Him I became equal to my circumstances.

Have you suffered with a lack of faith or impatience? Has a physical weakness made your infirmities like a door? Then open that door wide to the Lord Jesus Christ. Extend your faith to Him and give Jesus the opportunity to prove Himself in your weaknesses. Then you too will have the testimony that His grace is sufficient.

TODAY'S GEM: *The sufferings of this present time are not worthy to be compared with the glory which shall be revealed in us* (Rom. 8:18).

Old Testament Reading Ecclesiastes 10-12

Meditation. *And he said unto me, My grace is sufficient for thee: for my strength is made perfect in weakness. Most gladly therefore will I rather glory in my infirmities, that the power of Christ may rest upon me* (12:9).

In my very early days as a Christian I can recall a dear brother who regularly traveled over 200 miles just to disciple me. In looking back now I can see that I was so taken up with my born-again experience and Jesus was so real that it was hard for me to see the need to establish good, daily spiritual habits in my life. This brother had discipled a lot of young men. He knew that the emotional ride of our Christian experience could not carry us through the trials and testings of the Christian life.

What a wise and dear brother he was and such a strong Christian. However, lacking inner strength to discipline myself, I was just the opposite. When he suggested setting my alarm clock to rise early each morning and when he taught me how to have a quiet-time, I had no confidence in myself to maintain such a program. Although I loved the Lord Jesus (I really did), when it came to getting up in the morning an hour earlier, ugh! This brother introduced me to a daily Bible reading plan and the memorization of scripture. I could see the need to establish these habits, but to see the need and desiring to do them didn't cause it to happen.

Soon self-pity got hold of me, and I criticized his strength because I felt he was lacking in understanding of my weak nature. Nevertheless, he persisted and one day I realized my weakness could be an asset. Going to Jesus with my problem I discovered He had never intended for me to do these things on my own strength. I was to be a doer of the Word. What a wonderful experience to discover that when I acknowledged my weakness and looked to the Lord Jesus for the grace to be a doer of the Word, He never failed me. His strength actually became mine, and the previous thirty years of selfish undiscipline and the weakness of character it had built suddenly became an opportunity for a faith adventure. Now, after twenty years, I still maintain these same habits that have become my strength and foundation. Jesus became and continues to be my strength. He never removed my weakness, and I sense it is still lurking in the background; however, His strength continues to be perfected in my weakness.

TODAY'S GEM: Since Jesus' strength is perfected in your weakness, present yourself to Him as a vessel of His grace to show the power of God through you.

Old Testament Reading Song of Solomon 1-3

Meditation. *For we are glad, when we are weak, and ye are strong: and this also we wish, even your perfection* (13:9).

Paul was not disappointed or disillusioned by his weakness, and it was not that he did not persevere in prayer because he did. Paul sought deliverance from his weakness but never found it. Instead he found his strength in the Lord Jesus Christ. In today's writing Paul's joy was in his weakness as he openly confessed it. He didn't expect the self-sufficient or those who had built strength of character by their strength of will to understand his weakness because they take pride in their strength. However, he did advice those who are strong to press on to perfection and maturity in Christ.

To you who have achieved strength of character and show forth a maturity in your lives that we who are weak have never attained, be warned and read between the lines of what Paul was saying. He admired your strength but also recognized that it does not necessarily mean spiritual strength and maturity. It does show that you have your life disciplined and under control, but it does not necessarily mean that you enjoy a simple, childlike, trusting relationship with Jesus. That very strength could itself become a stumbling block. It in itself could be a weakness and stand in the way of a totally dependent relationship with Jesus. So Paul commended that kind of strength but encouraged those Christians to press on to develop a mature relationship with Jesus.

To those of you who find yourselves weak and undisciplined, read on to see what Paul was saying. He was not boasting out of self-pity. He was not using his confession of weakness as an excuse to refrain from the disciplines of discipleship, nor did he excuse his failures and blame them on his weakness. No indeed, he was glad and rejoiced in his brother's strength and also rejoiced in his own weakness. Neither natural weakness nor natural strength profits a person. God's best is that both entrust their weakness or strength, whatever the case may be, to the Lord Jesus Christ. The weak must find their strength in Jesus, that by doing what is impossible in the natural He might be glorified. The strong must entrust their strength to the Lord, not trusting in their own strength, nor leaning to their own understanding, but in all their ways acknowledge Him. They will need the wisdom and grace of God in an even greater measure if they are to glorify Jesus.

TODAY'S GEM: Weak or strong, *the branch cannot bear fruit of itself, except it abide in the vine* (Jn. 15:4).

Old Testament Reading Song of Solomon 4-5

Meditation. *But they had heard only, That he which persecuted us in times past now preacheth the faith which once he destroyed. And they glorified God in me* (1:23-24).

There was a time in my life when I was so ashamed of the past that I did not want to give my testimony about it. Even now I speak of the past with some hesitation. Indeed, there were those who had difficulty believing in my conversion but have come to see the reality of it only after my years of consistent Christian living. My whole attitude changed when I was led to understand just how much Jesus can be glorified through a testimony. But still I didn't find sharing any easier, skirting around the details deliberately, leaving some things a little vague to avoid the stark reality of some of those experiences. However, I struggled through the task of testifying, being motivated by the knowledge that it could glorify Jesus.

Paul said that God was glorified in him. The Jews had heard how he had abused the Christians, violating their homes and thinking he was doing God a service by casting these precious souls into prison. He deliberately set out to persecute the Christians without mercy, and his name became feared among the brethren. Now they recognized a work of grace in this man's heart and glorified God for it.

The very Messiah whom Paul had persecuted with ruthless, religious fervor had become his Messiah. He had found forgiveness at the Cross. The sacrificed Christ, whose blood he had once denied, was now his personal cleansing. He had a personal encounter with Jesus and had been baptized into His death. The same Holy Spirit that had fallen on the Church at Pentecost now dwelled within him. All had the assurance that a great work of grace had taken place in Paul's life, and he said, *"They glorified God in me."*

The power of the gospel in personal witnessing is shown by what God has accomplished in each of us. We can only make as much of repentance as it has meant in our own personal experience. How much you will make of the blood of Jesus in your testimony depends on how important that cleansing Blood is to you. Make certain that forgiveness and acceptance of it is your experience. If you lack power and depth of understanding of these truths, go to Jesus for the answer before you resort to the textbook. Be certain that your testimony gives God the credit. Do not speak of what you have accomplished but rather what God has accomplished in you. Examine and understand God's dealings with you in the light of His Word and let His glorification be your aim.

TODAY'S GEM: The past should be like a mirror reflecting the beauty of the cleansing power of Jesus Christ.

Old Testament Reading Song of Solomon 6-8

Meditation. *I am crucified with Christ: nevertheless I live; yet not I, but Christ liveth in me: and the life which I now live in the flesh I live by the faith of the Son of God, who loved me, and gave himself for me* (2:20).

How terrible and frightening it would be to read the Bible as a sinner and not understand the truth of it. The Bible clearly and irrevocably condemns sin and sentences the sinner to death. The love of God cannot and will not revoke the sentence of death on sin. The man who sins will surely die. The Bible tells us that all have sinned, and there is no one who has not. Who then can be saved? God has passed judgment on sin. The sentence has already been set with no appeal.

Imagine yourself in the courtroom of God with the sentence already pronounced. It was the last word spoken in your case, and the books are closed. Everything has a ring of finality about it as you await the execution. Suddenly the whole scene changes. Someone has come forward offering to be executed in your stead. He is without sin, without any personal guilt for sin, but has offered to become your substitute. If the Judge will allow Him to bear the consequences of sin, He will die on your behalf. An agreement is reached; a covenant is made. The execution takes place with the sentence of death no longer upon you. Now you are not only free from the consequences of sin but free from the sickness and pollution that once inhabited you. As you leave that place of death you meet the very One who was your substitute. Not only has He suffered death on your behalf, but He has also defeated and overcome it for all of us.

Basically this has already happened. Jesus stands before us offering to live a life in and through us that was previously impossible in the natural. The decision is ours whether or not to accept His offer and terms to turn our lives over to Him and live by His Holy Spirit. Is it any wonder that Paul could write, *I live; yet not I, but Christ liveth in me!*

Paul's life had led him to a place of shame and condemnation. Death awaited him until the day he met his Substitute and accepted His covenant. From then on he could say, *"Yet not I, but Christ liveth in me."* An exchange took place. Paul never confessed to a changed life, but because of one Man's death he received an exchanged life, which is eternal.

TODAY'S GEM: The verdict was death, and because He died now I live; yet not I, but Christ lives in me!

Old Testament Reading Isaiah 1-3

Meditation. *For as many of you as have been baptized into Christ have put on Christ* (3:27).

What a mystery Paul has presented in the above scripture. Allow me to reverse the order of verses twenty-six and twenty-seven to read: *For as many of you as have been baptized into Christ have put on Christ. For ye are all the children of God by faith in Christ Jesus.* Somehow you and I were present and even participated in the very death of Jesus Christ. We were part of that death upon the cross, not by blood, not by some heredity of the flesh, but by sin. Because of your sinful nature and mine Christ died; therefore, we can identify with Jesus and His death.

Today's text is not speaking about baptism in water but baptism into Christ and His death. In water baptism we submit our bodies to be engulfed, surrounded, submerged, and baptized in water. So, too, do we identify with Christ's death. It is total. All that sin was or is—its destruction and disfiguration of our human nature, all its consequences—has died, totally disappeared in Christ's death. It is not like a baptism; it is a baptism. It is a total immersion into what Christ has accomplished. It is not a likeness of death; it is death. When we are immersed into the death of Jesus Christ, it becomes our death, our dying to sin in our mortal bodies. Death can have no more dominion over us and has no sting.

When the angel of death comes to visit, just point to the cross and tell him that he is too late. We have been baptized into Christ's death and are waiting for the Lord Jesus to send His angel of life who will lead us through the valley of the shadow (not the real thing, just the shadow) of death.

Put on Christ, His righteousness, and resurrection power. Enjoy the love and favor Jesus has with the Father, because it is all yours. Eternity stretches before you. The life you now live is eternal and is of a godlike quality because it is the very life and nature of God himself. You don't have to try to live it because you are full of it if you are full of and baptized into Christ. Continue being full of His blessed Holy Spirit and you will go on living the life. Out of your innermost being will flow rivers of living water, and the result will be an overflow of that life to others.

Learning about Jesus is conducive to life but does not produce "the life." You will have and display only as much of Jesus' life as you let Him live in and through you.

TODAY'S GEM: You have been immersed in Christ, partaking in His death and resurrection, so walk in that newness of life.

Old Testament Reading Isaiah 4-6

Meditation. *And because ye are sons, God hath sent forth the Spirit of his Son into your hearts, crying, Abba, Father* (4:6).

He that hath the Son hath life; and he that hath not the Son of God hath not life (1 Jn. 5:12). God told us that because we are His sons the Spirit of God is living the life of Christ in and through us, manifesting that quality of life which Jesus called eternal. It is now to be our experience, not because of something we might have done to deserve it, but because we are sons.

Ours is a one-to-One relationship with the Father because we are His sons, not servants or hired hands. God will not dismiss us because of some failure. We have an inherited affection, a childlike love, because we are family. We are not like a servant whose life is divided between his serving and the privacy of a life outside of that service. We are the sons of God all day, every day, in every experience and relationship. God hath sent forth the Spirit of his Son because we are sons.

Do you really want to know God? Is it your heart's desire to know the Father who the Word says loves you with an everlasting love? Then let me suggest that you get to know the Spirit of the Son whom God has sent.

In the Scriptures we are told that the Holy Spirit of God will lead us into all truth. He will reveal the things of God and give us access to the very heart of the Father. What's more, He will glorify Christ in and through us. God never intended for us to try to put our lives together by determination and willpower. God's best for His heirs is for them to receive the Spirit of sonship. Jesus, the Son, received the Holy Spirit and lived a Spirit-filled life. The quality of life which He lived, the miracles performed, the death that He died, and His resurrection from the dead were all outward manifestations of the Holy Spirit living in and through the Son.

God has not withheld one good thing from us. Because we are heirs God has sent forth the Spirit of His Son into our hearts. Submit your will to His. Give Him freedom to be the Spirit of God in and through you, and see for yourself if He will not take every opportunity you give Him to glorify Jesus.

TODAY'S GEM: *For as many as are led by the Spirit of God, they are the sons of God* (Rom. 8:14).

Old Testament Reading Isaiah 7-9

Meditation. *If we live in the Spirit, let us also walk in the Spirit* (5:25).

It seems that Paul is making a very clear distinction between receiving the Spirit into our lives and our willingness or obedience to walk in the desires of the indwelling Holy Spirit. If I am to live within the freedom and protection of the civil law, then I must be obedient to its demands. If I drive my motorcar at 55 miles per hour I do not have to be looking in my rear-vision mirror or peering into the distance anticipating a speed trap. That is not for me, not when I can set my cruise control at the lawful speed and relax.

When we receive the Holy Spirit we should let Him be responsible for our lives. He knows what the will of the Father is for us and exactly how we can best be brought to a place of maturity. These earthen vessels have lived in rebellion for so long without the cleansing or the infilling of the Holy Spirit. They are used to doing their own thing and will try once again to exert their will over the indwelling Holy Spirit; however, they will only have authority if we give it to them. God's best is for us to be companioned by the Holy Spirit, to get to know Him as a person, welcoming, encouraging, and enjoying His company. Therefore, give Him freedom with your life.

The spirit of this world brings us into bondage to do his will, but the Holy Spirit will never exert His power or God-given authority over our will. Everything in His power will be done to persuade and bring us to a place of desiring to do the will of the Father. He in turn will provide all the heavenly resources to do it.

Yes it's scary; anything new and unfamiliar is. To walk in the Spirit, faith is required, faith to walk in obedience. Without faith we cannot please God. Let our walk in the Spirit and in obedience be the testimony to our sonship and to whether or not we are filled with the Spirit of God. Paul encouraged, or should I say commanded, that we who live in the Spirit also walk in the Spirit. So let us examine our own lives. Are we who profess to be filled with the Spirit walking a life initiated by the Holy Spirit? Or are we still doing our own thing and possibly asking God's blessing on it?

TODAY'S GEM: With full confidence place your life in the hands of the Father who will guide you by His Holy Spirit.

Old Testament Reading Isaiah 10-12

Meditation. *For he that soweth to his flesh shall of the flesh reap corruption; but he that soweth to the Spirit shall of the Spirit reap life everlasting* (6:8).

What great things man is capable of initiating and accomplishing under the power of his own spirit. The spirits of some men are religious, and they receive tremendous satisfaction from doing some great religious work. The test of whether a work is of God or man is the motivation behind it. If it is their hearts' desire to glorify God and not perform a good work for their own pleasure, then you can be certain it originated in the Father's heart.

A good example of man's religious spirit that originated in the flesh can be found in chapter 32 of Exodus. While Moses was on the mountain receiving the Ten Commandments from God, the Israelites had assembled around Aaron to persuade him to gather the prosperity God had given them as they left Egypt to build their own object of worship. They had even convinced Aaron that he was their God-given leader. When Moses returned with the commandments of God, which clearly forbade what they were doing, his face shone with the glory of God. The faces of the people also shone, but their faces reflected the excitement of the flesh, as they were carried away in total abandon and enthusiasm with their fleshly worship. They not only had an object to worship but they also had a license to do whatever they desired. The golden calf was expensive and beautiful, but it was a work of the flesh. *For he that soweth to his flesh shall of the flesh reap corruption.*

Wait on the Spirit, be patient, have faith in His ability, and trust Him to initiate some work of God in His own way and in His good time. If God has blessed you with the knowledge of His plans and will, be certain to wait on Him to initiate and bring His purposes and plans to birth. Beware lest your own spirit, your own religious desires and enthusiasm, initiate and motivate a "golden calf." Wait on and trust in the Spirit of God because he that *soweth to the Spirit shall of the Spirit reap life everlasting.*

Just because a whole nation followed the worship of a golden calf, that did not make it right. If you are to avoid being deceived, learn quickly to recognize the voice of your spirit and to distinguish the difference between it and the still, small voice of the Holy Spirit.

TODAY'S GEMS: Gather not to yourselves good deeds as idols, but let them be born out of your love for God.

Old Testament Reading Isaiah 13-15

Meditation. *To the praise of the glory of his grace, wherein he hath made us accepted in the beloved* (1:6).

As I travel throughout the country and tell people the message that God brought me to America to share, the number of people who hear and respond never ceases to overwhelm me. God clearly showed me that what I am to share with the people in this country is a simple, uncomplicated, childlike faith in Jesus Christ. Not that the people of God lack faith, however, sometimes in the life and growth of the Christian it is possible to misdirect it. Sometimes our faith is placed in teachings and teachers, or even worse in the Bible itself but ignoring the Author who is the Word made flesh and dwelt among us. People come to me continually confessing a fullness of the knowledge of God, but they have no personal relationship with the Lord Jesus Christ.

If we are a born-again people, then we are a people who have been chosen by God. Our heavenly Parent chose to adopt us. We didn't just stumble into the Family, making Him provide and care for us. God personally chose to parent and adopt us into His Family. He made us heirs of the Kingdom and will withhold no good thing from us.

God desires that we learn and grow in the knowledge that His ways are not ours. We cannot have too much understanding of the Word of God. It is God's intention for us to be wise in the Word, to know His ways, and to study the great godly principles in His Word. Through the Bible we are to have an intimate communication, that is, we are to get our guidance, direction, and, if necessary, our correction from it.

We are to be a people of the Book and a people who know their God, but here is where we must stop and examine today's text. None of these wonderful truths and no great spiritual experience, no matter how much we know, make us acceptable to God. When we come into the presence of the Father, we are not accepted because of our works, faith or great exploits. Always, to the very end of this life of ours, our acceptance before God is in the Beloved. We never outgrow the need of the Lord Jesus Christ. We are never complete without Him, only complete in Him. If you are to enjoy an uncomplicated Christian experience, your day must begin and end in Jesus. We are adopted by grace, praise God, but we are accepted in the Beloved, Jesus. So keep your relationship with Him an intimate one, getting to know your Friend more and more each day.

TODAY'S GEM: Jesus is the door to the Father, and we are acceptable only by going through that Door.

Old Testament Reading Isaiah 16-18

Meditation. *For he is our peace* (2:14).

I once heard a story about a great painting that hung in an art gallery. The artist had depicted a very stormy scene of lightning which lit up the vast darkness of the sky. You could almost hear the thunder, but the eye-catching point in the picture was a bird's nest firmly fixed to a strong bough of a tree, which was bent down with the fury of the storm. It was bent down just far enough to see some almost fully grown, little birds nestled into the warmth of their mother's body. It was obvious that this was not the first storm they had ridden out on that swaying bough. Even though the sky was black and lightning lit up everything around them, there was tranquility in that little nest. The harder the bough swayed in the storm, the closer the baby birds nestled to their mother. The artist titled his picture "Peace." As you gazed at that storm-filled canvas, what caught your eye was that little nest of birds at perfect peace. The stormy scene faded into the background as the calmness the artist intended to convey was felt.

Our lives can be like that picture because we are told that Jesus is our peace. If one of those little birds had been taken out of the nest, away from its mother, it would have experienced the full fury of the storm. Every one of us needs the Nest (Jesus) if we are to live and walk in His peace. Those who have built a daily quiet-time into their lives, closeting themselves away to know God, have a nest where the fury of the storm only brings them closer to Jesus. The storm must bow to His presence, for He is greater than storms, trials, tribulations, and fear.

To His disciples Jesus said, *"Peace I leave with you, my peace I give unto you: not as the world giveth, give I unto you"* (Jn. 14:27). In Ephesians Paul was not talking about the peace Jesus gives but that Jesus himself is that peace, which is perpetual. Later on in this chapter Paul talked about the peace Jesus brings, but, my dear Christian friends, in your daily quiet-time in the closet you can draw nigh unto Him who is our peace that passeth all understanding. Look not for peace but for the One who is that peace that triumphs in the most fierce storm.

TODAY'S GEM: In the darkest of nights and in the midst of a storm, nestle close to the One who calms the storm with a word. *Thou wilt keep him in perfect peace, whose mind is stayed on thee: because he trusteth in thee* (Isa. 26:3).

Old Testament Reading Isaiah 19-21

Meditation. *Unto me, who am less than the least of all saints, is this grace given, that I should preach among the Gentiles the unsearchable riches of Christ* (3:8).

Paul considered himself to be the very least of all the saints. This must have appeared true in the eyes of many in the light of his foolishness in persecuting the Church of Jesus Christ and his total ignorance of the Word of God, which was full of understanding and truth about the Messiah. Paul humbly received and appreciated the work of grace that sought him out on the road and brought him to his knees. It was that same grace which forgave him and cleansed him from all sin. To Paul grace revealed the Son, Jesus Christ, and gave him the privilege of making known to others what he called the unsearchable riches of Christ.

After Paul's encounter with and revelation of Jesus Christ much of the Old Testament must have come alive to him. He must have seen the sacrificial lamb as a type or shadow of the Lamb of God who would take away the sin of the world. From his writings to the Hebrew Christians it is apparent that Paul recognized the Old Testament heroes such as Moses, Melchizedek, and Joshua as typifying Christ.

The same grace that found Paul on the road to Damascus is available to you and me. It is available to cleanse us from all sin and to bring us into a wonderful relationship with the Lord Jesus Christ. By grace the Word of God can reveal to us all these wonderful types, shadows, and truths about Jesus. We need never be ignorant of who our Savior is. However, Paul speaks of grace that made unsearchable riches known to him. He did not discover them because of a great deal of searching, nor because of what he knew, but because of Whom he knew. The richness, which is the wealth of spiritual life that can be ours in Christ, becomes ours through fellowship with Jesus. Each day offers an opportunity to know Him if we are willing to share the incidents of each day with Him.

TODAY'S GEM: To really know and walk with the one, true God is to become heir to the *unsearchable riches of Christ.*

Old Testament Reading Isaiah 22-23

Meditation. *I therefore, the prisoner of the Lord, beseech you that ye walk worthy of the vocation wherewith ye are called* (4:1).

Paul preached equality in Christendom, where Jew and Gentile were alike and one in Christ Jesus. It was for this cause that Paul had been imprisoned; however, it is one thing to be imprisoned but quite another to walk as a Christian in those circumstances. Not only did much of Paul's writing take place in jail, but it was there that the Holy Spirit visited and was in continual fellowship with Paul, inspiring him to write. Are you lonely? Then, like Paul, in your loneliness find Jesus. In whatever situation you find yourself fellowship with Jesus is always available.

Before I was a Christian there was a time in my life when boredom or loneliness led me into mischief. I did not always want to do some of those things. Indeed, there were periods when, by exerting my will, I was well behaved and did not allow myself to be led into trouble. However, these times were short-lived, and I eventually slipped back into a pattern of misbehavior of which I am not proud. From all this I have learned that it is the company you keep that determines your behavior patterns.

It is amazing how my behavior has changed since I began walking with Jesus. Not long after my conversion I was going to a hotel to have a drinking session with the boys, but Jesus wouldn't go into the bar with me. So I turned around and went home to my wife with Him. It took a little while for her to get used to the change, but with the Lord I was in good company.

When we walk with Christ our behavioral patterns conform to His. What a hassle it is trying not to do something, but how much easier it becomes when we walk with the Lord. He is available every minute of the day, and His desire is to reveal Himself through each of us. If given the liberty, the virtues of Christ will be seen in our lives. If we are walking with Him we won't have to try to be holy because His holiness, lowliness, meekness, and longsuffering will be seen in us. Hang on, draw a little closer and open yourself up to Jesus; then you will walk worthy of your calling in Christ.

TODAY'S GEM: Our lives reflect the company we keep; so if your desire is to be like Christ, make Him your best friend.

Old Testament Reading Isaiah 24-26

Meditation. *Be ye therefore followers of God, as dear children; And walk in love* (5:1-2).

The spirit of the world would have us treat the Church like a social club or a place in which to gather around a preacher or a set of beliefs. In some places the bigger the church the more successful it is believed to be, and everything possible is done to make it a big success. However, Paul told us that we are to be followers of God, having a relationship with Him that leads us to walk in love.

It is possible to learn about God but still not be led by Him. Surely that is why Paul kept using the word "walking" in this chapter. He was exhorting us to walk in love as children of the light and to walk circumspectly (considering all the circumstances and possible consequences). What circumstance does God have you walking in at this moment? Where is He leading you? It is good to study His Word and go to church regularly to hear it. Then the knowledge of God can be stored in our hearts. However, we are out of balance if we just have knowledge but are not being led by His Word and walking in it, because God has called us to be His followers. It takes more than knowledge about God, more than a word from Him. Faith is a gift, a fruit of the Spirit. To become a follower of God and a doer of the Word faith is required.

As a baby Christian God wheeled you about in a pram. Nothing much was required for you to follow Jesus except resting in His presence. But now you have grown up and matured. Now it is time to walk with faith. Having established your relationship with the Lord Jesus Christ, allow yourself to be led by the person of the Holy Spirit who dwells within you. Go on being filled with the Spirit of God. The more freedom God has to manifest Himself in you, the easier it will be for you to be led by Him and to walk in His ways. Knowledge of where God is leading or why He has led you a certain way will not always be there. Faith is satisfied to follow and not require all the answers, just the directions. *Be ye therefore followers of God, as dear children; and walk in love.*

TODAY'S GEM: *Now faith is the substance of things hoped for, the evidence of things not seen* (Heb. 11:1). Therefore, as a child holds its mother's hand not worrying about its destination, place your hand in the Father's and be *followers of God*.

Old Testament Reading Isaiah 27-28

Meditation. *Put on the whole armour of God, that ye may be able to stand against the wiles of the devil* (6:11).

For most of us there comes a time in our walk with the Lord when we are led into a confrontation with the enemy. I can look back over my own walk with God these past twenty years and recognize times when I wasn't walking anywhere. It was a time to stand still, stand in His strength and in His victory. It was a time of standing my ground in Christ until the enemy yielded. He could find no chink in my armor because my head was covered. It wasn't that he did not entice and set subtle thoughts and suggestions before me, however, my helmet of salvation was firmly on my head. God has been good to me and has put into my heart and into my hand the shield of faith, so I refuse to give it up to the enemy. He has girded me about with truth and has prepared my feet to stand. There have been times when God led me nowhere and gave no new orders except to stand.

I am going to share something with you and pray that God will help you to understand this intimate sharing of my heart. There was an occasion when I had a vision, or it may have actually happened, I could not tell. I was awake and aware of where I was and that Satan had found my throat with his hands. As he squeezed my windpipe, for a moment fear gripped me. Then like a flash the realization suddenly came that there was no need to fear because that fear was also part of the enemy's attack. "Satan," I cried aloud, "you are defeated. Squeeze the last drop of air out of me if you will, for in that moment I will escape you and be in the presence of the Lord Jesus Christ. You will give me my heart's desire, for I shall see Him face to face!" Immediately Satan stopped the attack, and I sensed, not saw, the presence of the Lord Jesus Christ in the room.

Not everyone has to have such a dramatic encounter, but the enemy is real. That is why we are cautioned to put on the whole armor of God and stand. When it is God's time to move on again He will give us His word, and the enemy will retreat before the sword of the Spirit, which is the Word of God. There is a time to walk and be led and a time to stand in His victory until it becomes ours and the enemy yields.

TODAY'S GEM: When God leads us to stand we already have the victory. The battle, which is His, was won at the Cross!

Old Testament Reading Isaiah 29-30

Meditation. *Being confident of this very thing, that he which hath begun a good work in you will perform it until the day of Jesus Christ* (1:6).

Paul's confidence was in God knowing that He would not have begun a good work in the believers if He hadn't been willing to complete it. Paul also knew the deceitfulness of his own heart and the capabilities of the Holy Spirit to bring him to a place of understanding and of acknowledging Jesus Christ as Lord. Without violating Paul's freewill, the Holy Spirit had revealed Christ to him in all His glory until Paul could not resist and gladly confessed Jesus as Lord. Realizing the work of grace in his own life, Paul had absolute confidence in God to daily perform this good work of salvation in the believers until they were complete in Christ. Then they would reflect His glory, showing forth His likeness, expressing the mind of Christ and fulfilling His works.

If the Philippians were to have the same confidence Paul possessed, they would have to be filled by the Holy Spirit each day and be in continuing fellowship with Him. The life of Jesus was to be so lived in them that their conversation and manner of living would be worthy of the gospel of Christ. This time they were to *stand fast in one spirit, with one mind striving together for the faith of the gospel; and in nothing terrified by your* [their] *adversaries* (vv. 27-28).

Paul urged them to stand and in this instance to stand together with no competitiveness. Knowing this would not be easy, Paul exhorted them to strive—not self-striving but allowing God—exerting a little energy toward that end. I am sure these believers had to pray their way into the place God had chosen for them, dealing with a variety of hindrances that could keep them out of God's best.

We need not doubt God's ability to do the same thing today that took place in the early Church. By His indwelling Holy Spirit, God will bring us to a place of unity where we stand together in one spirit. However, it is conditional upon our response to the Holy Spirit. It depends upon our obedience to God's Word, our willingness to be led and to humble ourselves. Whatsoever He says unto us we are to do and then do it with all our might.

TODAY'S GEM: Unity can be ours if we are willing to be led of the Spirit and humble ourselves before God.

Old Testament Reading Isaiah 31-33

Meditation. *Work out your own salvation with fear and trembling. For it is God which worketh in you both to will and to do of his good pleasure* (2:12-13).

We are not responsible for our initial salvation experience because God himself initiated it. When the necessity of salvation was revealed to us, God's grace made it all possible. He allowed His Son to be the perfect sacrifice who saved us from the consequences of sin. There had to be a turning around and a turning away from our sin if salvation was to become a reality in our lives. It was God who made us feel this need for conversion.

Salvation is a continuing experience, not just once committing our lives to Christ. After we are justified by Jesus' blood through his once-and-for-all sacrifice, we then begin the daily walk of sanctification. That is why Paul wrote to the Philippian Christians telling them to work out their salvation experience with fear and trembling lest they failed to cooperate and to be doers of the Word. For them to enjoy and enter into a full salvation experience on a daily basis, they were to be responsive and open to the Holy Spirit of God dwelling within them. They were also to have confidence in God to make known His will to them until His will became their own. Once they had assurance of what God's will was, then they were to step out in faith and expect God's power—all His resources—to do His will.

Man does not have the means to initiate the will of God, but he does have the responsibility to make it his and then avail himself of God's grace to work it out in his experience. He can do this because all the resources of heaven are available to him. God will lead us every step of the way, but it cannot and will not happen unless we are obedient and go to the Father for grace. Then by faith in that grace we must step out and do it. It is also important how we accomplish the Father's will. Paul said, *"Do all things without murmurings and disputings"* (v. 14). God left us with great responsibilities in the exercising of our wills. Our daily salvation experience is secured by laying aside our own will and taking up God's with complete confidence in Him to will and to do. *For it is God which worketh in you both to will and to do of his good pleasure.*

TODAY'S GEM: Your responsibility as a Christian is to step out in faith and use your heavenly resources because *faithful is he that calleth you, who also will do it* (1 Thess. 5:24).

Old Testament Reading Isaiah 34-36

Meditation. *That I may win Christ, And be found in him . . . That I may know him* (3:8, 9, 10).

What made Paul a great man of God? He didn't campaign for any particular office in the Church, nor did he ask for any recognition of his greatness. His life was completely given to the propagation of the gospel of Jesus Christ. God had made him an apostle to the Gentiles. None of the other apostles shared his calling, and there was no school of training for what God had called him to do. Peter may have understood Paul's calling better than most since he had been in Cornelius' house when the Holy Spirit fell on the Gentiles; but this was not Peter's calling either.

What then made Paul the great man of God that he was, a man whose writings are still being read daily, probably being read more than any other book? I want to say that it was Paul's pursuit of the Lord Jesus Christ that made him so great. Everything he did, said, or wrote was simply an overflow of his fellowship with Jesus.

Paul had met Jesus on the road and had experienced that inner transforming experience that Jesus called the new birth. After that Paul never ceased to pursue Jesus and went away for long periods of time to be alone with the Lord. Paul, having tasted Jesus' love, wanted that love to be alive in him. He experienced the gifts of the Holy Spirit and enjoyed the manifestation of them in his life, but still he pressed on in his pursuit of Christ. Paul's mind became alive and fresh as he recognized that he was in touch with the very mind of Christ, but still Paul pursued more of Jesus. He bathed in the righteousness of Christ and enjoyed His peace, joy, patience, and love but still pressed on in his pursuit of more and more of Jesus.

It was like a race that must be run if he was to obtain the prize and win Jesus Christ. Paul expressed a desire, not to be righteous in himself but to be found in Christ, to walk with the Father. As he lived to care for and love the Kingdom, he was motivated by the Holy Spirit to know and do the Father's will. But all this was not enough. After writing about all these wonderful things and overflowing with the very fullness of Christ himself, Paul's heart was still beating for more of Jesus. There was a longing, an inner knowing, that there was still more, until his mouth confessed what the longing of his heart was: *That I may know him!* Knowing that intellectual pursuits or offices in the Church would not satisfy him, Paul realized that the world could not offer him more. Only Jesus could satisfy the longing of his heart. Paul's greatness was in his humbleness in the knowledge he possessed of Jesus Christ, and I doubt if he even knew it.

TODAY'S GEM: *And this is life eternal, that they might know thee the only true God* (Jn. 17:3).

Old Testament Reading Isaiah 37-38

Meditation. *Be careful for nothing; but in every thing by prayer and supplication with thanksgiving let your requests be made known unto God* (4:6).

Here is a scripture that you can practice and build your whole life around. You can experience the working out of it in your own experience as a never-ending, faith adventure that will please God. First Paul told the Philippian Christians to find their place in God and stand fast in the Lord. He urged them to help those who labored with him in the cause of the gospel. After standing fast in the Lord and helping Paul's co-laborers in the gospel, he then exhorted them: *Rejoice in the Lord alway: and again I say, Rejoice* (v. 4). This was to be accompanied with steadfastness, helping those who propagated the gospel of Jesus Christ.

Faith does not yield to anxiety or give way to worry; therefore, if these soulish, emotional things overcome us, then we must confess them to the Lord and receive from Him faith equal to our circumstances. This is where standing fast and rejoicing come in. Faith rejoices for that faith which is to be received, and it is praise that opens up a direct line with heaven, opening the heart of the Father through which faith can flow to you, filling your innermost being until all anxiety and fear have gone.

Now that you have opened the door, in your hand is a "hotline" to heaven. So make your requests known unto God, *by prayer and supplication with thanksgiving.* Do it God's way. Something is required of us because God's promises are conditional. Your motorcar will take you anywhere you want to go providing you do the right things in the right order. This is also true of God. This promise will take you through life and open a door to answered prayer, providing it is operated in context with God's directions.

Don't waste your time or God's by asking to be blessed. God wants to bless you, but He wants you to be specific. Tell Him what you want. If necessary even tell Him the color. Keep your requests before God and fellowship with Him over them (with praise and thanksgiving). Why, Paul even said, *"But my God shall supply all your need according to his riches in glory by Christ Jesus"* (v. 19).

TODAY'S GEM: Follow the directions in the Manual (the Bible), living the life that God has set before you, and the promises of God will never fail you.

Old Testament Reading Isaiah 39-40

Meditation. *We heard of your faith in Christ Jesus, and of the love which ye have to all the saints* (1:4).

As a man of God Paul had great faith in God's Word; the promises made to him became his experience by faith in Jesus. I feel a real need to qualify what I am trying to say. Paul did not take the promises of God and turn them into a formula in which to put his faith. No, his faith and trust were in the One who made the promise, Jesus Christ. That is why he could write to the Christians in Colosse that he had heard of their faith in Christ Jesus. We are to put our faith in Christ if we are to enjoy a trusting, faith relationship with Jesus; then we will not have doubts and fears over His Word. Paul simply wrote down promises that were made to him and were his experience when fellowshipping with Jesus.

Our vision of Christ and faith in Him would be less difficult if we would enlarge our understanding and press on to enrich our fellowship with Him. If we would seek Jesus day by day and fellowship with Him in all His glory, seeing His immeasurable stature, then faith in Him, His Word and promises, would become a very natural experience. It would simply be a product of our relationship with Him. Then, if Jesus would speak a word of promise into our hearts, our faith in Him would become faith in His Word, and instantly we would be ready to put it into practice.

Every now and again I go over the promises in the Scriptures that I know Jesus has quickened to my understanding. I examine myself to be certain that I have not neglected anything, because those promises are my signposts. They are His word to me, and my desire is that my life be centered on Him and what He is saying. To the servants at the wedding feast at Cana Jesus' mother said, *"Whatsoever he saith unto you, do it"* (Jn. 2:5). Their relationship with Jesus was simply one of obedience. They only knew Him as Master; therefore, obedience and faith in Him and the direction He gave produced a miracle.

Serve God's Word and be obedient to it, but by all means do not neglect the Author of the Word. Have faith in and build your life on Him. He in turn will live His life in and through you, and you will also be known as a disciple who has love for all the saints.

TODAY'S GEM: *For as by one man's* [Adam's] *disobedience many were made sinners, so by obedience of one* [Jesus] *shall many be made righteous* (Rom. 5:19). One does make a difference!

Old Testament Reading Isaiah 41-42

Meditation. *As ye have therefore received Christ Jesus the Lord, so walk ye in him* (2:6).

For you to receive the Lord Jesus Christ it took God-given faith, which created a vehicle or a channel to heaven through which God could extend His grace to you. None of us really deserved what took place in our hearts. This experience could not be bought or worked for. We simply accepted the opportunity to repent of what we were, sinners. Our hearts were at enmity with God and our spirits dead in trespass and sin. God's grace was extended to us through faith, and the Spirit of the Lord Jesus Christ became one with our spirits. A wedding or union took place where we were born again by the Spirit from above.

Now Paul was reminding these Christians at Colosse how to live victoriously in Christ when he said, *"As ye have therefore received Christ Jesus the Lord, so walk ye in him."* Let me again remind you that you have received Christ by the grace of God through faith. The grace that made this need known to you and through faith introduced you to the Lord Jesus Christ is the same grace that, through faith, is available to you to live the Christian life and to walk with the Lord Jesus as His disciple.

Paul said, *"And ye are complete in him, which is the head of all principality and power"* (2:10). Jesus calls us to walk *in Him* and reminds us that the salvation principle that saved us is also the principle in which we must walk if we are to go on being saved and to be triumphant over the adversary. We are to walk in Christ to defeat the old carnal nature that dwells within us and lives hoping and desiring to reign once again over our mortal bodies. However, we have given our bodies to Christ that He might reside within us. All that we are must be submitted to Him. Our old, troublesome nature has been exchanged for the very nature of Christ so that we now live availing ourselves of His strength, patience, love, and virtue. All of Christ is available for us to walk in. In which nature will you walk? In whose strength will you trust—yours or His? You have received Christ in the same manner by which you are to walk, by grace through faith. Establish yourself in Christ. Be rooted and built up in Him.

TODAY'S GEM: After marriage you no longer walk with singleness of mind or heart; the same is true when you become the bride of Christ. You are now one with His Spirit, *so walk ye in him.*

Old Testament Reading Isaiah 43-44

Meditation. *If then you were raised with Christ, seek those things which are above, where Christ is, sitting at the right hand of God* (3:1, NKJV).

If Christ has risen from the grave and has overcome death, then so have we because the scripture says *your life is hid with Christ in God* (v.3). The first victory Christ won for us was over death, which He conquered. Jesus entered the very bowels of hell and overcame on our behalf. Never will we suffer hell as the consequence of sin because Jesus has overcome! His blood has purchased our redemption and has won resurrection life for us. All He calls us to do is walk in it. Because we are a people who have received the Spirit of Christ into our spirits, we have been endued with power from on high! Jesus has sent His Holy Spirit to indwell and empower us. All the resources to live the resurrection life are ours in Christ. Hallelujah! It is no good telling God you can't because He knows it and never intended for you to try and live the life in your own strength. You are to live that resurrection life in Christ.

Paul goes to great lengths to spell out what that Christian life will be like when it is lived in and through Jesus. He lists virtues that couldn't be possessed or lived in the natural. Paul sets before us standards of conduct that would not only become law to us but would condemn us if we did not possess the life that Christ has invested in these earthen vessels. That very Life makes these virtues ours.

Now Paul points to another challenge, a higher form of life. Jesus has overcome hell and been given victory in the world, and now Paul tells us of a life in Christ in heavenly places where Christ is, *sitting at the right hand of God.* Paul said that we are to set our affections on things above, not on the things of the earth. *For ye are dead, and your life is hid with Christ in God* (v. 3).

There exists a relationship and a fellowship with Christ in heavenly places in the Holy of Holies. It is open to each of us right now, and He bids us to enter His courts with praise. In those courts are victories over principalities and powers. Jesus sets in order those things that are to be, and no power on earth can unseat them. As for us, we are to seek those things that are above.

TODAY'S GEM: As the sons of God, the power of heaven is available and can be manifested in the believer by the degree with which he walks guided by God's Holy Spirit. *For our gospel came not unto you in word only, but also in power* (1 Thess. 1:5).

Old Testament Reading Isaiah 45-47

Meditation. *Continue in prayer, and watch in the same with thanksgiving* (4:2).

It is good to be reminded that it was the Lord Jesus Christ who reconciled us to the Father. We had no relationship with Him because we were spiritually dead in our trespass and sin. Then by His sacrifice for sin, yours and mine, Jesus brought us into an eternal relationship with the Father. We have become more than converts or members of some denomination. We have become sons or daughters of God himself, therefore making possible a personal and intimate relationship. The questions are: What are we going to do with this wonderful opportunity, and how can we make the best of it? The how is answered for us in our text for today—*continue in prayer*!

I remember the first year of my infancy in Christ and being ignorant of so many things. For instance, I failed to recognize that my talking to Jesus each day was praying. It bothered me when I heard the beautiful prayers that church people made in the "King James" language. They were so unlike my conversations with Jesus that one dear brother approached me after a meeting. Having been asked to pray and not knowing what to do other than what I had been doing in my daily relationship with Jesus, I simply told Jesus all about it. The outcome was that this brother very lovingly told me that it was improper to talk to Jesus. He said that my prayer was theologically out of order and not to pray to Jesus but to the Father in Jesus' name. At this time I knew Jesus, but God the Father was a mystery to me, so in my struggle with all this I told my problem to a missionary from our church. This missionary made what appeared at the time the strangest reply. She said, "Tim, I hope you never learn to pray, but next time you're talking to Jesus would you mention my name?"

Let me again say that the question of how we have a personal and intimate relationship with God is adequately answered in today's scripture when it says to continue in prayer. Now what are we going to do with this wonderful opportunity we have? The answer is with you. Read what the Word says about prayer. You could also read some good books on the subject, but a whole lot is not going to happen until you involve yourself in a prayer relationship with Jesus. Experience is the key. The Holy Spirit would be delighted to fellowship with you in prayer and put you into a heart-to-Heart relationship since He is the best teacher and companion you could ever have.

TODAY'S GEM: Prayer is something to be practiced and experienced.
Old Testament Reading Isaiah 48-49

Meditation. *We give thanks to God always for you all, making mention of you in our prayers* (1:2).

Here is a beautiful little prayer experience you can have right now. After reading this, put your "Gems" down and go before the Lord with a quiet spirit. Give thanks and praise God for all those people you know and love, individually naming them. Let your thoughts dwell on each person for a moment. Then think of one particular person; name him or her before God saying, "Father, I want to thank you for (person's name)." Think of that person's good, God-given characteristics and name them one by one, thanking God for that person. Concentrate on some work of faith, labor of love or patience that he or she may have performed; then thank God for it. Pray for his or her continuing salvation experience and think of some of the things you would like to see more evident in your own life. Pray that God might also bless that person with these things. Keep away from negative thoughts and don't try to correct that person through prayer. Keep your prayers in the area of thanksgiving, rejoicing before God for specific things.

Now, having prayed with thanksgiving for those you love, try doing exactly the same thing for those with whom you have difficulty. In spite of your feelings name them before the Lord and verbally thank God for those good things in their lives. Thank God for their initial salvation experience and for any good experience you have had with them. Don't be feeble in expressing your thanks, but convince God of the sincerity of your actions. If your feelings—your soul life—do not conform and if your feelings are hindering this exercise, stop right where you are. Talk out loud to avoid doing this as a series of thoughts. Verbalize your prayer and rebuke your soul for its unwillingness to cooperate, reminding it that by an act of free will your life has been submitted, body and soul, to the Holy Spirit that dwells within your heart. Confess to the Lord Jesus Christ this reluctance and then by faith—faith with vigor and earnestness—step out determined to give thanks and praise for specific God-given virtues in that person's life.

Now having done all this, you are in for a surprise because your thanksgiving for them has opened up a channel to heaven through which you yourself can receive.

TODAY'S GEM: Since we reap what we sow, it is truly *more blessed to give than to receive"* (Acts 20:35).

Old Testament Reading Isaiah 50-52

Meditation. *For this cause also thank we God without ceasing, because, when ye received the word of God which ye heard of us, ye received it not as the word of men, but as it is in truth, the word of God, which effectually worketh also in you that believe* (2:13).

Here is another opportunity for a closet experience and being alone with God, giving Him thanks. Be grateful, rejoice, and express joy before Him for the word of God received. Let me try to make my point with an illustration. Imagine going to a restaurant for a steak. At this point you are really hungry as the aroma of the steak fills the restaurant, and if you had no appetite before you certainly have one now. As you sit there with your friend telling how hungry you are and how much you are looking forward to devouring that meat, you reminisce about other occasions such as this. Your juices are flowing, and you can hardly wait. However, talking about, smelling, and looking forward to it changes nothing until you have actually partaken of that food. If you were hungry enough and it is a good enough steak, you are going to have something complimentary to say with each mouthful. Physically you are going to be full and satisfied.

The above is a tangible example of what it is to hear and talk about the Word, have an appetite for and be exposed to it, but how different it is to receive God's Word, which is not only to be received but is to be experienced. Our text tells us that it is to effectually work itself into the lives of those who believe.

There is nothing better than thanksgiving to open your heart to God's Word and create an inner capacity to receive it so that it works effectually in your life. Thanksgiving is like an appetite that prepares the heart to receive the Word. Just as a bit of fat on a steak doesn't bother you because your eye is on the meat, neither should some impurities of man in his presentation of the Word. Lay aside the word of man and take the part that is truth because it is capable of manifesting life. Murmuring quenches the Spirit and robs you. Thanksgiving makes the Word yours and establishes it in your heart. Practice thanksgiving in your closet by taking a particular scripture and with eagerness and gratitude express your thanks.

TODAY'S GEM: The enemy and robber of thanksgiving is murmuring. It quenches the spirit of thanksgiving and prevents you from receiving the Word, making it ineffective in your life.

Old Testament Reading Isaiah 53-55

OCTOBER **15**   **Thessalonians 3**

Meditation. *For what thanks can we render to God again for you, for all the joy wherewith we joy for your sakes before our God* (3:9).

When we practice the ways of the kingdom of God in our prayer lives there is a special dimension of eternal life that becomes ours. Thanksgiving in prayer produces fruit. May I suggest to you that after you have successfully prayed—when God has heard your request and assured you that the very thing prayed for is yours—there is more. It is at this point most of us fail in our prayer lives and miss out on God's best. Most of us are so taken up with the answer that is the object of prayer that we neglect to adequately lavish thanksgiving upon God.

The answer to prayer usually meets some material or personal need in our lives. The answer in itself is a great blessing; however, I am trying to say there can be an even greater blessing to us personally. We can grow in a certain area of our spiritual lives if we not only accept the answer to our prayer but also practice thanksgiving. Out of ten lepers who were healed, only one returned to Jesus to give thanks and pour out his gratitude. This was much more than just a noble, well-meaning, or acceptable act of appreciation. This man had a real experience with Jesus that the other lepers who were also healed never had. For a few moments he had a heart experience with Jesus, and whatever took place between them added something to the life of this leper. Because he returned to offer thanks he had more than a healing. This leper didn't return to Jesus so he could get more, nor was his act selfishly motivated. He returned to give not to get, because it is more blessed to give than to receive. This poor, ragged, destitute leper had something to give and that something was thanksgiving.

Paul now opens another opportunity of real Christian experience to us to give thanks to God for the blessing that other Christians have been and are in our lives. There is a very special joy that is the fruit of such thanksgiving. Each of us can practice this since we all have or know somebody who has been a special blessing to us. Giving thanks for them before the Father and reminding Him of their love and generosity touches the Father's heart. He responds with joy, and when God begins to overflow with joy we become the recipients of pure and unadulterated, God-centered, God-given joy. Then there is a spiritual development that takes place within us, and we become more and more like Him. The person for whom we give thanks is blessed, God is blessed, and again we discover that it is more blessed to give than to receive.

TODAY'S GEM: *But this I say, He which soweth sparingly shall reap also sparingly; and he which soweth bountifully shall reap also bountifully* (2 Cor. 9:6).
Old Testament Reading Isaiah 56-58

Meditation. *But as touching brotherly love . . . ye yourselves are taught of God to love one another* (4:9).

We cannot despise one member of the Body and love another; to despise one of God's people is to sin against God himself. This sin will quench the Spirit and destroy our capacity to love God or the brethren. We can, however, despise and even hate the sin our brother may be into, but love the brother we must.

To write or talk about this principle is one thing, to practice it is quite another. Why do so many fail to achieve brotherly love that is uncomplicated, initiated, and made alive by the indwelling Holy Spirit? It is because they try to attain it by the power of their own wills and self-discipline. Some Christians have successfully attained a high degree of brotherly love in the natural; however, the spiritual man who hasn't developed this love in the natural to the degree that another man has cannot relate to this counterfeit because it is a work of the flesh.

The Scriptures tell us that we are to be taught of God—or should I say instructed by Him—to love one another. When God directs us to do something He also provides the resources. The first principle to learn is that we cannot fulfill God's commandments in the natural, and to do so is to put ourselves under the law. Our resultant relationship with God becomes a legal one instead of a love relationship. God is waiting for us to confess our inability to walk in His ways by our own willpower and to trust in the fellowship and power of the indwelling Holy Spirit to perform His word.

God desires that our inner motivation be pure and proper. The love that glorifies Jesus is supernatural. It is the same love that is shed abroad in our hearts by the Holy Ghost (fruit-of-the-Spirit love). Our motivation must not be to show off our Christianity but to glorify Jesus. We cannot afford to be passive, because doing nothing produces nothing. Our love for the brethren can increase more and more if we turn away from the temptation to find fault, because faultfinding destroys our spiritual ability and capacity to love.

Part of the purpose of the closet experience is to love our fellow Christian, and our daily witness is to be the fruit of that closet experience. Therefore, we should practice love, confessing it before the Father. In love we should pray for the brethren, desiring their prosperity, spiritually and materially, that they might have good health and abound in peace and joy. All that we desire for ourselves we should pray for them, then there will be an overflow from the Father. His Holy Spirit will abound with love for the brethren in and through us, and the very word God commands us to perform He will manifest in our lives by His grace.

TODAY'S GEM: Love of the brethren in the presence of the Father will result in His loving them in and through us.

Old Testament Reading Isaiah 59-61

Meditation. *Faithful is he that calleth you, who also will do it* (5:24).

I don't know who called you, but Jesus called me and really got my attention. I could not say that it was the authority in His voice any more than it was His love that drew me. If Jesus had said that He wanted to redeem me I wouldn't have understood a word of it. I just know that His presence made me feel badly about my life even though I do not think I had ever seriously thought about sin. I knew my life wasn't exactly pretty, but then whose was? It wasn't a matter of "if I died that night would I go to heaven or hell?" Jesus had called me, and there was an inner desire, which quickly grew, to know and follow Him.

Satan did everything he could to keep me from responding by even letting me see what a wretched sinner I really was. This was also conviction by the Holy Spirit, but the enemy put thoughts in my head that I was too bad for Jesus to accept me. According to his lies, Jesus would not want to keep company with me, and if He did I would mess it up anyway. He nearly had me believing his lies when he told me that this call to follow the Lord was just an emotional experience that would be over in a couple of weeks. He suggested that when the emotions of the moment had gone, so would my experience, and I would quickly slip back into my old habits and ways and be disillusioned, hurt, and sorry for myself. He almost had me convinced that it wouldn't work.

One thing of which I was convinced was that I had been called to this most meaningful and precious experience of my life; therefore, I was determined that nothing was going to rob me of it. Then Jesus and I came to a little understanding that He was to be equal to every situation that I would face. This is what I told Him in the midst of some difficult circumstances, "Jesus, if You're not equal to this situation, then You're not equal to any." Then the Lord gave me this scripture: *Faithful is he that calleth you, who also will do it.* He has remained faithful to His call. Never was there a moment, a temptation or disillusioning experience, to which Jesus was not equal. Never was there a time when He wasn't willing to be faithful to His call or willing to work it out in my experience. Faced with the consequences of Jesus' call on my life, I knew and still know that I can turn to my Lord and He will do it!

TODAY'S GEM: *He which hath begun a good work in you will perform it until the day of Jesus Christ* (Phil. 1:6).
Old Testament Reading Isaiah 62-64

OCTOBER 18   2 Thessalonians 1

Meditation. *Wherefore also we pray always for you, that our God would count you worthy of this calling, and fulfil all the good pleasure of his goodness, and the work of faith with power* (1:11).

In the Good News For Modern Man Bible this same scripture says that Paul and his co-workers would always pray for the Thessalonian Christians, that God would make them worthy of this calling.

Many years ago I read something that I believe was a prayer of Peter McCheynes. He prayed, "Lord, make me all that a redeemed sinner can be this side of heaven," and I have made this my prayer ever since. May God make me worthy because I certainly wasn't worthy of this calling when I was dead in my trespass and sin. However, there have been those who, praise God, have prayed that I might be made worthy of God's calling.

"Father, as others have prayed for me I now pray for every reader of 'Gems,' for every dear soul that holds this book and their Bible in their hands. I pray, Lord, that You do a great saving work within them, that they might be all that a redeemed sinner can be this side of heaven. May they be worthy of this calling and fulfill all the good pleasure of Your goodness."

The Christian life is not passive. God is always doing something in our lives, so let Him touch your heart today with the need to pray that God will make some dear soul worthy of His calling. God's creative work in us produces fruit, but we must be willing to cooperate by literally offering Him our hearts. Present your heart to God, trusting and knowing that He does know best. As we release our faith to Him He releases His grace to us, and the result is an outward manifestation of God's power in response to our work of faith.

God not only desires to call us, He also works in our hearts to make our calling evident to others. It is God's desire that His goodness, grace, and love be seen in us. There is nothing mediocre about God. He will so bring about a work of grace in our hearts that the wholesomeness of God, which is His holiness, will be seen in our lives. We will become such worthwhile and worthy creatures that none will doubt our calling.

Do not put any limitations on God. Let our prayer be, "Lord, make me all, all that a redeemed sinner can be this side of heaven!" Your calling assures you of God's willingness to perfect these things in your life.

TODAY'S GEM: Just as our calling was complete and total, so should our service be.

Old Testament Reading Isaiah 65-66

Meditation. *Whereunto he called you by our gospel, to the obtaining of the glory of our Lord Jesus Christ* (2:14).

When I was a young soldier there was an occasion when I volunteered for a special tour of duty in Korea. Specialists were needed from my engineering squadron, and I really wanted to go. What a letdown when I discovered my name was not on the list, and I had not been called. Looking back I now realize that there was nothing patriotic or virtuous about my intentions; I was just looking for adventure.

Now I can praise the Lord that when Dr. Billy Graham came to New Zealand in 1959 my name was on God's list. I didn't actually get to a crusade, nor did my radio allow me to hear him, but my name was on God's list just the same. He arranged for me to be called by the gospel of Jesus Christ. As the Lord spoke the gospel into my heart, it was clear and distinct, and I knew it was for me. There was a tremendous contrast in the life I was living and the life to which I had been called, but, praise God, He did call. My friend, give thanks and praise the Lord with me today that we are a called and chosen people!

God has chosen us for a distinct purpose. We will not suffer any disappointment if we will respond and walk in His call. God's people are to be a reflection of Jesus, possessing the mind of Christ and being filled with His love and compassion. He who has called will so establish us in Christ and establish Christ in us that His glory and righteousness will be seen. God's purpose for calling a people to Himself is *to the obtaining of the glory of our Lord Jesus Christ.*

Just as you give time to take care of your physical appearance each day, give time to meeting with Jesus in His Word. Then as a Christian you will reflect the likeness of Christ. Each day you will obtain a little glory and grow from glory to glory.

TODAY'S GEM: The purpose of man is the glorification of Jesus Christ in and through him.
Old Testament Reading Jeremiah 1-2

Meditation. *And the Lord direct your hearts into the love of God, and into the patient waiting for Christ* (3:5).

I really do not think Paul used idle words to communicate the life and truth that he sought to impart through his writings. It must have required much thought and prayer. He not only knew what he wanted to say, but it was his desire that his fellow Christians experience what he wrote. Paul wanted something to happen and prayed that it would. As his thoughts took on words you can rest assured that they were simply an expression of prayer. It is almost as though we could enter Paul's prayer closet and hear him making his request on this church's behalf. He was praying that the Lord would direct their hearts into the love of God and into the patient waiting for Christ. Paul knew that all these things would not happen without prayer, so this request was first of all made to the Father. Paul also knew it would not happen unless the Lord initiated this experience in their lives.

We Christians have not changed a whole lot. We talk about the potential of prayer and its power; we even read books about it and do just about everything but practice it. Let me suggest a life-changing adventure for you. Write down the names of some of your Christian friends—I would certainly be delighted if my name was included—and of course write down your own. Now pray by asking the Lord to direct their hearts (mine and yours also) into the love of God.

A little study or seminar or two might help you understand the love of God, but not a whole lot is going to happen until you go to the prayer closet and cry out to the Lord to direct each heart into the love of God. Keep doing this; place your request before Him morning after morning until some acknowledgment that He has heard and promises to answer is received. Don't cease from your persistent praying and begin praising Him until you know in your spirit that God has heard and has promised to answer.

What an experience you can have! Whatever was Paul's experience can be yours also. The love of God can be directed to your heart, initiated by the Lord himself. Patience in waiting will be yours as you persist in prayer. What might happen in the Church of Jesus Christ if some of you dear readers take up this challenge and pray this word into your experience! Why we would never be the same again!

TODAY'S GEM: To really know the Word is to experience it working in your life.

Old Testament Reading Jeremiah 3-4

Meditation. *Now the end of the commandment is charity out of a pure heart, and of a good conscience, and of faith unfeigned* (1:5).

Paul wrote that the end or goal of the commandment is love. Paul's desire was that the believer would enjoy a pure heart and a good conscience out of which love would flow.

Some years ago when I was a very young Christian, a friend who was also an elder in our church put his arm around my shoulder and suggested that I should be more loving. Unable to believe what I was hearing, I inwardly reacted to what he was saying. Hadn't I expressed love by working hard for the Lord? Hadn't God used me to lead many to Him? My family life and my relationship with my wife Marjorie were so different since Jesus had come into my life. What did this elder mean?

It wasn't long before I was telling the Lord all about it. Why if that elder could have known where the Lord had brought me from and where I now was in comparison, he would never have said that I needed to be more loving. Then the Lord began to speak to me about my attitudes and the motives behind some of the things I had done. Instead of speaking to me about how I felt toward people, God began dealing in the area of my heart and conscience. He spoke to me through the scriptures and arranged some circumstances that made it plain where my heart was. He was requiring the sort of faith that only works when we have a good conscience toward God and where it was almost impossible for me to do anything myself. Oh, there probably were some things I could have done, but I wanted to see God working in these circumstances more than I wanted the answer.

Somehow love flows best when it flows forth from a pure heart and a good conscience. When our faith becomes strong and alive, by His grace God can release a flow of His love. At the time the elder had spoken to me I had become very dogmatic about the Word and legalistic over my beliefs. My life was bound by self-imposed legalities. The law itself fails to produce tenderness of spirit, long-suffering, or gentleness. However, the heart will soon learn to reflect Jesus' love when it is unencumbered with the law, looking to Jesus to purify it, and when this is accompanied by a good, healthy, day-by-day relationship with the Lord. Give up trying to develop your own good conscience but instead expose it to Jesus daily.

Don't be secretive. Tell the Lord exactly the way it is, and see for yourself that your faith in Him will produce love out of a pure heart and a good conscience.

TODAY'S GEM: The intellect produces law without God's grace, but the purified heart produces love by the grace of God.

Old Testament Reading Jeremiah 5-6

Meditation. *For there is one God, and one mediator between God and men, the man Christ Jesus* (2:5).

There cannot be reconciliation between God and man without a mediator, which is the Lord Jesus Christ, who said that *no man cometh unto the Father, but by me* (Jn. 14:6). It was and is His desire to bring about a complete and total reconciliation between Father, Son, Holy Ghost, and man.

When first born again I quickly slipped into a very personal and uncomplicated relationship with Jesus. Without even understanding very much about His role as mediator, I willingly accepted the benefits of reconciliation. Jesus had assured me in His Word that reconciliation had taken place; therefore, I simply accepted what His Word said and praised God for my mediator, the Lord Jesus Christ. As time went by and I searched the Scriptures, the result was more and more knowledge about Jesus, and since my quiet-time with Him was consistent, an intimacy grew between us. It wasn't long before I discovered that I could be obedient and trust Jesus. So life became an adventure because Jesus was always available. No longer were the many things He required impossible, and through faith in Him I was led into many life-changing experiences. A richness became mine as I fellowshipped with my Jesus.

One day a realization came deep within my heart that I did not know the God to whom Jesus had reconciled me. Trying to comfort myself with such scriptures as *he that hath seen me hath seen the Father* (Jn. 14:9), somehow my inner spirit was not satisfied. As my mediator Jesus had reconciled me to the Father, Son, and Holy Ghost. Jesus I knew but the God to whom I had been reconciled was still a mystery. I also discovered how Jesus wanted to be the mediator in my life through a relationship with the Holy Spirit. Then I realized that the Father's relationship, which was so important and meaningful to Jesus, was to be mine also.

Legally a reconciliation had taken place, but my Mediator desires more than a legal reconciliation for His people. He wants a meaningful relationship to take place between the three persons in the Godhead and man. I realized that as my Mediator it was Jesus' desire that through Him I would have the same meaningful relationship (which was enjoyed between Jesus and me) with the persons in the Godhead—Father, Son, and Holy Ghost. This is His desire for each and every believer, so make room in your life for Jesus and not only ask but expect your Mediator, to bring you into the fullness of this experience. See if He doesn't enlarge your relationship with God.

TODAY'S GEM: Just as the curtain to the Holy of Holies, which is the presence of God himself, was torn in half, now open your heart to the Father and enter into the fullness of your priestly relationship with God.

Old Testament Reading Jeremiah 7-8

Meditation. And without controversy great is the mystery of godliness (3:16).

Today's scripture certainly has been my experience, and I wonder if it has been yours. As a young Christian I greatly admired the spiritual stature of the men of God that I heard or met and noticed that others did the same. There was a Bible teacher who came to our city about once a year. It wasn't long before students of the Word had developed some of his mannerisms. Not only did they use many of his very helpful and meaningful idioms, but they would say them in the same manner.

This was also true of a very famous and much admired minister in my country. You only had to be in his presence for a short time before sensing or feeling a godliness in his life. Many had been brought to the Lord because of this man's ministry, and these converts loved the Word, delighting in teaching and sharing it with others. In sharing the Word they took on all his little mannerisms. Listening to one of his admirers was like hearing the man himself. Even before actually meeting this man of God I had heard his admirers talking, walking, and even adopting his physical stature, but somehow it left me cold. It wasn't until meeting the man that I understood. What those who admired him really wanted was to walk in the same spiritual stature of godliness in which he walked.

Taking a man's knowledge of God's Word does not give us the same spiritual stature nor does adopting his mannerisms. A man's godliness, which is seen by men, is not something to be put on for the benefit of others. It is not the product of speech training but is the outward expression of the living Christ living by His Spirit in our lives. It is not just the result of a man's initial encounter with Jesus, but it is the fruit of a day-by-day experience with his Lord and Savior.

This man of God lived day by day with Jesus, and he didn't even have to emulate Him. Jesus himself produces godliness through each believer, treating us as individuals. Just as your salvation experience came to you in a unique manner prepared to meet your needs, that is the manner in which godliness is attained in each of us. We are unique, for we are His workmanship. What is to be seen of men is the godliness of the indwelling Christ manifesting Himself in each man's life. Then what appears a mystery becomes your experience when Jesus Christ becomes your life.

TODAY'S GEM: The mystery of godliness is Christ manifesting Himself uniquely through each individual.

Old Testament Reading Jeremiah 9-10

Meditation. *For every creature of God is good, and nothing to be refused, if it be received with thanksgiving* (4:4).

In God's dealings with Israel they were forbidden to eat certain animals. These laws were imposed on them so that the law might be a teacher through which man might discover the truth that he is a sinner in need of grace. Man had to discover the fact that if God was not in something nothing worthwhile could come out of it, and if it did not have God's blessing it could not bless man. In the Living Bible (a paraphrase of the Bible) today's scripture (verses 4 and 5) reads: *For everything God made is good, and we may eat it gladly if we are thankful for it, and if we ask God to bless it, for it is made good by the Word of God and prayer.*

I was born again into Jesus and then found myself in a church where I fellowshipped with a group of Christians who had a whole lot of dos and don'ts. One group of Christians contested with the other as to what they could or could not do. They proclaimed the grace of God but then imposed the law on their converts. It was very distressing for a young Christian who wanted to conform and walk in the ways of Jesus. We were constantly subject to all sorts of impositions that God had never put upon us. In writing to Timothy Paul explained that it is not what we eat that matters, rather it is our inner attitude, which should be one of thanksgiving toward God's provision.

While in the hospital some years ago, I still recall the day a nurse came in and out of my room, anxious about what she would do that evening. She was even a little crude in telling me that two boys wanted to take her out. Not leaving much to the imagination, she told me she didn't know which boy to go with. This nurse knew I was a Christian, and it looked as though she was trying to shock me. Calling her over to my bed, I said: "Nurse, you seem to be having some difficulty in knowing what to do. Can I present you with a rule that has helped me in making many decisions? If you can ask God's blessing on it then do it. If you can't it's not for you." She left the room a little red-faced but came back later to tell me she was going "home to mother."

If you are having difficulty in making a decision about doing or receiving something, apply this rule. Can you receive it as from the Lord with thanksgiving and ask God's blessing on it? If you can't it is not for you.

TODAY'S GEM: *The steps of a man are established by the* LORD, *when he delights in his way* (Ps. 37:23, ESV).

Old Testament Reading Jeremiah 11-13

Meditation. *Rebuke not an elder, but entreat him as a father; and the younger men as brethren; The elder women as mothers; the younger as sisters, with all purity* (5:1, 2).

There is a real need in the Church today to allow the Word of God to set our behavioral patterns. It is important, not only to our spiritual development but to the life of the Church, that we conform to these patterns set down in the Word by Paul's letter to Timothy. However, if we are to enjoy the spiritual benefits in the Church by conformity to the Word of God, then the Holy Spirit must both initiate the desire in our hearts and establish us in them. Our responsibility is to recognize in the Word the behavioral patterns that please God and then look to Him through prayer for the grace to live them. We must not give to the flesh the work that is rightfully the Holy Spirit's.

I feel certain that Paul was writing about more than social acceptance. In its better communities and finer expressions of social behavior, the world shows due respect to its elders, but Paul was writing about spiritual relationships. I can have a very beautiful fatherly relationship with an elderly, fatherly Christian or a motherly relationship with some dear elderly woman. The maturity that is theirs because of their years and the wisdom and knowledge of grace can make me appreciate them. A submissiveness to their paternal or maternal spirit can be used by God to develop certain aspects of our spiritual lives that He may have been unable to do in our own family relationships. However, some of us wouldn't have the faintest idea of how to treat a Christian brother or sister in brotherly love because we have never had the opportunity to experience it in the natural in our own family situations. But there is a special love that comes alive in our hearts when we are open to the Holy Spirit, allowing Him to work this love in and through us. To feel for a person, to reach out to them as a spiritual brother or sister and to experience the spiritual value of such an experience is I'm sure what Paul is writing about.

We would do well to see that Paul was speaking about spiritual relationships because there is life and love in them. In the Old Testament Jonathan and David had more than a natural friendship. In their endeavor to be obedient to God and as they fellowshipped in difficult circumstances, David and Jonathan enjoyed a spiritual, brotherly relationship that surpassed anything enjoyed or known in their natural family relationships. They would have gladly given their lives for each other. Why not ask the Holy Spirit to cultivate this experience in your life with all purity.

TODAY'S GEM: Love for the brethren is a grace and work of the Holy Spirit: *For whosoever shall do the will of my Father which is in heaven, the same is my brother, and sister, and mother* (Mt. 12:50).

Old Testament Reading Jeremiah 14-16

Meditation. *But godliness with contentment is great gain* (6:6).

Godliness is an expression of our attitude and activity toward God. Many young Christians are inspired to godliness when they see it in others. Their immediate response is to obtain an understanding of the Word, not always by reading the Bible but by reading books about godliness. These are usually books they feel will help them aspire to the image which they have mentally created. I am sure all of you will understand what I mean and understand that I am writing for those who have not already fallen into this trap.

Godliness does not become ours by building a mental image of the Christian we would like to be or putting on an outward show of grace as on some occasions we put on social graces. Godliness is the result of godly activity, a day-by-day pursuit of God himself. When your heart and affections are in pursuit of God and when a time is set aside each day to acquaint yourself with, listen to, and be with Him, then true godliness will be seen in your life.

Once there was a lady who tended roses. She not only grew them in her garden but also in a greenhouse, spending much of her time with them. As a result, when she left her rose garden and visited the little local store, with her came the fragrance of roses. Their fragrance soon disappeared, but while she continued to spend time with her roses their aroma was carried with her. Godliness is the fragrance of God and is only yours as you "keep company" with Him.

Paul's desire was that Timothy reflect the beauty and fragrance of God with contentment. Faith, trusting God with your circumstances and making adjustments to fit those circumstances, refusing to strive for a change in your life that God has not set before you, all this brings satisfaction. Contentment becomes yours when you accept what God accepts. External and material things do not breed spiritual satisfaction. Christian contentment comes by finding your place, wealth, recreation, and rest in God. Godliness and contentment will be yours as you continue the daily pursuit of God. Each day you will bring it with you from the prayer closet.

TODAY'S GEM: The fragrance to be brought from your prayer closet each day is godliness and contentment, which are part of the bouquet of a Christian whose fulfillment is in God.

Old Testament Reading Jeremiah 17-19

OCTOBER 27 2 Timothy 1

Meditation. *For God hath not given us the spirit of fear; but of power, and of love, and of a sound mind* (1:7).

As he continued to instruct Timothy, Paul was aware that the prince of this world is always trying to put something on us that will again bring us into bondage. He goes about like a roaring lion seeing whom he can devour, and unfortunately there are Christians who leave themselves wide open, almost inviting his attention. Paul made it very plain that fear is not from God.

Some time ago I joined myself to a small group of God's people. The size and nature of this body enabled me to be very close to them. It was not very long before I detected a spirit of fear in this group and sought the Lord as to what manner I should minister to them. The above verse of scripture has been put to music, so I taught these people this scripture in song. They sang and sang it until it became part of them and until the words and melody got down into their spirits. In the morning they even awoke singing it. Whenever they had a moment of fear they would lay hold of this verse and be reminded that God's gift was not fear but power, love, and a sound mind. One girl who was a night watchman in a large factory told me how she overcame her fears with this scripture in song. She also told me that she had successfully led another person into the same experience of deliverance that this scripture had brought her.

What we listen to affects our emotions. If we listen to every thought that comes into our minds, we would soon be in confusion. If we listen to those thought patterns that are negative and capable of producing fear, then we will be fearful. The Scriptures direct us to bring the imaginations of our minds into captivity to the gospel. The important thing is that we sift our thoughts and decide what to receive and what not to receive. Listening to and filling our minds with the Word of God, meditating on it, will enable the Word to produce its own fruit in our lives. It will not produce fear but produce power, love, and a sound mind. Today may you receive that power, love, and sound mind as the result of our meditation scripture.

TODAY'S GEM: Practice living the Word and it will live in you.
Old Testament Reading Jeremiah 20-22

OCTOBER 28   2 Timothy 2

Meditation. *The Lord knoweth them that are his* (2:19).

In the Body of Christ I have met some lonely people, those who find it difficult to know their place in the Body and those who feel neglected. Surely this scripture is the answer. *The Lord knoweth them that are his.* In today's writing let me suggest a little spiritual and practical exercise for all of us to engage in, even if we are not in the above category.

What is there special about you? How do you style your hair? If you do it for Jesus it doesn't go unnoticed. How about your eyes? Some people have the most attractive eyes. If Jesus knows you then you are more than a number, more than just another convert because He even knows the color of your eyes and probably looks to see if there is a twinkle and whether they reflect His image. Jesus also knows your height, shape, how you dress, and walk, and whether you love or are too hard on yourself. Every minute detail our Lord knows, and He cares about each one of us.

Knowing what your thoughts are, what motivates you, and what your affections are toward Him means that He knows you better than you know yourself. He possesses knowledge of how you should choose your friends, marriage partner, and your employment. However, Jesus is not a computer that has been fed facts and is matching information with information that might have been wrong when it was fed into the machine anyway. What is best for you, in what situations you might fail, and in what situation you would best succeed, those are all part of God's understanding of you. He also realizes what environment is needed for you to grow and come to a place of maturity. Paul knew all this when he instructed Timothy how to live the Christian life and what things he was to master and overcome and those things which he was to watch out for.

Let me suggest that you get alone with God. Use your quiet-time perhaps and present yourself to Him. Ask the Lord for yourself what He likes about you, or you may ask Him about your attitude toward some situation in which He has put you. Discover for yourself the one thing of which you can be absolutely certain and that is that Jesus knows you better than you know yourself. He also knows you better than you know Him.

TODAY'S GEM: With the knowledge of God comes the understanding of our total and complete acceptance in the Beloved just as we are.

Old Testament Reading Jeremiah 23-24

Meditation. *This know also, that in the last days perilous times shall come* (3:1).

In a conversation with a minister friend the other evening, I was asked if God had been speaking to me at all about preparing for the last days. Coincidentally, just a week before this I had been asked what I thought about storing food in preparation for these days. It seems that everywhere I go this question keeps popping up as God's people ask themselves the question: "What can I do to be equipped or prepared to face these perilous times in the last days about which Paul has written?"

Well, I do not have all the answers, but perhaps that is good. How can we expect to walk in Paul's predicted perilous times and receive directions, perhaps life-saving directions, and to have confidence in our guidance if we can't hear what the Lord is saying right now about preparation? If we are deaf to God's guidance and direction now, what makes us think that we are suddenly going to start hearing then? Do we have to wait for perilous times before we develop a personal hearing and obedient relationship with God? Now is the time to develop a daily walk with the Lord, learning to listen and getting to know ourselves and our weaknesses. If we are unable to hear the Lord speak to us in the good times, we certainly will not hear Him when times get hard, not unless we do something about it right now. If we have difficulty trusting God and being obedient today, we are not going to suddenly become obedient. Now is the time to learn to trust and obey.

By all means store food if this is what you are hearing the Lord say to you, but let me sound a word of caution. Do not put your faith in these external or perishable possessions. Center your faith in those things that are eternal. Develop your faith in Jesus' ability to communicate and your ability to hear, to follow, and be obedient. Work these things into your daily experience by a quiet-time relationship with Jesus, and you will walk when others fall. You will be part of God's answer to the perilous days instead of one of God's casualties.

TODAY'S GEM: *And the rain descended, and the floods came, and the winds blew, and beat upon that house; and **it fell not**: for it was founded upon a rock* (Mt. 7:25, emphasis mine). Jesus is the Rock.

Old Testament Reading Jeremiah 25-26

Meditation. *Notwithstanding the Lord stood with me, and strengthened me . . . And the Lord shall deliver me . . . and will preserve me unto his heavenly kingdom* (4:17, 18).

I never have been a very strong person—obedient, yes—but constantly, daily in need of the Lord Jesus Christ to stand with and strengthen me. In foreign countries (so far away from home) I have been subjected to being led away by police to be held and questioned, and, on one occasion, separated from my wife and daughter, not knowing what was happening.

Then there were the times the Lord told me to give my money to a pastor, a missionary, and a widowed lady. On each occasion it was all the money my family and I had. There were no savings, nothing to fall back on, or somebody to go to who might help. Jesus was in control, directing me to give and give all while He stood with me. His standing there strengthened me in the inner man, or I would have failed Him.

Marjorie and I once stood by the bed of our dying son when Jesus directed us to let go of the situation and hand our son and his life over to God. Never expecting to see our son in this world again, we left his bedside in obedience to the Lord's still, small voice. However, Jesus stood there with us and changed the whole situation. He strengthened us and delivered our son.

In my early days as a baby Christian there were some bad moments. Our house caught on fire, we were plagued with sickness and suffered many things, but notwithstanding the Lord stood with us. Today someone needed a little reminder of that fact. Some dear soul is hurting, bewildered, and in need of direction; however, in the midst of your conflict let me remind you where to focus your eyes. Do not focus them on the problem because it will surely overwhelm you. Wipe away the tears, my friend, and look, because notwithstanding the Lord stands there.

Jesus will be with you in this conflict, and He will still be there when other difficulties assail you. If He is there when you are having your quiet-times and having spiritual mountaintop experiences, if He is there when everything is going well, then you can rest assured that He will be there when the circumstances are not so good. Let us learn to see Jesus with the eyes of faith and trust Him. Build into your spirit that inner knowing that without exception the Lord stands with you, and He will preserve you unto His heavenly kingdom.

TODAY'S GEMS: *Commit thy way unto the LORD; trust also in him* (Ps. 37:5). *For he hath said, I will never leave thee, nor forsake thee* (Heb. 13:5).

Old Testament Reading Jeremiah 27-28

Meditation. *In hope of eternal life, which God, that cannot lie, promised before the world began* (1:2).

I have learned to appreciate the word hope and what it means to our salvation experience. We use it in an entirely different context today when we talk about hoping for something. If we are hoping for a thing to happen, it may or may not. It is almost interchangeable with wishing. There is nothing positive about the way we use the word hope today.

This was not true for Paul. When he said he had a hope in eternal life, he had something to hold on to. He could look down the way a little and see God building eternal life—God's quality of life—into his experience. Paul was not wishing. There was no possibility of God withholding from him the eternal life hoped for if he walked in Christ. Faith had already served Paul well. By faith he had seen, heard, was motivated to believe and had received Christ as his personal savior and companion. He was baptized, and by faith he identified with the death of Jesus Christ. Indeed he was baptized into Jesus' death. By faith Paul walked in the Lord's cleansing blood. Repentance became his continuing experience, and there was a continuing infilling of the Holy Spirit which Paul spoke about in Ephesians.

From Paul's position in Christ, maintaining a pure heart and a good conscience, he saw eternity stretching before him. Eternal life with all its benefits, cleansings, keeping powers, and ability to save to the uttermost was his one day at a time by faith. The more he appropriated the more he saw and the more he was able to hope. Paul knew it was only a matter of time when more and more of the Kingdom would be his.

Paul's hope was not in wishing for more of the Kingdom. His hope was in the knowledge that it was already his. There was no principality or power that could separate Paul from the hope that was within him. He could not appropriate heaven or the reality of life after death by faith, nor could he appropriate the vision of the gathering before the throne or the banquet feast with the Lord Jesus Christ. These were realities hoped for, and he had faith in Jesus to make these "hoped-for" realities his.

TODAY'S GEM: *Now faith is the substance of things hoped for, the evidence of things not seen* (Heb. 11:1).

Old Testament Reading Jeremiah 29-30

Meditation. [Jesus] *gave himself for us, that he might redeem us from all iniquity, and purify unto himself a peculiar people, zealous of good works* (2:14).

As a Christian each day of your life begins as a result of Jesus having given Himself for you. Yesterday was a very special day for me. Nothing was planned; it was just that my wife and I did a lot of neat things together. This would not have been possible if Jesus had not given Himself for us. Now that most of my family of six children is grown, we have had some opportunity to enjoy our grandchildren. However, we realize that it would not have worked out that way if Jesus had not given himself for us, because everything worthwhile in life began when I realized that that was what He had done for me.

In looking back at my first experience as a Christian, I must admit there were many doubts and fears as to whether that new life in Christ could continue. There were times when I was certain it was all over, but He who began that good work by giving Himself for me had no intention of not finishing that work of grace. Jesus just keeps on redeeming us from all iniquity.

I am sure you know that it is quite an experience to break the habits of many years. Things that had always been acceptable in the past suddenly became out of place in that new life in Christ, but He continues to redeem us from them. Changes have taken place in each of our lives, and we are just beginning to settle down to appreciate the good work Jesus has done.

Outward habits that could not fit into our new life in Christ have gone because He has redeemed us from them. Then we discover something else happening as our inner feelings and thought processes are touched by the living Christ who dwells within us by His Spirit. Our desires, thoughts, and inner motivations center on Jesus as He begins to purify His people. Interest in the things that were once so important to us is lost. There was a time when we worked for comforts, rewards, money, and position but not now. Our motives are purified, and our hearts and love for Him are not divided. Because of this purification we must appear peculiar to the worldly Christians who are busy gathering unto themselves. They try to hide their intentions, to put on a religious cloak, but their good works give them away. However, our zealousness in good works comes from a purified heart.

TODAY'S GEM: As we allow Jesus to purify our inner thoughts and motives, our lives and works will be the overflow of a Christ-centered life.

Old Testament Reading Jeremiah 31-32

Meditation. *That being justified by his grace, we should be made heirs according to the hope of eternal life* (3:7).

Just being reminded that I am justified by Jesus' grace will make today a different day for me. I really don't have a legal mind, but I do understand that my marriage could never have been blessed the way it has if it had not had a legal beginning and foundation. In our love for one another my wife and I enjoy a freedom because of a legal, covenanted relationship. It won't make or save our marriage but does give us a liberty in our relationship which we could not have had otherwise.

To be justified before God by His grace gives us a freedom, a liberty to build into our lives a covenanted relationship with the Lord Jesus Christ. To be justified by grace makes that freedom of relationship legal. No man can take it away, and death cannot terminate it. *What therefore God hath joined together, let not man put asunder* (Mk. 10:9). If we are justified by grace, and we are, then the moment we confess our sin believing in the saving grace of the Lord Jesus Christ and receive Him and His forgiveness, He brings us into reconciliation with the Father. Then and only then (the moment we are born again) our names are written in the Lamb's book of life. Our new-birth experience is recorded, and we are adopted. Praise God, all is legally sealed for our justification. We can never be any more or any less justified than we are right now by God's grace. Now the work begins because we are being made heirs according to the hope of eternal life.

In my fellowship with Christians over the years I have noticed how those who are solid, unshakable, and constantly unfaltering also have a solid, unshakable hope. They know where they are going and are not living as if they need the things of this world forever. Their hope in eternal life is alive. It is real for them right now as they are seeing more and more of their inheritance in Christ. Their faith is solid in their legal justification, and they are cooperating with the Holy Spirit in obedience to the Word. The Living Word is theirs, and they are being made heirs, enjoying a lively hope because eternal life is within them. It is all within their reach.

TODAY'S GEM: Through the New Covenant we are legal heirs to our inheritance in Christ, which is to be realized right now.

Old Testament Reading Jeremiah 33-35

Meditation. *Yea, brother, let me have joy of thee in the Lord* (20).

There was a time when I was more involved in child evangelism. The children would give themselves to Jesus, have a real born-again experience, and then at some time in their experience you would tell them you were their brother. Their little faces would light up, and the realization that you were their brother in the Lord would really touch them and you. I must confess that my feelings are somewhat the same while writing these "Gems." I really feel for you and have no hesitation in baring my heart before you because I am sensing your brotherly and sisterly love.

There is a joy in the Lord that is mine from the sheer privilege of sharing my life in Christ with you. You who are lonely and see very few people, I praise God I can enter your homes and hearts to comfort, encourage, and remind you that it would never have been like this if Jesus had not cared. What a joy is mine in being able to set before you this wonderful life in Christ that can mean so much more when it is a brother or sister in Christ sharing it with you.

How much then does this love mean to Jesus, our elder brother? Our hearts are at His disposal. The hand that holds this pen is available to Him, and it is His Holy Spirit dwelling within me that stimulates and makes alive that love. Our big brother Jesus is not slow to tell of His love for us because He desires an intimate, brotherly or sisterly relationship. It is His joy to know that He can set before His brothers and sisters His written word, just as surely as Paul's letter was set before Philemon. Jesus looks for and delights Himself in our response to His Word. He has a right to expect our obedience but approaches us in love, hoping that we will respond in love. For us to respond out of obligation would be distasteful to Him.

We were once the runaway, the unprofitable servant, but now Jesus can look into the face of the Father and say: "Father, look at this brother or this sister. Rejoice with Me in their love for You and their love for one another. I have given them back to the world, for they are the salt of the earth." My dear sister or brother, rejoice with me in Jesus' love and the love of the brethren. Let this love be shed abroad in our hearts by the Holy Ghost. "Yea, brother and sister, let me have joy of thee in the Lord!"

TODAY'S GEM: Like the prodigal son we were lost but now found; therefore, let us enter into an intimate relationship with our elder brother Jesus.

Old Testament Reading Jeremiah 36-37

Meditation.   [God] *Hath in these last days spoken unto us by his Son, whom he hath appointed heir of all things, by whom also he made the worlds* (1:2).

Whatever a man sets his heart on has a tremendous influence on his life and shapes or forms his character. The business world has very successfully proven this principle. Set your heart on making dollars, adopt a positive attitude, discipline yourself, and you will make money. At the same time these disciplines and desires are character forming. So be careful because vanity, pride and fear might become the fruit of your efforts.

Every desire of the heart, good or bad, that I know of leads to a dead end, bar one. When that goal that you thought would be a crowning success is obtained, it becomes empty and flat and usually has some pretty bad side effects on your character. However, I said every desire bar one. God is booming it out at us, spelling it out in capital letters, that in these last days He, God, has spoken to us in the person of His Son. God's Word is final. There never will be a greater and plainer communication from Him. If we cannot or will not hear, there is no other plan that God might produce to communicate. You and I live in the last days, and in these last days God has spoken to us through His Son.

If we are to hear what God is saying, there must be a turning away from all other desires so that our hearts' desires become centered on God. Everything we do, say, and are must be the product of who He is. He is like a tuning fork to our lives. Everything must come into line with God, and that is the result of centering our lives on Him. The fruit of this will be the development of a God-honoring, God-built character. Had we given way to and set our hearts on other desires they would have ruined us, but now if God would allow us these desires they will occupy a balanced place in our hearts. They will become secondary to our true desire, which is Christ; however, they can safely share the heart, providing they are His heart's desire also.

All the questions you have about guidance, ethics and morality will fall into place in your experience in a very natural and peaceful way when your heart's desire and your pursuit is not these topical questions but Jesus Christ himself. God's best and final word to you and me is: Put God first!

TODAY'S GEM: To be in tune with God put Him in the center of your life (on the throne).

Old Testament Reading Jeremiah 38-39

Meditation. *For which cause he is not ashamed to call them brethren* (2:11).

The Christ (Jesus) with whom we can have fellowship even at this very moment was once made lower than the angels. He who from the beginning was with God is equal to God and, as the writer to the Hebrews says, is God himself. He laid aside His glorious divinity that was His before the world was in existence, and Hebrews 2:9 says that Jesus *was made a little lower than the angels for the suffering of death . . . that he by the grace of God should taste death for every man.*

By His death Jesus took our sin to the grave. He buried himself in the sufferings of death that He might destroy the sin principle and the judgment that had bound us to death. Overcoming death on our behalf, Jesus so completely destroyed it that death itself became a crown of glory and honor to Him. Down through the ages the multitude of believers has applauded this great mystery and mastery over death, and generation after generation honors and praises Him for that deliverance.

Jesus marched down the corridors of time, gathering to Himself the sin of God's people. Every one of us has had to lay our sin upon Jesus. That sin principle controlled our lives and sought to destroy us and indeed would have destroyed us. The Bible says *there is none righteous, no, not one* (Rom. 3:10). Jesus took upon himself that which sought to destroy us and carried our sin into the place of death. Then, crowned with glory and honor, Jesus was raised from the vileness of sin to become our captain, our leader, turning away from that sin principle and leading us in His glorious light.

Jesus presents us to the Father saying: "See, I have cleansed them. I have led them out of death and into eternal life." Jesus stands proudly before the Father seeing only the perfecting work of the cross, the cleansing of the shed blood. I can almost hear Jesus with much affection saying, "Look closely, Father, for these are My brethren." There is no shame at our former sin as Jesus presents us with joy to the Father as His brothers and sisters who are complete in Him.

TODAY'S GEM: He has made us one with the Father, acknowledging us as His brethren!

Old Testament Reading Jeremiah 40-42

Meditation. *Wherefore, holy brethren, partakers of the heavenly calling* (3:1).

As a young Christian it really did something for me to know that Jesus considers me a brother and refers to me as one of His brethren. I especially remember in Matthew's Gospel when Jesus was told His brethren were outside wanting to see Him. *But he answered and said . . . who are my brethren?* (Mt. 12:48). *For whosoever shall do the will of my Father . . . the same is my brother* (Mt. 12:50).

From yesterday's devotional I am reminded how you and I became Jesus' brethren and His joy at being able to present us to His Father, but today I read how we are His holy brethren. Glory to God! Get hold of this truth, and it will make your day. Jesus not only considers us brethren but Paul said that we are holy—His holy brethren—made holy by Jesus' cleansing blood. In the Old Testament the command or demand of the law was that *ye shall be holy; for I am holy* (Lev. 11:44). Under the law we could never have attained to holiness or fulfilled it, but now in Christ we are holy because He is holy. Jesus has taken our sin, washed us in His blood, and made us to be one with Him and the Father. Again let me say, because Jesus is holy we are holy. We are partakers and participants; in that is the life of the gospel. As brethren in Christ, Jesus' heavenly calling becomes ours. Whatever He is we are also.

There was a time in our lives when we lived in sin, were bound by it, and lived in a world of sin. The sin nature was alive within us, but now that is not so. Now we live in Christ, participating in His heavenly calling. The nature of Christ lives in us. Yes, we abide in the world but just for a season as sojourners, a people who are passing through. No longer do we consider ourselves brethren to those who are not in Christ and are of the world. *And now I am no more in the world, but these are in the world, and I come to thee. Holy Father, keep through thine own name those whom thou hast given me, that they may be one, as we are* (Jn. 17:11).

We are Jesus' brethren, His holy brethren. As we become one with Him who is holy, we take on His holiness, and we are holy as He is. The more your mind dwells on Jesus' holiness and who He is, the more you will outwardly manifest what you are in Him.

TODAY'S GEM: As joint heirs with Jesus Christ we are what He is and share in His heavenly calling.

Old Testament Reading Jeremiah 43-45

Meditation. *For we which have believed do enter into rest* (4:3).

The first verse of this chapter reads, *Let us therefore fear, lest, a promise being left us of entering into his rest, any of you should seem to come short of it.* At the very outset we should understand the rest that the holy brethren enjoy is God's rest, which is the reward of those who appropriate it by faith. God worked six days in the creation of the world and then rested from His labors. Man's first day as man was God's day of rest. From the very beginning God's best for man was that he might enter into His rest.

Man had nothing to do with the creation of the world. The work was finished. God created, saw that it was good, and, upon completion of His labors, God introduced man into what He himself had created. Creation belongs to the Father not to us. We can enjoy it for a season and then pass on.

There is, however, a rest in Christ. After having completed the work of redemption by His death and resurrection, Jesus sat down on the right hand of God, His work of reconciling us to the Father completed. There is nothing you and I can do; the work of redemption is finished. All that is left for us is to by faith enter into the rest that is already His.

We can deceive ourselves into thinking we have to do all sorts of good works, but deception comes because of a lack of faith in what Jesus has done. Faith lays hold of what He has accomplished, believes in it, and enters into His rest from the finished work upon the cross. From this place of rest in Christ by faith, Jesus can then manifest His life within us. Rest produces the manifestation of the indwelling life of Christ, which gives us a testimony. From our place of rest in Him He will give us victory over temptation. Principalities and powers will bow to Jesus' presence and His life in us. Many wonderful and beautiful experiences will be ours as we remain in His rest. Our wills become one, and from that place of rest we begin doing the will of the Father. Guard carefully, my brethren; fear lest you should come short of God's best, which is His rest.

TODAY'S GEM: It is finished. Now enter into God's rest by faith.
Old Testament Reading Jeremiah 46-48

Meditation. *Who can have compassion on the ignorant, and on them that are out of the way; for that he himself also is compassed with infirmity* (5:2).

Praise God that we have a High Priest who can have compassion. In our heads we know this truth and probably confess it over and over again to others, but do we sense and feel the compassion of Christ in our hearts? When we are feeble and our weaknesses get in our way, interfering with doing God's will, do we come to Him and partake of His comfort and compassion? Our weakness can be turned into strength if we will trust Jesus in the midst of it.

When we lack understanding and are mindful of our ignorance, do we go to Jesus and share the pain of our ignorance in order to draw His understanding, love, and compassion from the warmth of His heart? If so, we have learned to use our infirmities well. However, the temptation is to use our weakness and feebleness to justify our inability to walk in God's will. This leads to disaster, disobedience, and sin. Jesus himself was not without infirmity. He was in the garden of Gethsemane praying when he cried out to God from His infirmity. Asking that the cup might pass from Him, Jesus prayed vigorously until great drops of blood appeared on His forehead.

Jesus did not tell His Father that He was not equal to what He had been called to walk in so He could be excused. The Father knew Jesus, in His humanity, was not equal to the situation and that He would have to come to His Son in that weakness so He could be Jesus' strength. I am sure the Father felt His Son's weakness and yielded a heart of compassion to Jesus until He could resist the will of the Father no longer. Jesus laid aside His own will to take up His Father's.

Jesus, our High Priest, has experienced infirmity or feebleness. He has been there and has felt the shame and hurt of it until He cried out to the Father in near defeat. Jesus knows and feels your infirmities. His heart is open to you, and He waits for you to come to Him in your weakness to find His compassion and strength. This is all part of our completeness in Christ.

TODAY'S GEM: As Jesus commended His Spirit into the hands of the Father, so should you commend yours to Christ.

Old Testament Reading Jeremiah 49-50

Meditation. *Which hope we have as an anchor of the soul, both sure and stedfast, and which entereth into that within the veil* (6:19).

We who have the hope have been nominated by Jesus to be His brethren. He has encouraged us to leave behind the principles of the doctrines of Christ, which are foundational truths. Because the foundation for our faith should have been solidly laid in Christ, we can now press on with Him into a whole new realm of Christian truth and experience.

The writer to the Hebrew Christians sees them as a ship anchored in the bay with Jesus like that unseen anchor. The sailors go about their duties totally unconcerned for the stability of their ship because out of sight beneath the waters they know that anchor is not only there but there to hold. They know the nature and structure of the anchor and its ability to hold the ship securely. Even when a strong wind blows through the rigging of the ship and the seas heave that vessel around, their faith—or I should say their hope—is in that unseen anchor that remains sure and steadfast.

Our Anchor, or Leader, is no longer wandering around Israel in a gospel dispensation. He has ascended. He rests in still waters and has disappeared out of sight within the veil. The next verse says that Jesus is the forerunner and has entered in on our behalf. Jesus has become a high priest forever after the order of Melchisedec and now desires that we know Him in His never-ending office. Jesus desires for us to have our hope in Him as the anchor—Christ within the veil—and that we no longer be anxious or concerned about our salvation experience, for we are established in these foundational truths. He now bids us to know and fellowship with Him, living our lives with our lines cast and anchored in the place of rest and victory that He has won for us. Within the veil we can triumph and overcome; so let us follow our Forerunner and enter in.

TODAY'S GEM: Your foundation is Christ as your lord and savior. Now continue to build your Christian experience by entering into fellowship with your Great High Priest within the veil.

Old Testament Reading Jeremiah 51-52

Meditation. *Wherefore he is able also to save them to the uttermost that come unto God by him, seeing he ever liveth to make intercession for them* (7:25).

From the days of Aaron there was a continual succession of priests. The whole system was limited as to its character according to the ability of the priest. With nothing permanent it was full of weaknesses as priests came and went; however, all this has now been changed by this man Jesus because He continues forever, having an unchangeable and permanent priesthood.

Our salvation experience is centered in the Lord Jesus Christ, our Great High Priest who will never die and will never pass His office on to another. He lives forever to make intercession for us. In the world we live in very unstable times, but in Christ we have stability because He never changes. It is the responsibility of Jesus' office to intercede on our behalf. We can be certain that He will never tire of this responsibility and never grow too old. Because Jesus lives forever He is able to pray to the Father continually on our behalf.

I find myself constantly counseling brethren who complain that Jesus is not always as near to them as they would like. They say that the feeling of His nearness, which they had enjoyed in the past, is lacking. Jesus' answer is for us to draw near, enter in, and meet with Him within the veil.

I very seldom ask the brethren to pray for me. There was a time when I did, and there are many times when we must. However, I am a little slow in going to the brethren when I can go to Jesus directly and have Him make intercession on my behalf. We are called to live our new life in Christ within the veil, availing ourselves of His office of great high priest.

Our coming to Jesus enables Him to save and to save to the uttermost. If we are fainting a little in our faith, then coming to Him means He can fulfill His promises. Are you hurting? Are you plagued by failure, or is sin robbing you of your joy? Then come to Jesus that He might intercede and save you to the uttermost since He lives to make intercession for you.

TODAY'S GEM: Come boldly into the throne room, for Jesus liveth to make intercession for His brethren.

Old Testament Reading Lamentations 1-2

Meditation. *Now of the things which we have spoken this is the sum: We have such an high priest, who is set on the right hand of the throne of the Majesty in the heavens; A minister of the sanctuary, and of the true tabernacle, which the Lord pitched, and not man* (8:1-2).

Each day we have been reading this letter to the Hebrew Christians and have been led somewhere in our spiritual understanding. Only by the Spirit can this letter be understood, and only by the Spirit can we be led into the experience of it. Our intellects could never comprehend this mystery that is unfolding systematically before us.

Moses built a tabernacle that was a type or replica of a tabernacle in heaven and was a place of sacrifice where the blood continually flowed. It was also an expression of praise and cleansing, a place where priests were continually ministering and were constantly before God on behalf of their people. For the people to respond and participate, on their part it required obedience to the law and the legalities of the tabernacle.

Now the writer to the Hebrews speaks of another tabernacle—a sanctuary in heaven where Jesus, our Great High Priest and King, ministers unto the Lord our God with praises and holy sanctified worship. There is nothing legal about it or the intercessions being made. Jesus, as priest, has offered His sacrifice. There is a continual flow of the Blood cleansing all who, by the Spirit, have the right to participate.

Jesus left the disciples, took up His office in the heavenly sanctuary, and sent His Holy Spirit, which is the Spirit of the sanctuary, to us. This tabernacle not made by man but by the Spirit of God extends into our very hearts so that we, you and I, can have access by the Spirit into the heavenly sanctuary and be brought into the presence of the Father by our Great High Priest. We have been born again by the Spirit from above that we might participate in the heavenly function of this holy sanctuary. Make a place for vocal praise in your quiet-time experience. By faith you have an opportunity to enter into the greatest mystery of all time. It is hidden from the legal or intellectual mind, but, by the Spirit, an extension of the heavenly sanctuary becomes yours in your heart.

TODAY'S GEM: The true tabernacle is in the heart of man where the Spirit of God dwells.

Old Testament Reading Lamentations 3-5

Meditation. *The Holy Ghost this signifying, that the way into the holiest of all was not yet made manifest* (9:8).

According to the Old Covenant, in the temple worship only the priests ministered in the holy place, and before them hung the great curtain or veil. They practiced their priestly duties before this veil which hung or stood before them as a great sentinel separating them from the Holy of Holies or holiest of all where the very presence of God dwelled. God did not dwell in their priestly practices but behind the veil. Their sacrifices made on behalf of the people, the lamp that was tended so it would never go out, and the shewbread prepared and placed on the table—all these religious practices were conducted outside the presence of God. This was the way the Holy Spirit showed that the way into the Most Holy Place had not yet been revealed. The way to the Holy of Holies was never made open except for one selected priest who was very carefully prepared, sanctified, and dressed for the occasion. Once a year, probably once in a lifetime, he would actually enter into the presence of God who dwelled in the Holy of Holies and was seated on the mercy seat between the cherubim.

Under the New Covenant the veil has been removed, and by revelation the Holy Spirit leads us into the Holy of Holies. What the Holy Spirit could not do under the Old Covenant He can now do under the New. Jesus himself has taken His place in the Holy of Holies, which is the sanctuary not made by human hands. He has sent the Holy Spirit to us that He might communicate to our spirits and by revelation lead us into the sanctuary, which is the very presence of God. We are no longer to practice our religion under law outside the dwelling place of God but are to enter boldly into His very presence.

The Holy Spirit once signified that the Holy of Holies was not open to God's people under the Old Covenant. He now signifies—nay, He bids us with joy—that we are to enter this very holy place into which He will lead us. Therefore, all our Christian practices, the very life of Christ that we live, have the fragrance of and their origin in the heavenly sanctuary. Let us open our hearts to the Holy Spirit, the keeper of the sanctuary, that having removed the veil He might lead us so we may dwell where Christ dwells and be full of this heavenly mystery, which is our oneness in Christ Jesus in the sanctuary.

TODAY'S GEM: Under the Old Covenant the Holy of Holies was closed to us, but now we can boldly enter into God's presence and be one with Him in Christ.

Old Testament Reading Ezekiel 1-3

Meditation. *Let us draw near with a true heart in full assurance of faith* (10:22).

What can these words mean to us unless we take God at His word and draw near with a true heart and a full assurance of faith? He has made it very plain that the work of redemption was sufficient to allow us to enter with Jesus, our Great High Priest, into the Holy of Holies, which is the presence of God. One blood sacrifice by Jesus cleansed us from all sin. By writing these truths in our hearts, He has given us an inner witness of the spirit that they are true. He has given us a new heart and sent the Holy Spirit to introduce us to the realities of these truths so we might enter into a new and living way.

Now Jesus himself calls us to draw near. As soon as the reality of His blood sacrifice—His death upon the cross—is written in our hearts, He calls us to move on. We then become concerned about our sanctification and enter the holy place where the priests are continually ministering to the Lord. There is much activity; lamps are continually being filled and a variety of services and ceremonies are performed as unto the Lord. Praise God, now under the New Covenant we can have more than just a legal experience. Now we can have an everlasting heart experience. Yet Jesus again says, "Draw near."

Until the Holy Spirit reveals to you the truth that the curtain is no longer there and that you need not linger in foundational experiences, there is no understanding. There is just an inward desire or restlessness as your inner spirit desires to move on and draw near. Then the Holy Spirit comes, and with faith in your cleansing you enter in with boldness. The sanctuary then becomes your home. There is spiritual harmony and your heart rests in this sanctuary experience. Now Jesus becomes more than savior and reconciler. He performs His office of Great High Priest and King in your heart. So hearken and be encouraged. The King of heaven bids you to draw near with a true heart. Do you hear that? He bids you to draw near!

TODAY'S GEM: The Great High Priest bids you to enter the sanctuary into the very presence of God because the Blood sacrifice was and is sufficient for your cleansing.

Old Testament Reading Ezekiel 4-6

Meditation. *And let us consider one another to provoke unto love and to good works* (10:24).

Let me begin your day with a story. A lady went off to a seven-day, Christian, summer camp. While she was away nobody bothered to water and care for her grass in the same manner she would have if she had been home. Each day it died just a little until by the end of the seven days of scorching sunshine the grass was almost dead. Immediately upon her return she lovingly watered her grass, and it was amazing how quickly it recovered.

Just seven days of quiet-time, seven days of getting alone with God and entering into a valid experience of pressing on and drawing near to Him, brings about a life-changing experience. Setting aside time to fellowship in the heavenly sanctuary permeates your inner life with its holiness. The peace and joy, praise, and worship and the presence of the indwelling Christ in your heart life can initiate all sorts of wonderful manifestations of God. They initiate the most wonderful manifestation that surely is the greatest—God's love, sanctuary love.

With so much going on in your heart, you are going to have to share. Others are going to see the change and will be asking questions. You cannot meet with Jesus in the sanctuary every day and not have some changes in your life. So out of love consider others' needs. Provoke them into seeing that to be saved is to be a doer of God's will. Jesus did, and He continues to do, the will of the Father. For every believer God's will is for them to have a sanctuary experience of entering into the Holy of Holies and knowing the Lord Jesus Christ as their High Priest. Provoke others by encouraging them to set aside time each day to enter into a relationship with the Holy Spirit, who will lead them into a meaningful, life-changing experience. Encourage them in love. Don't give up until they are quiet-time practicing Christians, and in their lives you will, as the scripture says, be able to see in them your good works.

TODAY'S GEM: Love can initiate a life-changing experience in others by sharing a heart experience with them.

Old Testament Reading Ezekiel 7-9

Meditation. *But without faith it is impossible to please him: for he that cometh to God must believe that he is, and that he is a rewarder of them that diligently seek him* (11:6).

Having reminded us of these mighty men of God who had great faith, Paul said that when the promises of God were set before them *they were persuaded of them, and embraced them: and confessed that they were strangers and pilgrims on the earth* (Heb. 11:13). The promise of a heavenly city and a king had so changed their lives that to them their earthly experience was a pilgrimage. They were strangers to everything outside of the promise. Even so, the Word tells us that they all died in faith not having received the promise.

Those men lived waiting, believing and looking forward to the day God's promise would be a reality, but we live in a day of grace when these promises can be ours right now. By the working of the Holy Spirit in our hearts we can experience what these men longed for. By faith they saw the coming of the messiah, but we have the opportunity to embrace that Messiah and confess Him as our own lord and savior. They diligently sought after the promise and were rewarded for their diligence and faith, but we have the opportunity to seek out and enter into a meaningful relationship with the One who had set the promise before them. These were things they only dreamed of but are now found by those who will diligently seek Him.

What more can God do? He has sent His Son Jesus that His shed and sacrificed blood might prepare us for such a relationship. In turn, Jesus has sent the Holy Spirit so we might be led into the Holy of Holies, which is the very dwelling place of God himself. Jesus has persuaded us of His love, and by that love He has embraced us by confessing His love for us on the cross. His will is that we might diligently seek Him. If we lack any good thing, even faith, Jesus will reward with faith those who seek Him.

Believer, Jesus offers us so much, such rewards and love beyond our understanding. Through a little diligence, a little time for Jesus in the sanctuary, He will give us His Holy Spirit to dwell within us, and we will have the "sanctuary joy" of pleasing Him.

TODAY'S GEM: We are but pilgrims on the earth, but the promise is ours, and God is *the rewarder of those who diligently seek Him* (rewards beyond measure!).

Old Testament Reading Ezekiel 10-12

Meditation.   *By faith* (11:20).

By faith Isaac blessed his seed, and it was the word of promise made to his father Abraham that kindled faith within him. Even though he did not live to see the promise fulfilled, Isaac lived by faith and died believing the promise. By faith in the same promise Jacob blessed Joseph's sons, seeing in them the promise of a great nation. It was faith that saw a people of God and a mighty Deliverer, a Messiah!

Joseph, while dying, also saw the reality of things to come by faith. He saw a people of promise. When they were but a family he saw a nation. So intense was his faith in the promise that he gave commandments concerning the disposition of his body after death.

In the midst of a people of promise Moses was born at a time when they suffered great affliction. He was baptized into faith by his mother, who saw in him only what the eye of faith could have seen. Her faith was a channel through which God saved Moses' life.

When Moses became of age, faith in God and his people, who were now suppressed and suffering, caused him to come to a place of decision. He not only refused the comforts of the world but he refused to compromise with its spirit. Moses chose to be one with a people who were suffering because they were the people of the promise. From the people and the spirit of the world Moses separated himself unto the God who had made to a people the promise of being a great nation. There certainly was no evidence of the promise, and there was nothing great about the people of God and their circumstances. All they had was the promise.

Faith enabled Moses to leave his comforts, his home, the Egyptian people who loved him, and the people he wished to identify with who had rejected him. Faith helped Moses endure and led him to seek and ultimately find the invincible God who had made the promise. Moses expressed faith in the works of God and even kept the Passover because he had faith in the blood and a healthy fear of God.

My dear friends, these men of faith walked in the expectation of a promise yet to be fulfilled, but we are a people who have that very promise and have entered in. All their expectations are now ours to experience. While In worship Moses had only a type of the heavenly, we have the reality of it. With what intensity will we separate ourselves from the world and give of ourselves to live in the fullness of the promised Christ, living by faith to do His will?

TODAY'S GEM: We are the people of the promise that has already been fulfilled. So enter in!

Old Testament Reading Ezekiel 13-15

Meditation. *Wherefore seeing we also are compassed about with so great a cloud of witnesses, let us lay aside every weight, and the sin which doth so easily beset us, and let us run with patience the race that is set before us, Looking unto Jesus the author and finisher of our faith* (12:1-2).

What a great witness of faith precedes this verse. It is like a cloud of witnesses acclaiming that by faith they have run the race that has been set before us and now fill the seats in the arena, watching and waiting to encourage us in our race by their example.

It is time to be serious and recognize that we are involved in a life and death contest. Even though we have been born again and the Holy Spirit of Jesus lives in our hearts, we are in mortal combat. The spirit of this world seeks to lure and seduce us away from Christ. The devil just never gives up seeking out our weaknesses and pampering us until we are surrounded by such comforts and indulging in self-centered occupations that there is no way we can run a race. It is not very long before our hearts' desires are for the things of this world, and we even participate in deceiving ourselves into thinking that this is God's prosperity. The seriousness of pursuing Christ is gone. We even have answers for those who dare to quote such scriptures as *whosoever he be of you that forsaketh not all that he hath, he cannot be my disciple* (Lk. 14:33).

For those of you who have forsaken all and have laid aside every besetting sin, you are committed to run the race. The words *"let us lay aside, let us run,"* suddenly become alive with meaning. God never did call us to run alone. Separation does not mean loneliness. It means separation unto Him. He who is the author and finisher of our faith is the One who paces us. He doesn't run around any of the hurdles we take but instead jumps over them with us. Is the going hard? Jesus is right alongside pacing us every step of the way. Did you make a mistake and take a wrong turn? He is there with you to lead you back into the race. If you feel like giving up He will encourage you. If you lack the strength to run, His strength is sufficient. *Lo, I am with you alway, even unto the end of the world* (Mt. 28:20).

TODAY'S GEM: The race is ours to run in God's strength, for He is not only the author but the finisher of our faith.

Old Testament Reading Ezekiel 16

Meditation. *Let brotherly love continue* (13:1).

The writer to these Hebrew Christians made little mention of the love of God, but he now mentions the love of the brethren. In the preceding scriptures Paul has led us into such beautiful pastures and has enticed us beyond our present spiritual experience to enter into the heavenly sanctuary where we fellowship with our Savior. He is the Christ exalted to the right hand of the Father, ordained to the eternal office of Great High Priest, crowned king and gloriously attired in righteousness, made equal to rule and reign with the Father and assured that every knee shall bow to His name. This man, Jesus—all man from the top of His head to the soles of His feet and surrounded with all His glory—looks to us in love. He bids us in love to draw near and whispers into our hearts one word, "brethren" (holy brethren).

How can we not love those whom Jesus loves? How can we not be hospitable and entertaining or remember the persecuted brethren behind the iron curtain and other countries of the world? Even our marriage relationships can't help but take on a more beautiful meaning when we have spent time in the sanctuary with the Man who loves us with an everlasting love. It is a love that will not let us go, for God is love. The fragrance and spirit of the sanctuary is love, perfect love. It is like a fragrance that hangs on the air. As Jesus says, "Draw near," our hesitations suddenly melt before the spirit of love that authored the words. Every gesture, every word Jesus speaks is full of love and causes our empty and dry hearts to leap in response and to open to this stream of everlasting love which bursts forth from the sanctuary.

Do you desire to know the love of God shed abroad in your hearts by the Holy Ghost and to be filled and continue to be filled with love for the brethren? Then spend much of your time in the sanctuary. You will never again feel the need for love because the love that comes from the Father as you spend time with Him will saturate you until it overflows from you to others. The brethren will be recipients of your continual love. No, there was no need for the author to write about love because he knew if he could lead you into the sanctuary you would become an epistle of love.

TODAY'S GEM: The fragrance of the sanctuary is love that will permeate your very being.

Old Testament Reading Ezekiel 17-19

Meditation. *Let the brother of low degree rejoice in that he is exalted* (1:9).

Jesus has a very special love for the poor. He said, *"Blessed are the poor in spirit: for theirs is the kingdom of heaven"* (Mt. 5:3). Jesus cannot leave the poor really poor. Are you feeling your lack of this world's necessities and in the eyes of others are you poor? Is there little for your table and even less for the other comforts of life? Do you feel your poverty and wish that it could be different? You cannot have an encounter with Jesus, be taken in as His brethren and remain poor because He sets His kingdom before you to explore. You have the same opportunity as anybody else because Jesus has exalted you. He has lifted you up and out of the filth and sin of this life to dwell in heavenly places with Him. He can and will open your eyes to an inheritance that will make the poorest of circumstances trivial. Should you be given the most glorious mansion on earth it would seem of such little value. Its glamour would come so far short of the inheritance that awaits you in heaven that your heart would not even miss a beat because it is set on things above. The Lord Jesus Christ has named you His brother before the Father, making you a son and an heir. One glimpse of that heavenly inheritance and your spirit would become alive with so much of heaven that even the richest worldly circumstances would become unbearable.

Jesus can reach out to the poorest lost soul in a drunken stupor, the prisoner, and the junky. I know because I have lived in the darkest and most degrading society and have seen Jesus reach out to the heart that is open to Him. Lonely, caught up in self-pity, or just feeling neglected? He can reach out to you; so open your heart to Jesus and be drawn into the sanctuary. Let the Blood of Jesus flow, be cleansed and look around through the eyes of faith. If you allow Him, the Holy Spirit can reveal to your spirit the Lord Jesus Christ in all His glory so He can be exalted. To those of you who know, have seen and have been there, I say recapture your faith. Take hold of it. Dwell again in that holy place with Jesus.

TODAY'S GEM: *For what shall it profit a man, if he shall gain the whole world, and lose his own soul?* (Mk. 8:36).

Old Testament Reading Ezekiel 20-21

Meditation. *Hearken, my beloved brethren, Hath not God chosen the poor of this world rich in faith, and heirs of the kingdom which he hath promised to them that love him?* (2:5).

The Living Bible (vv. 5-6) in its paraphrase says, *Listen to me, dear brothers: God has chosen poor people to be rich in faith, and the Kingdom of Heaven is theirs, for that is the gift God has promised to all those who love him. And yet, of the two strangers, you have despised the poor man.* James makes it plain that it is not the way of the kingdom of God to despise a man because he is poor. At the same time if we honor a man and prefer his company because of his wealth or social standing we are carnal, and pride controls our lives. According to Romans 2:11 *there is no partiality with God* (NKJV).

To the poor man God says, "I choose to make you rich in faith," probably because the poor man is not encumbered. He is not as preoccupied or anxious about his wealth or social standing as the rich man. My heart goes out to the rich man because Jesus commented on how difficult it would be for a rich man to enter the kingdom of heaven.

I recall a little African folk story where a certain mission station was bothered by monkeys stealing their supplies, particularly peanuts. They set a trap by putting peanuts in a narrow-necked jar big enough for a monkey's hand to be put in but not big enough to be pulled out with a handful of nuts. When a monkey had his hand full of nuts he could be caught. The animal certainly could not let the nuts go to extract his hand because his greed would not let him.

God knows that the poor man does not have a conflict of interest. He might be dissatisfied with the status quo and looking for something, but he is so thirsty that when he comes to the well of salvation he just drinks and drinks. When faith is required to enter in and he discovers the Author of faith is willing to give to him that faith without measure, well, he just can't get enough. When that faith releases the kingdom of heaven to him and he finds his wealth, his eternal life, you can rest assured that he will hang on to that faith and become rich in it. My poor brethren, if you have nothing else but faith you are rich indeed.

TODAY'S GEM: The best things in life are free. *If the Son therefore shall make you free, ye shall be free indeed* (Jn. 8:36).

Old Testament Reading Ezekiel 22-23

Meditation. *But the wisdom that is from above is first pure, then peaceable, gentle, and easy to be entreated, full of mercy and good fruits, without partiality, and without hypocrisy* (3:17).

In his first chapter (v. 5) James wrote: *If any of you lack wisdom, let him ask of God, that giveth to all men liberally . . . and it shall be given him.* The world offers us a kind of wisdom, but it is contaminated with self. "What's in it for me?" is usually at the center of it. Our mailboxes are full of worldly wisdom telling us how much we can save if we spend. Big mail order businesses are established, growing fat and rich off those who seek the wisdom of the world, but the world doesn't have it. It has just deceived itself into thinking it does. The wisdom of the world cannot deliver a man from sin or set him free, nor can it give or show the way to eternal life. No man has come to Jesus by the wisdom of the world.

James told us that there is a wisdom that is not like the knowledge of the world, for that knowledge is no wisdom at all. There is a wisdom that is from above, and if any man lacks it, let him ask of God. Brethren, it's free! It may require a little time because you are going to have to go to God for it, but it's there for the asking. As James told us, *be ye doers of the word, and not hearers only* (1:22).

How can you know which wisdom it is, whether from the world or from God? First of all it depends on where you have received it. It is not dependent upon what you know but Whom you know. If you received your wisdom from Jesus you can trust it, have faith in, and act upon it because it is then the wisdom of God about which James was speaking. Godly wisdom has certain characteristics. Today's scripture tells us that it is pure with no conflicting motives. A peace will accompany it, and you will not be fearful of not getting your own way or of it not working. Godly wisdom produces a gentleness in your faith and will give you an inner confidence in it. Easy to be entreated, you won't feel threatened by it and will be able to see the godly fruit and even the mercy of God in it.

Godly wisdom is different all right, but it is yours for the asking. *But let him ask in faith, nothing wavering* (1:6).

TODAY'S GEM: *The fear of the* LORD *is the beginning of wisdom* (Ps. 111:10).

Old Testament Reading Ezekiel 24-26

Meditation. *Submit yourselves therefore to God, resist the devil, and he will flee from you. Draw nigh to God, and he will draw nigh to you* (4:7-8).

We have little or no understanding about the first 30 years of Jesus' life. It probably wasn't a whole lot different from the upbringing of any other boy whose father was a carpenter. Since He was the eldest in the family, we can assume He had responsibilities. There came a time when Jesus had to make a decision to leave His trade and home to step out in faith, trusting God to lead Him each step of the way. James would have been very familiar with those years. Suddenly Jesus ceased to be the carpenter and head of the family as the eldest brother, and this must have been difficult for James to understand. The transition was marked by several remarkable experiences.

First of all, Jesus submitted Himself to John the Baptist's call to Israel to repent, be baptized, and prepare for the coming messiah. Jesus immediately did this, and John the Baptist pronounced Him the fulfillment of prophecy, the messiah. Then the Holy Spirit descended upon Him as God confirmed what was happening with an audible voice from heaven. Afterward Jesus removed Himself for 40 days from the crowd that had been prepared by John for His coming. The very first thing Jesus did in way of preparation for His ministry was to have an encounter with Satan, who tempted Him in every conceivable way. To the outside observer not understanding God's will, there was very little difference between God's will for His Son and Satan's offer. Satan also wanted to make Jesus a prince and exalt Him, but Jesus denied the enemy his desire so He might not do Satan's will nor His own but the will of the Father.

Space does not permit me to follow this through sufficiently to say that there should be times in our Christian growth experience when we leave everything in which we are physically and spiritually involved to go away alone and remain with God, submitting ourselves and our thoughts to Him. This is a very humbling experience. By doing so we are saying: "God, I am here. I am totally committed to doing Your will and therefore submit myself to You." The enemy is defeated when you turn away from and deny him his desire. To experience the victory over the devil by turning around and fleeing is only half of the total experience. To enter into the fullness of this experience and enjoy God's ultimate and best is to resist, flee and then draw nigh unto the Lord.

TODAY'S GEM: Each encounter with Satan can become an act of drawing closer to God.

Old Testament Reading Ezekiel 27-28

Meditation. *And the prayer of faith shall save the sick, and the Lord shall raise him up; and if he have committed sins, they shall be forgiven Him* (5:15).

As a young Christian I can remember being asked if I believed in healing. At that time there was so much I didn't know about God or His Word that there was no way to give an intelligent opinion, but I didn't have any real reason not to believe in healing.

The more I read the Word by following this same reading plan of going through the Bible each year, the more the Bible, its spirit and life, became part of me. Intellectually I never did come to a place where I had to make a decision about believing or not believing in healing. As the Word became part of my very life, the tenor of the Word itself became my heart experience. It never did become necessary for me to make some great decision concerning this truth.

The Holy Spirit of God dwelling within my heart assured me that God heals. If He healed in the past and if His Word promises healing, then as long as His Word and promises remain He will fulfill them. We can only conclude that God must also heal today.

If we are to be honest with ourselves, the real question is not does or will God heal and is it for today, but the question is will we pray? Ponder these scriptures in chapter five of James: *Is any among you afflicted? Let him pray* (v. 13). *Is any sick among you? let him call for the elders . . . and let them pray* (v. 14). *Confess your faults one to another, and pray one for another, that ye may be healed. The effectual fervent prayer of a righteous man availeth much* (v. 16). *Elias was a man subject to like passions as we are, and he prayed . . . he prayed again, and the heaven gave rain* (vv. 17, 18).

The big question is this, as the people of God will we pray? It is our praying that brings us into the realm of spiritual reality. It is through prayer that we touch the heart of the Father and bring about changes. Not a whole lot happens in the kingdom of God unless we pray. The Holy Spirit is looking for the heart on its knees that He might quicken and inspire, yes, even initiate prayer that will be heard in heaven.

TODAY'S GEM: *And it shall come to pass, that before they call, I will answer; and while they are yet speaking, I will hear* (Isa. 65:24).

Old Testament Reading Ezekiel 29-31

Meditation. *Blessed be the God and Father of our Lord Jesus Christ, which according to his abundant mercy hath begotten us again unto a lively hope by the resurrection of Jesus Christ from the dead* (1:3).

Who but God would have or could have planned such a wonderful, eternal experience for us? He created one man and then set before him the task of discovering and naming all that He had created. Only God could have produced a woman to be man's helpmate and friend to love and want to live with for eternity. God's creative ability goes beyond our wildest imaginations. Who could have even thought of the complexities and mysteries of life that He has set before us or His plan for eternal life in Christ Jesus?

In our rebelliousness and stupidity we rejected it, but even then God was not put off, offended, or wanting to give up on us. He reached out to us with mercy tempered with His love, and through the Lord Jesus Christ God gave us a lively hope, an inner assurance that just as He raised Jesus from the dead so too will He raise us. God has set before us a life so abundant and full that only He, bless Him, could have devised such a plan and then make it work in our experience.

With such a lively hope made possible through the Lord Jesus Christ there can be no fear of death. Who can fear it when we have such an assurance of resurrection and eternal life? With Christ's death upon the cross and our identification with that death there is no judgment for sin to face. His blood continues to cleanse us from all sin. Why, even the bondage or habit that bound us to that sin nature is broken, and we are free. Yes, free!

Since there is no death, no judgment, no bondage, but only a living, eternal hope, then what are we going to do with this supernatural, eternal life that is ours? Are we going to put it away until we may need it? Are we going to show it off only on Sundays and maybe at midweek meetings? Or are we going to lay hold of it with both hands and live it? I think Peter's opening remarks were simply an expression of that which was heard on his lips constantly because it expressed the life lived in his heart. *Blessed be the God and Father of our Lord Jesus Christ.*

TODAY'S GEM: Living God's quality of life now makes and keeps alive our hope in the resurrection.
Old Testament Reading Ezekiel 32-33

Meditation. *But ye are a chosen generation, a royal priesthood, an holy nation, a peculiar people; that ye should shew forth the praises of him who hath called you out of darkness into his marvellous light* (2:9).

No Christian need suffer from an inferiority complex or have any doubt as to who he is. Satan would love to rob and cheat you even of your identity or entice you into believing you are something other than what you are, which is that which the Bible says you are. If we would read today's verse over and over again until it got down into our spirits, we would find an inner change taking place in our lives. Because of that inner change the circumstances in which we live would change. That is why it is so important to have a daily Bible reading program, especially a plan that takes you through the Bible each year.

You are what the Word says you are, *a chosen generation*. If that's not enough it also calls you royal, *a royal priesthood*. Put it all together and we become *a holy nation, a peculiar people*. There is no doubt about it, we are different. Whatever we were before Christ we are not that now. We are different, and Peter makes the purpose plain. We are to be a people to show forth the praises of Him who hath called us.

One of the greatest weaknesses and sins in our lives is our unwillingness to be what we are or to be and do what we are called to do, and that is to praise God for who He is. He has called us out of darkness into His *marvellous light* that we might be children of light. Therefore, live like children of light. Praise God, shower your affections on Him, love Him and live for Him. The more we live as God's peculiar people and the more we develop our praises, the more we become like Him, finding our identity by accepting and living what the Word says we are.

The place to develop and grow in praise and to become what the Word tells us we are is in the quiet-time. It is a place and a time set aside to be alone with God each day. The more you practice your Christian experience before Him, the more you will live the life before others and be to yourself and to them what the Word says you are.

TODAY'S GEM: Find your identity in Christ and be what God says you are—*a chosen generation, a royal priesthood.*
Old Testament Reading Ezekiel 34-35

Meditation. *For the eyes of the Lord are over the righteous, and his ears are open unto their prayers* (3:12).

There is not a whole lot we ourselves can do to be righteous, but righteous we must be if we are to have the Lord watching over us. There is a scripture that tells us we are the righteousness of God in Christ (2 Cor. 5:21). The key to being righteous is to be in Christ and accept His righteousness as our own.

God is watching over you and that alone should be a comfort. If you are the righteousness of God in Christ, He has an eye for where you are and is never going to let you out of His sight. God will be watching what you are doing and looking for an outward expression of that righteousness. When you fail Him He only sees the intent of the heart. Searching and examining the desires of the heart, God seeks that heart which delights in doing His will, and He watches over it.

The really neat thing in knowing that we are God's righteousness because we are in Christ is that it gives us the ear of the Father, whose ears are open unto our prayers. Why then do we seem to come so far short of God's best for us? We are surrounded by sick, lonely Christians and Christians in need. Does that mean there is something wrong with their righteousness? No! No! There is nothing lacking in God's righteousness that is ours in Christ. The lack or failure is not in His righteousness but on the part of God's people to be righteous and pray.

God waits, listens, and is available to us. His ears are open to hear our prayers, but we fail to put into practice and to lay hold of these opportunities to pray. We are convinced that we are the righteousness of God in Christ but are preoccupied with being everything other than what He has called us to be. If we would pray, we would become the envy of the world. If we would humble ourselves and pray confessing our lack of prayer, the Body of Christ would take on a dimension of God not yet seen. God's ears are open and waiting to hear our prayers.

TODAY'S GEM: We stand before the Father clothed with the righteousness of the Son.

Old Testament Reading Ezekiel 36-37

Meditation. *But the end of all things is at hand: be ye therefore sober, and watch unto prayer* (4:7).

I think Peter may have been feeling like many Christians are feeling throughout the nation today. He felt that God's patience with His people was running out when he wrote about evildoers, busybodies, and a lack of practicing Christianity. He reminded them of the need to have fervent charity among themselves and to be hospitable to one another. It wasn't too long after Peter wrote this letter of the judgments of God on Israel that it actually came to pass. One Bible commentator said that about ten years later the Temple and Jerusalem were destroyed. There was great suffering, and Israel never recovered from it.

Chapter six, verse thirteen, of Genesis sounds familiar. *And God said unto Noah, The end of all flesh is come before me.* That was God's word to Noah and was followed by the instructions to build an ark that would deliver the righteous. It has always been that way. God has always released warnings of things to come to the hearts of men, not to frighten them but that they might listen and discern the times in which they live and be prepared. The first and very best preparation is to prepare our hearts before God, to establish such a faith relationship with Him in prayer and to have our lives so in order before Him that we can easily be led through such trials by the Holy Spirit. So Peter wrote, *be ye therefore sober, and watch unto prayer.*

The bottom line is going to be your relationship with God. Therefore, learn to trust Him right now. Let your faith experience be uncomplicated and develop your spirit to be sensitive to the Holy Spirit. Be sure you know you are in the place God would have you be. Hold lightly the prosperity God has given you and be certain you have forsaken all to follow Him.

Lastly, let me repeat myself. Prepare your heart. Don't look to others to do this for you. By all means take their teaching, but there may be a day when they are not available any more. Then you will have to stand alone in your own experience. So establish yourself right now.

TODAY'S GEM: Recipe For End-Time Preparation: To your quiet-time with God add one full measure of faith, sprinkle heavily with obedience, and garnish with an intimate knowledge of God. Yield: One mature Christian preserved for eternity.

Old Testament Reading Ezekiel 38-39

Meditation. *The elders which are among you I exhort, who am also an elder, and a witness of the sufferings of Christ, and also a partaker of the glory that shall be revealed* (5:1).

Peter, addressing himself to the elders, reminded them that he had been a witness to the sufferings of Christ. There was no way he could have forgotten because his whole life had been turned around. However, few men were saved because of seeing Jesus Christ in His suffering upon the cross for their sin. When the works of the Father that Jesus came to do were completed, His sufferings faded into the past because of His glorious resurrection. Death couldn't hold Him, and sorrow gave way to joy when He stood in their midst.

Jesus took a short time preparing His disciples for His ascension to take His place at the right hand of the Father. Jesus promised them that the moment He took up His position in heaven the very Spirit of heaven, the Holy Spirit, would be sent to them. People started getting saved when Jesus' disciples were filled with the Holy Spirit and they proclaimed the message of the gospel—Jesus' sacrifice for sin, His death, resurrection and ascension into heaven.

Whatever Peter was before—bold and maybe brash, certainly impetuous—didn't seem to matter. This man who had witnessed the sufferings of Christ now spoke forth from a transformed life. He spoke about the life of the indwelling Christ in such a way that a people who, as a nation, were about to face disaster could triumph over the days that were ahead of them.

Peter talked about being a partaker of the glory that shall be revealed. He had come to grips with a life that no man could take away from him. Peter had learned the secret of the indwelling life of Christ, which would never fade away, nor could man take it away. Once he had run for his life but now he had forsaken all to follow Jesus. No man could rob him of his wealth or life because it was hidden in Christ where no man could touch it. It is not knowledge of Christ crucified that saves us but our being crucified with Him.

TODAY'S GEM: No man can take away from you what you have and are in Christ.

Old Testament Reading Ezekiel 40

Meditation. *Whereby are given unto us exceeding great and precious promises: that by these ye might be partakers of the divine nature* (1:4).

I love this scripture and pray that you will meditate upon it all day. God's best for us is to be partakers of the divine nature. Oh, we have a nature of our own, but no matter how much we pretty it up with clothes, makeup, social graces, etc., God's estimation of it is that it is like so many filthy rags. We may have never committed any outlandish sin but that nature is capable of it. The Bible tells us that *the carnal mind is enmity against God* (Rom. 8:7), and surely that is enough to recognize its worthlessness. Our carnal nature is petty and selfish and loves to have its own way. It is very clever to put on the appearance of being religious and indeed can be very religious. But now we are called to be partakers of the divine nature, which is the very nature of Christ living within us.

Then how can we have this divine nature living within us? How might we be partakers of the divine nature? This can be accomplished very simply by receiving the exceedingly great and precious promises. The more you live in the promises—reading and meditating upon them, praying them into your experience, and working them out in your life by the grace of God—the more the spirit of the promises becomes yours. As the spirit of the promises becomes yours, the divine nature, which is the life of Christ living within you, is manifested. Your carnal nature then dies, and the divine nature living its life through you takes over and becomes the only expression of your life. It is the spirit of the promise, the spirit of the Word that brings life. Not only must it bring life but it must also become our life.

You, my friend, have been given *exceeding great and precious promises: that by these ye might be partakers of the divine nature.* Search them out; devour them. Get the life and spirit of them into your spirit and your heart; then you will observe the presence of the divine nature.

TODAY'S GEM: God's promises are heavenly food on which to feed and produce a heavenly nature.

Old Testament Reading Ezekiel 41-42

Meditation. *The Lord knoweth how to deliver the godly out of temptations, and to reserve the unjust unto the day of judgment to be punished* (2:9).

Jesus made it clear that we are to make temptation a matter of prayer. The godly or righteous are not exempt or especially preserved from temptations. Even Jesus had to face them at the very outset of His ministry. Temptation itself is not sin, yielding to it is. *There hath no temptation taken you but such as is common to man: but God is faithful, who will not suffer you to be tempted above that ye are able; but will with the temptation also make a way to escape, that ye may be able to bear it* (1 Cor. 10:13).

Yesterday we read that we are given *exceeding great and precious promises: that by these ye might be partakers of the divine nature* (1:4). The scripture in first Corinthians (10:13) is one of those promises. In ourselves we are not equal to battle temptation, nor has God left us to face temptation in our own strength. He promises us grace to live the Christian life. The Lord knows how to deliver us out of temptation, and when assailed by it we now know and have a promise that is equal to our need. As the promise becomes ours, the spirit of the promise becomes alive in our hearts, motivating us to become victorious. Then the divine nature feeds and grows on it and we have the victory. Our old nature, which is carnal, is put to death by being continually overcome by the exceeding great and precious promises and by continual defeat.

Temptations themselves cause us to call on God's grace and to use the promises effectively. Then we can see and know that *all things work together for good to them that love God, to them who are the called according to his purpose* (Rom. 8:28).

Do not shun or run from temptation, but immediately turn to the Lord expecting the victory. Then rejoice in the growth of the divine nature. Never doubt the Lord's ability or intentions because He knows how to deliver the godly out of temptation.

TODAY'S GEM: Temptations can be turned into victories just by using God's promises and calling on His grace.

Old Testament Reading Ezekiel 43-44

Meditation. *Wherefore, beloved, seeing that ye look for such things, be diligent that ye may be found of him in peace, without spot, and blameless* (3:14).

Everywhere I go throughout the world there is a very real sense of things not continuing as they are. Scientists predict a crisis, a coming to an end. Non-Christians are reading the signs of the times and know that the world cannot continue as it is. Some groups are very seriously trying to prepare for whatever it is that will bring about a complete breakdown in the world. I know of one Christian group who has built an underground, nuclear complex enabling them to survive a nuclear war because they believe that God would have them minister to the survivors. Many people are storing large quantities of food, sensing the necessity to prepare for what the Bible calls these last days.

I think they are right. As Christians we should be searching the Scriptures and seeking the Lord's direction so we might be better prepared for those things that lie ahead of us. Peter spoke of things to come, and the early church was prepared. At least its leaders spoke to the people, forewarning them. As far as Peter was concerned it was obviously important that the people prepare their hearts. So he told them to be diligent in order that they might be found without spot and blameless. Peter foresaw the coming of the day of the Lord and on that day the heavens dissolving in fire. *The heavens shall pass away with a great noise, and the elements shall melt with fervent heat, the earth also and the works that are therein shall be burned up* (v. 10). *Nevertheless, we, according to his promise, look for new heavens and a new earth, wherein dwelleth righteousness* (v. 13).

Whatever the future holds for you and me, our security and trust must be in the Lord Jesus Christ, not in our preparations. By all means prepare but our priority is to prepare our hearts with all diligence. Scripture tells us: *If we confess our sins, he is faithful and just to forgive us our sins, and to cleanse us from all unrighteousness* (1 Jn. 1:9). The blood of Jesus continues to cleanse, but only sin confessed is sin forgiven. We are to avail ourselves of the cleansing blood daily, keeping our hearts pure. Then should the Lord come to us He would find us cleansed in the Blood without spot and blameless. The heart that knows the continuing cleansing of the Blood is at peace and can face death. Make some practical preparations by all means, but it is "heart preparation" that will enable you to stand in the day of the Lord.

TODAY'S GEM: The protection of the Christian is to draw closer and closer to Him who saves, Jesus Christ the Messiah.

Old Testament Reading Ezekiel 45-46

Meditation. *That which we have seen and heard declare we unto you, that ye also may have fellowship with us: and truly our fellowship is with the Father, and with his Son Jesus Christ. And these things write we unto you, that your joy may be full* (1:3-4).

John was not writing theology or theory about God; he was writing Christian reality about a Christ that was as human as he was. John explained that he had seen with his own eyes all the things they had heard about Jesus. John had actually heard with his own ears that about which John and others had written. They could have fellowship around all those things John had declared unto them, whether it was about Jesus' birth, His family, His ministry, miracles, death, or resurrection.

After years of proclaiming Jesus as Messiah, watching over the churches and attending to their needs, in his old age John then presented the heart of the gospel—the mystery of God—when he said, *"Our fellowship is with the Father, and with his Son Jesus Christ."* We may have envied John his wonderful experience of living and traveling with Jesus. Had we been John I'm sure we would have treasured every word Jesus had said, sharing with others these wonderful truths. However, John made it plain that his real joy came from the present fellowship he enjoyed with the Father and the Son. We can read about the three years Jesus devoted Himself to preparing the disciples with the truth that would be proclaimed to the uttermost parts of the earth and of His great concern for the people of God. However, at that moment John said his joy was made full by the fellowship that was his with the people of God, those who shared in his fellowship with the Father and the Son.

Nothing has changed. We must read and study the Word and be enlightened about the character of the Father and the Son and their uniqueness. The Word is what helps us to appreciate their faithfulness to fill our hearts and lives with the spirit of the Word and to develop within us the divine nature. But our real joy of Christian living that will be established deep within our hearts by the day-by-day fellowship we have with one another reflects the fellowship we enjoy with the Father and His Son Jesus Christ.

TODAY'S GEM: The fellowship we share with others is a mirror reflection of our relationship with God.

Old Testament Reading Ezekiel 47-48

Meditation. *My little children, these things write I unto you, that ye sin not. And if any man sin, we have an advocate with the Father, Jesus Christ the righteous* (2:1).

In today's reading John is speaking to those who are young in the Lord. However, in the previous chapter he makes it quite clear that he is speaking to those Christians that he has fellowship with in the Father and the Lord Jesus Christ. John writes to those with whom he is in fellowship so they will not sin.

For some time my wife and I lived in a community with a group of very young Christians whose spiritual growth was our responsibility. Because of their previous circumstances they were unable to go out and earn a living; therefore, Marjorie and I completely trusted the Lord to provide for us so we could in turn provide for them. We literally prayed in every item of food item by item and had the exciting experience of seeing God miraculously provide for two years.

However, every now and again the food would suddenly stop appearing, and even though we had special seasons of prayer with fasting it made no difference. Then somebody in the fellowship would come under conviction of sin and openly confess it. We would join with them in their confessions as if they were our own, seeking grace and forgiveness for the offending brother or sister. The fellowship we enjoyed with one another was the fruit of our fellowship with the Father and the Son, who was our advocate in presenting our petitions to the Father. A cleansing that we all felt and that was beneficial to all would then take place. The sin had been dealt with in mercy and love by the Blood. The proof that Jesus had been a successful advocate and that a cleansing had taken place was clearly seen by the immediate restoration of a continual flow of food.

The need to pray for our physical needs and have God provide our food in this manner created a very sensitive communion or fellowship with God, and it was a very simple matter for Him to get our attention. Our hearts were kept pure before the Lord, and sin was not allowed to remain in our fellowship. What a comfort it was to know that Jesus, our advocate, was always available, always willing to intercede on our behalf so His righteousness might reign and rule in our fellowship.

TODAY'S GEM: Jesus not only delivered us from our sinful nature but He now lives to make intercession as our advocate to the Father.

Old Testament Reading Daniel 1-2

Meditation. *Behold, what manner of love the Father hath bestowed upon us, that we should be called the sons of God: therefore the world knoweth us not, because it knew him not* (3:1).

I have been among people of the world who have wanted my friendship and sought to keep company with me. Then I have watched their discomfort, not conviction, just an awkwardness *because they knew him not* (Jesus). The saddest thing to see is the worldly Christians, the born-again believers who, although they have received the grace of God, have such a desire for the things of the world. The world has gotten hold of them until their values are not our values. Our pursuits differ, and they too are very discomfited by us. They *knoweth* us not.

What manner of love is this that the Father hath bestowed upon us, that we should be called the sons of God? Somehow it doesn't bother me one little bit what worldly people call me because by the Father I have been called a son of God. Therefore, I do not seek to be what the world calls me to be, nor do I consider it of much value. The Father has whispered into my heart His word. He has written it there with all assurance, calling me a son of God. To the world I must appear to have little going for me because I do not seek its praises or approval. The worldly Christian works harder and harder to gain the world's wealth, but I have no need of it. They personally know nothing of sonship and the Father's practical provision. Therefore, the world knoweth us not.

The world looks at and judges us by what they see, not knowing that *now are we the sons of God, and it doth not yet appear what we shall be: but we know that, when he shall appear, we shall be like him; for we shall see him as he is* (v. 2). Oh beloved, now are you the sons of God! Do not let yourselves fall into the trap of the world that judges by appearances. God has called you sons and has made you to be sons unto Himself by the redemption of the Lord Jesus Christ. The spirit of the world would see contradictions and seek to confuse us, but the Spirit of God reminds us that *the world knoweth us not. Now are we the sons of God, and it doth not yet appear what we shall be: but we know that, when he shall appear, we shall be like Him*!

TODAY'S GEM: Do not judge by its appearance what God has not yet finished.

Old Testament Reading Daniel 3-4

Meditation. *Herein is our love made perfect, that we may have boldness in the day of judgment: because as he is, so are we in this world* (4:17).

One day our works and lives must bear examination (1 Cor. 3:11-17). What foundation did we lay? What material was used, and will it stand the test of fire? *If any man's work abide which he hath built thereupon, he shall receive a reward* (1 Cor. 3:14). My friends, Jesus Christ and His love for us must become the very foundation of our lives. We love Him because He first loved us. The strength of this building or tabernacle (your strength) must be the indwelling Holy Spirit of Christ because *greater is he that is in you, than he that is in the world* (1 Jn. 4:4). The mystery that our strength is the Holy Spirit of Christ living within us overcoming the world means that the world is no match for us. Within us is the Holy Spirit who can shed abroad in our hearts the love of God that passeth all understanding. What trial can overcome that?

That which is to make us perfect is love. Then, on the day when we, as Christians, are judged by these works, we will stand before Him with great boldness because our confidence will be in His love that perfected us. It is the kind of love that casts out fear and enables us to keep His commandments, loving one another as He has loved us. If God dwells within us then so does love, for God is love. The heart that loves by grace is loved of God. The love of God makes us to know the Word that became flesh and dwelt among us, because as he is, so are we in this world.

John went on to say, *If a man say, I love God, and hateth his brother, he is a liar: for he that loveth not his brother whom he hath seen, how can he love God whom he hath not seen?* (v. 20). It is better that we judge ourselves and not our brother by his words. Examine yourself to see if there is any bitterness or wrong attitudes such as envy and jealousy. For some reason if we cannot constructively judge ourselves by the Word then we must listen carefully to what comes out of our mouths in private conversations. We can then examine what we say and measure it against the love of God. How do our words measure up? Are they an expression of God's love? If so, by His love God is perfecting a work in us that will remain for eternity. If our words are not an expression of God's love, we should confess the sin of bitterness or whatever we perceive that is standing in the way of God's love that is building what is contrary to His desires. Praise the Lord, today is a day of cleansing for you so you may stand in the day of judgment with great boldness.

TODAY'S GEM: Let the love that Jesus gave us as our foundation shine through each of us. *Know ye not that ye are the temple of God?* (1 Cor. 3:16).

Old Testament Reading Daniel 5-6

Meditation. *Everyone who believes that Jesus is the Christ has been born of God, and everyone who loves the Father loves whoever has been born of him* (5:1, ESV).

One day when Jesus came into the coasts of Caesarea Philippi, He asked His disciples, *"Whom do men say that I the Son of man am?"* After a variety of answers Jesus went on to ask, *"But whom say ye that I am?"* When Peter answered Him and said, *"Thou art the Christ, the Son of the living God,"* Jesus answered Peter and said, *"Blessed art thou, Simon Barjona: for flesh and blood hath not revealed it unto thee, but my Father which is in heaven"* (see Mt. 16:13, 15-17).

It is God the Father who reveals the Son to us. The Scriptures tell us that God draws us to the Son or gives us to the Son. Satan and his demons know who Jesus is, and the Word says they tremble. However, John is talking about more than knowing who Jesus is. Like Peter, John is talking about knowing Jesus as the Christ—the anointed one, the messiah. It is one thing to know that Jesus saves people from sin and its consequences but it is quite another thing to know and believe that Jesus saves each of us personally from it. If Jesus is your messiah whom you are trusting to save you, then He saves by inhabiting you. His Spirit descends from above and becomes one with your spirit. A spiritual wedding has taken place, and by this union He dwells in your heart by His Holy Spirit. This is your new birth and is what being born again means. You cannot help but love Jesus, for love is both the natural and spiritual response to the Christ who has taken up residence within your heart.

John was saying that if you love Him who has saved you to the uttermost and by whom you are born again, then you will love others who share an identical experience with you. You do not even have to try because your purged and cleansed heart will immediately respond. Your spirit recognizes other believers, and there is an immediate, effortless love for those who also are begotten of Him. God has established this love for the brethren in our hearts, but it is up to us to maintain it and to keep our hearts pure before Him. When our dislikes and resentments get in the way, we are to confess them and receive forgiveness. Anything other than an attitude of love toward other believers is never justifiable. We must love them as God has loved us.

TODAY'S GEM: *If we love one another, God dwelleth in us, and his love is perfected in us* (1 Jn. 4:12).
Old Testament Reading Daniel 7-8

Meditation. *Look to yourselves, that we do not lose those things we worked for . . . He who abides in the doctrine of Christ has both the Father and the Son* (vv. 8-9, NKJV).

There is so much that God wants to do for us. His desire is to manifest Himself and His love within each believer and to make us new creatures in Christ, creating a new nature in us that will reflect the glory of Jesus. Our minds cannot conceive the half of what God has in mind for us, but all that God can do is conditional on our doing the right things. We are to be obedient to His every desire and to overcome our own will with all its selfishness and desire to have its own way. Then we can yield ourselves to the will of the Father. The greatest hindrance of which I know to our spiritual growth is not the world or the devil, although both tempt us, it is our own self (our flesh). Yet God goes on trusting, having faith in us to do all sorts of wonderful things for Him.

Look to yourselves, John wrote. He knew that the promises of God are conditional. He also knew the generosity of the Father and His desire to prosper us. Why, if we walk and abide in the doctrines of Christ, both the Father and the Son will inhabit us by making our hearts their dwelling place. The Word of God is so full of His promises. He wants us to prosper in health and in our love for one another. His desire is that we lack no good thing. God is available day and night. He is faithful, promises to supply our every need, and intercedes for us. Yet with God wanting to bestow upon us even more than we can think of or ask for, John finds it necessary to caution us to look to ourselves, that we lose not those things for which we have worked.

After cautioning us John gives the antidote that will save us from any possibility of backsliding. The Christian who will eventually fail is the one who lives asking for God's blessing on His self-initiated actions, praying for God's provision to do his own will, putting his faith in his own ability to live the Christian life. The answer lies in looking to ourselves, distrusting in our ability to fulfill the purposes of God and therefore abiding in the Father and the Son. Then all our faith and hope will be in His ability to save us to the uttermost. Learn quickly that you can't but God can. It is not I that lives but Christ that lives within me (Gal. 2:20). Didn't Jesus himself say, *"I can of mine own self do nothing"*? Having submitted our own will to His, we can now do all things through Christ who strengthens us.

TODAY'S GEM: *And I give unto them eternal life; and they shall never perish, neither shall any man pluck them out of my hand* (Jn. 10:28).

Old Testament Reading Daniel 9-10

Meditation. *Beloved, I wish above all things that thou mayest prosper and be in health, even as thy soul prospereth* (v. 2).

Because of John's love for Gaius John would not have wished him anything but God's best. Even as his soul was prospering so too John desired that he would enjoy good health and that all would go well with him. If this was God's best for Gaius then prosperity must also be His very best for us. However, the first and foremost prosperity that we must enjoy is that of the soul. God can only cause us to flourish materially in proportion to our spiritual prosperity, and the real question is, can God trust us with prosperity? It is not a matter of will He or won't He. It is a matter of will we do the right things with the wealth He gives us?

What motivates our desire for success? Is it a selfish motive, or is it out of greed or pride? Will we remain humble and totally dependent upon Him should He prosper us, and will our true motives be that we might glorify the Lord Jesus Christ? Will we take our successes and do the right things with them? If you have first of all prospered spiritually and your soul is totally surrendered to the indwelling Holy Spirit so you live to do His will instead of serving the flesh, then your answer will be yes to all of these questions.

In their flight from Egypt the children of Israel knew material wealth. When Moses left them to be with God on the top of the mountain, their lack of spiritual prosperity caused them to give way to selfish desires. Their God-given material wealth was used to build a golden calf, a god of their own making, to fulfill their religious fantasies. Putting a motorcar into the hands of a ten-year-old child isn't prosperity, it's suicide. *But seek ye first the kingdom of God, and his righteousness; and all these things shall be added unto you* (Mt. 6:33).

TODAY'S GEM: The character of prosperity is two-sided. To those who possess spiritual maturity it can be a blessing.

Old Testament Reading Daniel 11-12

Meditation. *Jude, the servant of Jesus Christ, and brother of James, to them that are sanctified by God the Father, and preserved in Jesus Christ, and called* (v. 1).

Jude was Jesus' half-brother and introduced himself first of all as the servant of Jesus Christ, one who had been set aside (sanctified) by God the Father. Meditating upon this verse, I can't help wondering how much of our lives is set aside to serve the Lord Jesus Christ. Are only those who leave secular employment to go into full-time ministry sanctified or set aside? And how many of us have been set aside by God the Father to serve the Lord Jesus Christ? Has He set before us some service? If so, what has our response been?

Jude reminded those who are set aside by the Father that they are to serve the Lord Jesus Christ because they are preserved in the Lord. His desire was that they keep the faith pure and remain consistent to the original simplicity and pattern that had been set before the saints. They were exhorted to contend with those things that would rob them of a true relationship and experience, and this could be accomplished if their set-aside lives were preserved in Jesus Christ. Surely the greatest privilege we can have in the kingdom of God is to humbly and submissively serve the King. Can you imagine being called into His presence or having a message sent to you for some service and saying, "Not today, it doesn't fit in with my schedule"? No wonder Jude desired that we be preserved. What if you were asked to serve but decided you didn't like the way it was being done or that it just was not for you? I am sure by now you recognize the attitude of the flesh from which Jude desired us to be preserved. What rewards are lost or how much spiritual growth is hampered by our fleshly responses? Reflect on the joy of which we rob ourselves when the servant side of our divine nature is neglected.

As servants set aside by God, He offers us a whole dimension of Himself. We are being offered fellowship and spiritual growth as the result of dealing with our selfishness and pride. Faith and adventure that glorifies Jesus is seen at its best in His service. Be assured, my dear Christian friend, that not too long after having read this you will be confronted with the opportunity to serve; therefore, may you be preserved in the Lord Jesus Christ.

TODAY'S GEM: If the Son of Man, who is God himself, came to be a servant of man, how can we be anything less?

Old Testament Reading Hosea 1-4

Meditation. *I heard behind me a loud voice, as of a trumpet . . . I saw . . . One like the Son of Man, clothed with a garment down to the feet and girded about the chest with a golden band. His head and hair were white like wool, as white as snow, and His eyes like a flame of fire; His feet were like fine brass, as if refined in a furnace, and His voice as the sound of many waters . . . His countenance was like the sun shining in its strength* (vv. 12-16; NKJV).

John was on the isle of Patmos, a place of exile, which was rocky, treeless, and constantly inhabited by Roman prisoners. He was separated from those he loved in the Lord; yet in this barren, uncomfortable situation Jesus came to him. John had known Jesus intimately for the three years he had spent with Him as His disciple. Then again after Jesus' death he had the joy of having fellowship with Him after His resurrection. Over the years since Jesus' ascension to the Father and His subsequent gift of the Holy Spirit, John had again learned to fellowship with the Lord in the same manner in which he exhorts us. Through meditation and prayer he enjoyed a heart-to-Heart, spirit-to-Spirit relationship with Jesus, and that is exactly what he was doing when Jesus appeared. *And when I saw him, I fell at his feet as dead* (v. 17).

In his Gospel John wrote these words that Jesus said to Thomas and the other disciples, *blessed are they that have not seen, and yet have believed* (Jn. 20:29). When I was an infant Christian I saw a picture of Jesus hanging on a hospital wall. Captivated by it, I bought one to put in my home. I loved that picture, and it was very important to me. But somehow over the years the picture lost something as my feelings toward it changed. Searching my heart to understand, I discovered a very wonderful thing. It was my habit to read the Bible through once a year, and from the Word the Holy Spirit had been taking descriptions of Jesus like the ones John used. Jesus' likeness and an expression of Christ had been planted in my spirit by the Spirit of the Word so that what I saw with my eyes couldn't measure up to what I saw in my heart.

Let me encourage you to meditate upon the Bible's expressions and descriptions of Christ. See for yourself that it will surpass any artist's brush.

TODAY'S GEM: Within each of us is the ability to see Jesus as the Holy Spirit helps us piece together each scripture to form a picture of Christ.

Old Testament Reading Hosea 5-8

Meditation. *Nevertheless I have somewhat against thee, because thou hast left thy first love* (2:4).

Jesus was pleased with the church of Ephesus. He was pleased with their works, patience, attitude toward evil, and the way in which they had dealt with false teachers that He called liars. Jesus commended them for their patience and persistence; however, He cautioned them about leaving their first love.

Allow me to share one of my initial responses to my first love for Jesus. As a baby Christian my greatest joy came from mowing the church grass, whistling hymns as my old drinking buddies drove by. Seeing the joy I derived from serving Jesus in this manner, my wife Marjorie bought me a motor-mower. Since we didn't own a motorcar it had to be pulled behind my bicycle, or I had to walk with it the distance of about a mile to the church. The grass barely got a chance to grow because I just couldn't keep away. This is my earliest recollection of doing something for Jesus, and that which stands out most in my memory is the attitude of love I had for Him. It was this attitude of love that motivated me.

After some years of being a Christian I was going to a Gideons' camp meeting, which I loved to attend and to fellowship with the members. For the first time I noticed that something was missing in my attitude toward this ministry; and my attitude toward my other responsibilities was no different. Something had changed inside me, and I became concerned about my testimony. What might people think if I didn't do these things? After all, I had an image to maintain. I also began to notice that I was doing many things begrudgingly. My thoughts returned to that time when, as a baby Christian, I had mowed the grass for Jesus. I then reflected on the absence of that love for the Lord and my love to serve. It bothered me, and I repented of my sin. Changing my attitudes, I returned to the freedom of serving Jesus out of my love for Him, not just out of love for serving and being useful. Returning to the simplicity of that childlike love for my Savior, I began enjoying another life-changing experience.

TODAY'S GEM: *If the Son therefore shall make you free, ye shall be free indeed* (Jn. 8:36).

Old Testament Reading Hosea 9-11

Meditation. *Behold, I stand at the door, and knock; if any man hear my voice, and open the door, I will come in to him, and will sup with him, and he with me* (3:20).

Jesus said some hard things to the seven churches. He was standing in their midst examining their works and the attitude of their hearts, knowing if they were not corrected, chastened, and purged in the area of their weaknesses that they would be unable to overcome and would eventually fail. Jesus' interest in His Church is eternal. He is committed and refuses to give up on us, laboring with us forever, even to the end of the age. However, it is a two-sided coin. Though there is no doubt about Jesus' commitment to us, it is our commitment to Him and to His Church that is in question. Jesus told the churches: *I know your deeds, that you are neither cold nor hot. I wish you were either one or the other!* (v. 15, NIV). Get in or get out, Jesus is telling us. "If you are in, then come to Me. Buy from Me the substance that you will need that will stand the test of fire. I will clothe you if you come to Me. I will anoint your eyes so you can spiritually see why I have nothing but riches and wealth if you will do the right things." That is the substance of what Jesus is saying in this letter.

Then Jesus extends a very beautiful invitation to the Christians in the Laodicean church. "Behold," He says, "now that I have your attention, I want you to know it is not My desire to be far off. I want to enter into an intimate relationship with you. I've been trying to get your attention, but you really must learn to listen. Learn to hear My voice."

"If any man hear My voice—has the ears to hear and the faith to invite Me into a very close and intimate relationship—I will come into such a personal fellowship with him that it will be as close as two people eating together. I will feed you, and you will feed Me. We will both benefit from this fellowship." Jesus goes on to say that the next step is to overcome our inhibitions, our besetting sins, and all those things that would waylay us. Then we can follow Him to the throne room and sit with Him there.

Jesus has extended the invitation but we must make the time. This is the purpose of the Gems ministry. What is your answer?

TODAY'S GEM: Jesus requests the presence of all true believers to overcome and *to sit with Him on His throne*—R.S.V.P.

Old Testament Reading Hosea 12-14

Meditation. *Thou art worthy, O Lord, to receive glory and honour and power: for thou hast created all things, and for thy pleasure they are and were created* (4:11).

Continuing on from yesterday's teaching, Jesus is saying: "If you will open the door of your life to Me that I might come into every area of it, then I will open the very door of heaven and invite you into the throne room itself. Nothing in heaven will be withheld from you." *After this I looked, and, behold, a door was opened in heaven* (v. l).

One morning very early after studying this chapter with a friend, we were kneeling in his kitchen praying. What happened cannot be explained, but I know that I was no longer conscious of my surroundings. A sea of glass like unto crystal was what I was seeing. How can this experience be interpreted or adequately described? I just know I was so overcome with the presence of love that was welling up within me. My whole physical being seemed to be going through some change as over and over I was saying: "Thank you, Jesus. Thank you, Jesus."

Jesus had supped with me many times since extending to me that first invitation, but that day, kneeling on the kitchen floor, He must have done what He said in verse one—opened a door in heaven. I didn't see or hear any more than I have described but somehow the verse that has been chosen for today's meditation has its place in that experience. I feel completely at home with that verse and want to sing it. The spirit of that verse seems to have somehow entered my heart and remains there as a constant reminder that He led me through the open door into His throne room.

I am not inviting you to seek extraordinary experiences. My invitation is for you to open your life each day to Jesus and seek Him in response to His invitation and His desire that you have a more intimate relationship with your God. As you make the time for Him, He takes time with you. Who knows, you may hear yourself singing as you enter into His throne room— *"Thou art worthy, O Lord, to receive glory and honour and power!"*

TODAY'S GEM: God only comes through an open door, and in return He opens all of heaven, so *seek, and ye shall find; knock, and it shall be opened unto you* (Lk. 11:9).

Old Testament Reading Joel

Meditation. *Saying with a loud voice, Worthy is the Lamb that was slain to receive power, and riches, and wisdom, and strength, and honour, and glory, and blessing* (5:12).

What a marvelous anthem of praise John must have seen and heard in his vision. The Living Bible paraphrases verses eleven to thirteen saying: *Then in my vision I heard the singing of millions of angels surrounding the throne and the Living Beings and the Elders: "The Lamb is worthy (loudly they sang it!), the Lamb who was slain. He is worthy to receive the power, and the riches, and the wisdom, and the strength, and the honor, and the glory, and the blessing." And then I heard everyone in heaven and earth, and from the dead beneath the earth and in the sea, exclaiming, "The blessing and the honor and the glory and the power belong to the one sitting on the throne, and to the Lamb forever and ever."*

John gives us a little glimpse of heaven. It is obvious that every knee is going to bow and angelic beings in a multitude that cannot be numbered are going to add their voices to the voices of God's redeemed. The elders are going to be right up front raising their voices and proclaiming power, riches, wisdom, strength, honor, glory, and blessing.

Surely these are more than the words to a song of praise inspired by the Holy Spirit. The song itself excels all others, and there never will be sung a greater anthem than this. But my heart says to me there is more. This is the day of acknowledgments. Heaven and earth have joined together to shower their praises upon the Lamb of God who sits upon the throne and to bestow upon Jesus, or at least to acclaim, that which God the Father has bestowed upon Him. Today the Son of man, who is the Son of God, receives what was rightfully His inheritance. With great honor He receives it in the presence of His redeemed and amidst the praises of the hosts of heaven. Angels will gather from the four corners of heaven, and the saints will assemble in heaven and on earth to witness this tremendous, never-to-be-forgotten acclamation and the bestowing upon the Lord Jesus Christ His full inheritance. No wonder the redeemed sing—His inheritance is also theirs. We too will share, yes, we will enter into Christ's glory with Him!

TODAY'S GEM: *Eye hath not seen, nor ear heard, neither have entered into the heart of men, the things which God hath prepared for them that love him* (1 Cor. 2:9).

Old Testament Reading Amos 1-3

Meditation. *And white robes were given unto everyone of them; and it was said unto them, that they should rest yet for a little season, until their fellowservants also and their brethren, that should be killed as they were, should be fulfilled* (6:11).

I remember an occasion in New Zealand when a missionary home on furlough was driving her jeep on a reasonably safe road through a very large gorge. The river paralleled the road through the gorge, and there was hardly a time when it was not directly below the road. At some crucial point in the road there was an earthquake and the missionary was killed as the road rolled and heaved, shaking the jeep and driver into the raging waters of the river below.

Later the sister of this missionary decided to visit the mission station where her sister had worked to see the kind of missionary work she had been doing. The sister told the story of how she was walking along a very primitive track with the native people ahead of her leading the way and others behind her. A little sad and feeling the sorrow of these people, she thought she heard a voice. It sounded like her sister's voice saying to her: "Why are you so sad? I am more alive than you are."

The Bible leaves us in no doubt as to where our loved ones are who die in the Lord or die in His service. Just think of those martyred saints who suffered, especially in our day, those behind the iron curtain and in China. Indeed, we live in a generation when the suffering of the Body of Christ surpasses anything else in the history of the Church. Clothed in righteousness, these martyred saints wait. After their much suffering they rest and wait until their brethren, their fellow servants, join them. One day we will see these saints face to face and share eternity with them. We may even hear of their exploits and faithfulness and will be able to share in and see their eternal reward. At the moment perhaps they are more alive than we are.

TODAY'S GEM: *The things which are seen are temporal, but the things which are not seen are eternal* (2 Cor. 4:18).

Old Testament Reading Amos 4-6

Meditation. *And he said to me, These are they which came out of great tribulation, and have washed their robes, and made them white in the blood of the Lamb* (7:14).

Whatever suffering has been the saints' portion during trials and tribulation it is obvious there is a very special eternal reward awaiting them. How can this reward even be measured? They will be clothed in white robes that will glow with the beauty of the washing of the blood of Jesus Christ. All heaven and eternity will acknowledge and acclaim the beauty and pricelessness of these robes. What could be more intimate or more perfect than a robe washed in Jesus' blood and given to the saint who has come forth out of tribulation? The robe will lovingly cover the scars, the brokenness, and the imprints of the saints' suffering for Christ.

Jesus has gathered them close to Himself, and they have the privilege of serving Him day and night before the throne in His temple. He that sitteth on the throne, the Lord Jesus Christ, who can identify with their sufferings and who also bears scars of suffering and tribulation, shall dwell among them. There will be a sweet sensitive fellowship between them, and they who knew what it was to hunger will hunger no more. Thirst will no longer torture them, nor will the heat of day ever again add to their sufferings.

Jesus the Lamb will be in their midst and shall feed them. Every suffering member of the Body of Christ will find a special place and comfort. The saints, Jesus, and the throne—all will be one. So closely related will they be that there will be no more suffering, no more crying out from fear, loneliness, or pain. Their hearts will be knit together by their sufferings. The Lord Jesus Christ for whom they suffered and who in turn had suffered and died for them will personally lead them to living fountains of water. God himself shall wipe away all tears from their eyes. A very distinguished people this shall be, standing out in heaven as a special people with a special place in the heart of Jesus. What a privilege it is to contemplate living for eternity with such saints!

TODAY'S GEM: Covet this place and reward in heaven, for *whosoever will lose his life for my sake, the same shall save it* (Lk. 9:24).

Old Testament Reading Amos 7-9

Meditation. *And when he had opened the seventh seal, there was silence in heaven about the space of half an hour* (8:1).

What was the silence? Was heaven shocked at what was about to happen to the earth, creation, and its inhabitants? Man is not the only one that inhabits the earth. Before man was created by God and the earth became man's home, Satan, the fallen archangel, had set up his demonic empire here on earth. From the very beginning he was bent on destroying that which God had created. With sin he has contaminated every good thing on earth that God has made. His legions of demons reduce man and rob him of the life that was his before the fall of Adam.

John was about to witness the judgment of God upon this demonic empire. Hell was not created for man, although rebellious man, who will not accept the salvation that is his by the blood of Jesus, will end up there. God made hell for fallen angels. What John saw he saw. So why should I try to interpret it? Frightening but true, the end is what John saw. He felt and experienced the silence, the hurt of heaven. Thirty minutes of silence—all praise and worship ceased. The activities of heaven came to a grinding halt. All stood, just stopped whatever they were doing, and for thirty minutes there was no sound.

John must have heard his own heart beating as he felt the rising anticipation of this great end-time event. He had been carefully instructed to record everything he saw. I am sure he had been especially careful to try and capture every detail of the moment; so he wrote, *there was silence in heaven about the space of half an hour*.

How could John stand it? How could he see all these end-time things and not faint in his heart? He would not have had time to study them, but he must have wondered where he would be in the midst of all this. However, I would like to think that he was past caring. Grace through faith had brought him this far. He had outlived his contemporaries and had come this far by simple obedience and trusting the grace and love of the Lord Jesus Christ. What he saw was death to sin and life to righteousness. That same grace and love that was sufficient to meet his needs will also be sufficient to meet our needs.

TODAY'S GEM: *The righteous cry, and the* LORD *heareth, and delivereth them out of all their troubles* (Ps. 34:17).
Old Testament Reading Obadiah

Meditation. *And it was commanded them that they should not hurt the grass of the earth, neither any green thing, neither any tree; but only those men which have not the seal of God in their foreheads* (9:4).

God has gone to tremendous lengths to make provision for fallen man, and it is the desire of His heart that not one of us should perish. No wonder the Word says He loves us with an everlasting love. God carefully planned for a reconciliation allowing His very own Son Jesus to suffer the indignities and abuse the prince of this world would heap on Him. If that wasn't enough, the Son of God tasted death for every man.

Having brought about a reconciliation and having adopted us into the family of God, making us acceptable in the Beloved, Jesus now extends Himself again that we might not only live and enjoy the eternal life He has won for us but also develop it and prepare ourselves to stand in the days ahead.

The Lord's whole purpose of visiting John on the isle of Patmos, instructing him in the writing of these letters and revealing to him those things that were yet to come, was that the people of God—the Church of Jesus Christ—might be prepared to face whatever the future held for them. However you interpret these scriptures or whatever you do with them, you cannot get away from the fact that Jesus wanted us to be prepared. This is His provision for His people. We are to be forewarned, and our Christian growth experience must include whatever preparation is necessary. It is to be done now so we will stand in these days that John recorded.

There is to be a great judgment. God will pour out His wrath upon the earth, and all that are not of the kingdom of God will be in torment and devoured. There will be those who have refused God's grace and so hardened their hearts against Him that death and hell will seem more acceptable to them than God's wrath. As for you and me, where we will be is not the question. The questions are: Will we see these prophetic, God-given predictions as His provision for us to prepare our hearts and lives before Him? If we should face such days, do we have absolute assurance that we will stand? It will be too late to answer those questions then. They must be answered now. We will not have a pure heart then if we do not have one now.

TODAY'S GEM: The best preparation for future trials and conflicts is to live by God's grace and cleansing today.

Old Testament Reading Jonah

Meditation. *And I saw another mighty angel come down from heaven, clothed with a cloud: and a rainbow was upon his head, and his face was as it were the sun, and his feet as pillars of fire* (10:1).

Surely this mighty angel John was describing was Christ. Before all these events set forth in Revelation can befall the earth, Jesus Christ himself—the mightiest man the world has ever known—will stand in the midst of it all. Whatever God the Father is doing in heaven or on earth, you can be certain that His Son, who is also God, will be in the midst of it. Who could better know and do the will of the Father than the Son? Amid the judgments of God all heaven and earth, all powers and principalities, will bow to Jesus as King of kings and Lord of lords.

John saw Jesus descend like one of the angels and stand in the midst of these events in all His magnificence. To describe Him John said that His head was surrounded by an aura or rainbow. This produced such heavenly beauty and was possibly to remind us of the flood, which was God's previous judgment upon sinful man. On this previous occasion of judgment God provided an ark for His righteous people. Today Jesus is our ark, our place of safety, and there is no other provision by God. John wrote that if we are to be saved by the Son in these times it will be because we know His salvation experience and know Him right now.

As soon as I read that Jesus is to be in the midst of all this, I was encouraged. The thing for us to do is develop our relationship with the Lord now, then when difficult or impossible times come we will be familiar with His ways and know His voice. Our spirits will be so sensitive to Jesus that should He appear in the midst of calamity we will be drawn to Him. No matter how bad things are around us, we will have eyes for Him and see Him as He is. We will feel safe and secure by Jesus' presence. Should His face shine like the sun it would not cast fear into our hearts; indeed it would only enlarge our adoration, love, and sense of security. If His feet appeared like pillars of fire consuming unrighteousness, we would welcome the opportunity for the least unrighteousness in us to be consumed.

We too have an opportunity to gaze upon the Son through the eyes of faith and eat the book out of His hand. What will we do with this obvious God-given opportunity to prepare?

TODAY'S GEM: Not all was revealed to John, but what will we do with what was? Will it inspire us to be prepared?

Old Testament Reading Micah 1-3

Meditation. *And the seventh angel sounded; and there were great voices in heaven, saying, The kingdoms of this world are become the kingdoms of our Lord, and of his Christ; and he shall reign for ever and ever* (11:15).

Nobody in his or her right mind would favor war, which is ugly and hurtful. What John had described is not unlike a war between the kingdom of heaven and the kingdom of this world. Those spiritual powers on earth that have been set up by fallen angels and demons will fall to the hosts of heaven and be destroyed. In those days man will either stand with the spirit and prince of this world and perish because of it, or he will be totally separated from this world order and will have found his place in the kingdom of God.

Our scripture to meditate on today proclaims the victory of the kingdom of God. All heaven and earth will hear the cry go out: *The kingdoms of this world are become the kingdoms of our Lord, and of his Christ; and he shall reign for ever and ever!* Will this be good news to you?

Everything that is not of the kingdom of God will be destroyed. In reality I guess nobody wants these events to take place because we are so attached to relationships in the world that we do not want them to suffer. By ingenuity we have built places for ourselves in the kingdom of this world, but all will fall to the forces of heaven.

Now is the time to turn loose of anything that is not of the kingdom of God. If we love those who are not of God we will pray for them and do what we can. As part of our preparation and faith in John's predictions of the things to come, we should warn our loved ones who are not part of God's kingdom. It is our duty, by God's Spirit, to turn them away from the hold the world has on them by turning them to the Lord Jesus Christ and His salvation experience. Then they can prepare their hearts for these judgments of God by separating themselves from their sin. They will no longer be sinners and therefore at enmity with God. We are to separate ourselves from the sin of this world and look forward to the coming of the Kingdom, which is the reigning of Christ, and rejoice in His ultimate victory!

TODAY'S GEM: We are but pilgrims; therefore, let us separate ourselves and, according to His promise, *look for new heavens and a new earth, wherein dwelleth righteousness* (2 Pet. 3:13).

Old Testament Reading Micah 4-5

Meditation. *And I heard a loud voice saying in heaven, Now is come salvation, and strength, and the kingdom of our God, and the power of his Christ: for the accuser of our brethren is cast down which accused them before our God day and night* (12:10).

Satan carries the war to heaven itself. Not only is the earth seared by war and death but also Satan furiously makes war on Israel and seeks to destroy her seed (her child), which surely is the Church. God intervenes and delivers Israel and her child. Michael gathers his angels together and casts the devil out of heaven, and again the cry of victory goes forth. John writes: *And I heard a loud voice saying in heaven, Now is come salvation, and strength, and the kingdom of our God, and the power of his Christ: for the accuser of our brethren is cast down, which accused them before our God day and night.*

The saints will all share in this great victory, and the next verse tells how they will overcome the accusations of the devil. It says: *And they overcame him by the blood of the Lamb, and by the word of their testimony; and they loved not their lives unto the death.* The end has not yet come, and Satan is loosed upon the earth.

One day these things that John saw will be history. They will be but a testimony of the past; however, before they can become that we will be required to live through these events. They won't surprise us, and we cannot complain that we were not prepared. Not only are we expected to prepare our hearts and lives to face these events, but we are also expected to know how we are going to overcome. Well the Scriptures tell us not only what might enable us to overcome but how the saints—that is us—actually overcome by the blood of the Lamb. Let's not have any reservations about this truth, for it is God's provision for us to overcome. Our faith must be in the blood of Jesus Christ. Our sin (our unrighteousness) must be covered by the Blood, and we must have a testimony of faith in that Blood if we want to sing the victory song with the saints.

TODAY'S GEM: Let's refuse to listen to men's ideas and imaginations about the life hereafter and listen and allow the Word to prepare us for these events that are to come.

Old Testament Reading Micah 6-7

Meditation. *And all that dwell upon the earth shall worship him, whose names are not written in the book of life of the Lamb slain from the foundation of the world* (13:8).

I'm glad Jesus went to the trouble that He did to let John know about the end times and what we, the saints of God, will be called on to face. As for me I am especially happy that we can turn to the end of the Book to discover how it all turns out, and that is exactly what Jesus wants us to do. Not only does He want us to know how it will all turn out, but He wants us to be certain to prepare ourselves by building an unshakable faith, a day-by-day trust in His ability to save us to the uttermost. We are to be sensitive to His indwelling Holy Spirit and be obedient to what He is saying, not what our flesh is demanding of us.

When the Antichrist comes, the Word tells us that Satan will give him great power. He will have the power to perform miracles, and all the world will go after the Antichrist to worship him. He will murder Christians and Jews, and we will have to face confusion and fear. Obviously we will have to know the difference between a God-given miracle and that which is the power of Satan.

Our text makes it quite plain that those saints whose names are written in the Lamb's book of life will not worship the Antichrist. There is no doubt that we who live in these last days will face some very perilous times where trials and testings will abound. If we think for one moment that we will be able to overcome by our strength of character or dogged determination, then we will fail. The weak, those who can face the fact right now that they would fail if it were not for God's grace, will overcome. We must learn to trust Him in our weaknesses and be faithful to His will and Word right now. Satan can wipe out your good intentions and your will any time he wants to, but he cannot wipe out or overcome God's will in your life.

If you are living to do God's will and not your own, and if you are depending on His grace to do His will and overcome the desires of your flesh, then you will indeed overcome. If you who are born of the Spirit of God will be led of the Spirit, then you will overcome. Do these things now and you will be able to do them in more difficult circumstances. And your name will be among these whose names are written in the Lamb's book of life.

TODAY'S GEM: Learn to yield to God and be led by His Holy Spirit today and you need not fear tomorrow.

Old Testament Reading Nahum

Meditation. *Here is the patience of the saints: here are they that keep the commandments of God, and the faith of Jesus. And I heard a voice from heaven saying unto me, Write, Blessed are the dead which die in the Lord from henceforth: Yea, saith the Spirit, that they may rest from their labours; and their works do follow them* (14:12-13).

Have patience, my friend. We may not possess complete understanding of what John saw and wrote, but we can be certain that we can trust Him to add to our understanding as it is needed. We must be careful to keep our hearts open to this word and not close our minds on something because we are offended or because it doesn't fit in with our speculative teaching.

For instance, verses nine through eleven are hard to hear but hear them we must. *And the third angel followed them, saying with a loud voice, If any man worship the beast and his image, and receive his mark in his forehead, or in his hand, the same shall drink of the wine of the wrath of God, which is poured out without mixture into the cup of his indignation; and he shall be tormented with fire and brimstone in the presence of the holy angels, and in the presence of the Lamb: And the smoke of their torment ascendeth up for ever and ever: and they have no rest day nor night, who worship the beast and his image, and whosoever receiveth the mark of his name.*

My heart almost faints as I read the ultimate fate of those who refuse the gospel of Jesus Christ. How small and insignificant is our suffering for the gospel's sake in comparison with the eternal suffering of the rebellious. There have been those whom God has allowed to see this hell in a vision or a dream, and it has inspired them to proclaim the gospel. Knowing the fate of the lost has been their inspiration and has motivated them to spread God's Word with tremendous love. I don't want to preach hell, but we cannot read the Bible, committing ourselves to reading it through each year, without having to face up to the reality of God's complete plan of salvation for man and creation. Lest we be deceived it is not good for our growth to just relate to the truths we like but ignore the rest. Face the facts as they are written. By all means cry for the lost, Jesus did. Keep before you not only that to which you have been saved but also from what you have been saved.

TODAY'S GEM: Your righteousness lies in the cleansing blood of Jesus Christ who *is able . . . to present you faultless before the presence of his glory* (Jude 24).

Old Testament Reading Habakkuk

Meditation. *And they sing the song of Moses the servant of God, and the song of the Lamb, saying, Great and marvellous are thy works, Lord God Almighty; just and true are thy ways, thou King of saints* (15:3).

I am not always certain that I want to read about the judgments or the wrath of God that will be poured out upon man. However, I am reminded that in His Word God has said that His ways are not our ways. Now today's scripture assures me that God's judgments are just and true. Another thing I have learned is not to sit in judgment of God's Word. His Word is to judge us; we are not to judge it. In questioning what God has said we make a terrible mistake. This was the subtleness of Satan in the garden when man forfeited his right to walk with God. He questioned God's word. "Did God say…?" There is a certain freedom that comes into our lives when we submit ourselves to God's Word and patiently wait on the Holy Spirit to quicken to our understanding those truths we need to know.

We don't need to become protective or defensive of God's Word. It can stand on its own two feet and has managed to hold its own against the greatest of scholars for many centuries. When we find that the Word does not have to be justified or proven right or wrong and we can just submit ourselves to its truth, then we come into a place of complete trusting and freedom. If the contentious intellectuals must have answers, then they would do better in going to the Author of the Word instead of His students.

Freedom to believe, receive, and walk in God's Word brings a new song to our lips, and we find ourselves singing the scriptures and exalting the Lamb: *Great and marvellous are thy works, Lord God Almighty; just and true are thy ways, thou King of saints.* The more of the Word we have in our lives the more spiritually alive we become and the more sensitive to His Word.

If it is necessary for God to judge and pour out vials of His wrath upon the earth, then it is necessary. I will not make that judgment and will patiently wait upon the Lord for understanding of His works and ways, accepting by faith that God knows best.

TODAY'S GEM: *Woe unto him that striveth with his Maker!* (Isa. 45:9).

Old Testament Reading Zephaniah

Meditation. *Behold, I come as a thief. Blessed is he that watcheth, and keepeth his garments, lest he walk naked, and they see his shame. And he gathered them together into a place called in the Hebrew tongue Armageddon* (16:15-16).

John heard the instructions given for the wrath of God to be poured out upon the earth in the form of plagues, which produced sores upon the men who had the mark of the beast and upon those who worshiped his image. The sea turned into blood, and every living soul died in the sea. The rivers and fountains of water also turned to blood as God's judgments continued. The sun became so hot that men were scorched with fire, and yet there was no repentance in the hearts of men. A great darkness invaded the land, and men were in such pain that they gnawed their tongues, blasphemed God, and did not repent of their deeds.

Then John saw three unclean spirits come out of the mouths of the dragon, the beast, and the false prophet to gather the kings of the earth together to battle the forces of righteousness at a place called Armageddon.

In the midst of these terrible plagues Jesus will come, not unlike when Moses waited to lead God's people out of Egypt. Quietly, like a thief in the night, He will come to gather together those who have kept their garments spotless and have trusted in His blood. You will remember how the children of Israel sat throughout the night, trusting in the blood of the lamb that was upon their doorposts, while Egypt wailed in its misery and death. In the midst of these end-time afflictions, our Lamb—Jesus Christ—will come to lead His people out of this great darkness.

The Scriptures tell us that the place Jesus will gather these rulers is called Armageddon. You can stand on the Mount of Megiddo today and look across its great, flat, fertile plains. It is here that you find the pass across the mountains that connects the continent of Europe with the continent of Africa. It is one of the most fought over pieces of land in history. All land troops will have to make their entrance from the north to the south; however, this is the place the last great battle on earth will take place. It is a very moving experience to stand on Mount Megiddo and gaze upon this biblically significant place where Jesus will gather us together one day to lead us out as surely as Moses led his people out of Egypt. However, this time the enemies of God, the kingdom of this world, will face complete and total defeat.

TODAY'S GEM: *Because thou hast made the LORD . . . thy habitation; There shall no evil befall thee, neither shall any plague come nigh thy dwelling. For he shall give his angels charge over thee, to keep thee in all thy ways* (Ps. 91:9-11).

Old Testament Reading Haggai

Meditation. *These shall make war with the Lamb, and the Lamb shall overcome them: for he is Lord of lords, and King of kings: and they that are with him are called, and chosen, and faithful* (17:14).

What would it have been like to stand where John stood and to see all these amazing sights? To see the suffering, death, ugliness, and foulness of it all until your stomach could stand it no longer, or maybe it wasn't that way at all. There were the enemies of heaven who had waylaid and defiled man and were bent on destroying every good and righteous thing that God had ever done. Perhaps for the first time John saw and understood the power of these mighty demonic forces that have plagued man for thousands of centuries and have sought to destroy him.

From the fallen angels God has taken away the right to worship Him. They forfeited that right when they worshiped Satan as their prince and king. To man God has given the freedom and privilege to worship Him in their stead, and this must surely make them angry. Man will be raised up and led by the Lord Jesus Christ to destroy this foul and evil kingdom that Satan has set up. Satan knows the potential of man's soul and contends with God for it.

In a sense we all live a little of Job's experience. Satan has liberty to harass and does everything he can to hold man to his fallen nature and prevent him from coming into an understanding of the truth and life that is his in Christ Jesus. The enemy continues to deceive the lost and accuse the brethren. In the light of this and by God's grace I think I could find the stomach to be part of this great army. It is the army of the called, the chosen and faithful led by the Lord of lords and King of kings. It will put down and destroy this great, sinful, revolting power, which is this kingdom of demons that has established itself on earth. With Jesus leading us into battle and victory assured by the things John saw, I find myself becoming excited about the new life that will be ours as the kingdom of God is established on earth as it is in heaven.

Yes, I want to be part of that kingdom and to march with those liberating forces of Jesus to show off my garments that have been kept spotless by the blood of the Lamb. Wow, I can almost taste the victory!

TODAY'S GEM: Victory in Jesus today is our assurance of victory in Jesus in the end.

Old Testament Reading Zechariah 1-3

Meditation. *Rejoice over her, thou heaven, and ye holy apostles and prophets; for God hath avenged you on her* (18:20).

Today's reading shows a city of sin destroyed. Satan has set up his kingdom in the hearts of men; however, he could not control the great cities of the world such as Babylon unless man had desired and allowed it.

In Jeremiah 17:9 the Bible tells us that *the heart is deceitful . . . and desperately wicked.* A child does not have to be taught to sin because this is a natural inclination. The sin principle or sin nature is inherited as the result of the fall. Imagine what the cities of the world would have been like if it had not been for the influence of the gospel of Jesus Christ.

Every city of the world is under the curse of sin because they were born in sin. By His grace God delays His judgment and extends the gospel of salvation to all who will listen. However, the day will come when God will look at His creation, see what the prince of this world has accomplished in and through the hearts of men by his fierce bondage to sin, and step in to totally destroy everything that will not have a place in the kingdom of God.

As Christians, we need to face the reality of what we have been saved from and what we are saved to inherit. The blood of Jesus Christ has cleansed us from all sin and has saved us from its consequences. God's ultimate plan is to put away all sin by striking at its very root and destroying every evidence of it.

For those who want to face the reality of God's judgment and wrath, what will our reaction be? How will we handle it when He turns to us and says, *"Rejoice over her . . . for God hath avenged you on her"*? Will we see justice in His hand of judgment and rejoice at the realization that apart from God's grace we too would have been consumed and destroyed? Will we accept that God knows best and recognize the power of sin? Will we see its ability to destroy man and that God in fact is being merciful when He destroys it? Will we breathe a sigh of relief when those sinful things of the world in which our flesh took pleasure are destroyed so we will be tempted no more? My friend, will we so abhor sin that upon its destruction we will be able to rejoice from the very depths of our innermost beings? If we have come out from among the world and forsaken all to follow Jesus, then we will rejoice. Rejoice and be glad today that you are numbered among those who will rejoice.

TODAY'S GEM: When God's judgments are poured out upon the earth, don't be like Lot's wife who looked back.

Old Testament Reading Zechariah 4-6

Meditation. *And after these things I heard a great voice of much people in heaven, saying, Alleluia; Salvation, and glory, and honour, and power, unto the Lord our God* (19:1).

Not being a sadist, I do not want to see my fellowman destroyed. Nor, for that matter, does God desire that any should perish. However, God has not left us ignorant, and His intention that all who sin shall surely die can be read in the Word.

The other day someone told me that he had been reading Romans 6:23, which says, *for the wages of sin is death; but the gift of God is eternal life through Jesus Christ our Lord.* This man said that if he could have eternal life, which is free, then why should he work for the wages of sin, which is death.

Well, I am awfully glad John was able to see what was going on among the saints of God in heaven when all those heavy judgments and the destruction of sin were taking place. It is as if John was watching the fall of Babylon, the armies of the Lord being assembled, and the cameras moving in to focus on a rejoicing people who were delirious at their good fortune to be among the eternally saved instead of the judged and eternally damned. They were a people who had experienced for themselves the cleansing of the Blood and knew by experience what it meant to be and feel clean. Never again would sin bind them or have any hold upon their lives, and now God's plan for the end times was being set into motion by God's mighty hand of authority to which all heaven and earth must bow.

No, it is not the end of life that we are seeing, but the end of sin. A cleansing was taking place. As a new order of life, which is eternal, was being established, sin and death were to be no more. Creation will also be set free from the curse of sin, and the blood of Jesus Christ will purify, yes, cleanse everything upon the earth. No wonder there will be heard a great voice of much people in heaven, saying, *"Alleluia; Salvation, and glory, and honour, and power unto the Lord our God!"*

As for me, I am practicing my alleluias now, and I'm looking forward to singing with that great heavenly choir. Eternity and all it holds for us is the most exciting, yes, the most exhilarating reality imaginable, and it is all mine, promised by the Father, and mine in Jesus Christ!

TODAY'S GEM: Today I am one day closer to the most exhilarating reality of eternal life, a world without sin!

Old Testament Reading Zechariah 7-9

Meditation. *Blessed and holy is he that hath part in the first resurrection: on such the second death hath no power, but they shall be priests of God and of Christ, and shall reign with him a thousand years* (20:6).

The life about which Jesus was writing is the life that awaits us in Christ and far exceeds anything our imaginations could conjure up. Satan is to be expelled from the earth and locked up by an angel in the bottomless pit. For 1,000 years he will be locked away, and the Word says, *he should deceive the nations no more, till the thousand years should be fulfilled* (v. 3).

Then John saw thrones on which were sitting those who had been martyred for their faith, those who had refused to worship the beast or receive his mark upon their foreheads or in their hands. These reigned with Jesus for 1,000 years. Get hold of this, they lived and reigned with Him for 1,000 years! How can our intelligence grasp what He is saying? We are so conditioned to living for today and looking forward to 70 or 80 years of life, but John saw the faithful living and reigning with Christ for 1,000 years, which is only the beginning of eternity. No wonder John said, *"Blessed and holy is he that hath part in the first resurrection."*

Now that we are born again how seriously are we taking our Christian experience? I suppose it depends upon what value we put on God's offer of eternal life and whether we are living as if this is the only life we have to live. It also depends on whether we are looking forward to and preparing ourselves for the eternal life that John described. It is obvious from what John wrote that it does matter how we use the life we have. The people of God who will reign and rule with Jesus are those who have been faithful to Him and have refused to participate in a world system even though it cost them their lives.

I think if we are to be assured of a place in Christ's kingdom that John saw in his revelation, then we must be assured of a place in His kingdom right now. It is not a matter of will I or won't I have a place, but am I living in the Kingdom now? Am I preoccupied each day with things other than the Kingdom, or do I have time to listen and to live my life for God? Does Jesus direct my life, and do I live for Him now? If not, why should I suddenly start living for Him after death when I don't live for Him today?

TODAY'S GEM: The place to sort out our lives and put them together in Christ is the prayer closet (the quiet-time). If it doesn't work there it won't work anywhere else.

Old Testament Reading Zechariah 10-12

Meditation. *And I saw a new heaven and a new earth* (21:1).

I'm excited! John saw what the end was to be, and I want to be part of it. I want my God-given desire to motivate me into doing the right things and being whatever it is that God has called me to be. My greatest desire is to see and be part of the new heaven and new earth.

John saw the holy city coming down from heaven and called it the new Jerusalem. Through his writings we are given some idea that its size was as large as Texas. He said it was new and had an eternal freshness about it, an air of excitement and purity like a bride adorned for her husband. Then a voice out of heaven called it the tabernacle or dwelling place of God, where God will dwell with men and they shall be His people. God himself shall be with them and be their God. There will be no death, no tears or sorrow, for the former things are passed away. He that sits upon the throne will make all things new. *He that overcometh shall inherit all things; and I will be his God, and he shall be my son* (v. 7). We are not sons because we have overcome but because Jesus overcame death and sin on our behalf. Now, as sons and daughters, something is expected of us—through Him we are to be overcomers.

After seeing the first heaven and earth pass away John described what he saw. That in itself is enough to melt me and fill me with a Holy Ghost desire to have a place in this new Jerusalem, this heavenly city where God reigns, rules and lives with His people.

"God, I'm not exactly sure what lies ahead of me in this life. I can only live it today one day at a time, but this I am sure about: Whatever I need to overcome today, whatever You have in mind for me to overcome, I ask You in Jesus' name for wisdom and the grace to overcome it.

"Father, I am not going to make ignorance an excuse and risk missing out on the victory. So I pledge myself to meet with You daily so I might know and do Your will. I will need grace to maintain my pledge, for without You I can do nothing. Holy Spirit, companion me in my commitment and enable me to be completely and constantly yielded to You. Father, hear my prayer, for my heart's desire is to live in the new Jerusalem that John saw with You. I make this request in Jesus' name."

TODAY'S GEM: My goal for eternal life is to live with Jesus now, here on earth, and in the new Jerusalem for eternity.

Old Testament Reading Zechariah 13-14

Meditation.   *And the Spirit and the bride say, Come. And let him that heareth say, Come. And let him that is athirst come. And whosoever will, let him take the water of life freely* (22:17).

John's revelation has made my heart and spirit desire the things about which he was writing. By revelation I came to an understanding of salvation, but more than this I saw in my spirit Jesus crucified for my sin. Gradually, over the years a great love for Jesus has developed in my heart as I walked with Him, sought to be obedient, and have tried to live according to His will.

The Word has made Him many things to me, and I'm sure Jesus is all of these things to you. He is the fairest of ten thousand, the bright and morning star, even the lily of the valley, King of kings, and Lord of lords. Oh, I could go on and on. To overcome and to live faithful to Him has been my desire and goal. I have always wanted to be so totally yielded to His Holy Spirit that I might be constantly available to Him. But now, after reading John's revelation that life is offered to the faithful and to all that will overcome, being totally yielded becomes so much more desirable. If I knew nothing more than the fact that Jesus would be at the center of it all, filling me with His presence and glory, it would be enough for me to pursue Him to the very end.

Because of what John saw he promises us a lifestyle in eternity that almost leaves me delirious for the fulfillment of it. Sin will be no more. I will not need to be on my guard against the wiles of the devil because the curse shall be no more. The gates of the heavenly city shall never shut, and the glory of Jesus will so fill it with light that there will be no darkness. We shall actually see Him face to face, and how proudly and with what joy we shall bear His name on our foreheads. New songs of praise shall burst forth from our lips as worship with all purity and holiness shall flow from our hearts. Everywhere we turn we shall see and be part of His glory!

Oh, I feel the spirit of the bride yearning within my heart, and I identify with these words of scripture—*the Spirit and the bride say, Come. Even so, come quickly, Lord Jesus!*

TODAY'S GEM: May I live today for the sole purpose of living tomorrow with Jesus in eternity.
Old Testament Reading Malachi

An Exciting Adventure
In Faith

Tim Ruthven's life was one of whole-hearted devotion to Jesus. It stands as a testimony to the miracle-working power of God. His walk was humble and childlike, believing in the miraculous. Simply put, he was a friend of God who dared to believe every word written in the Bible; therefore, he saw many miracles happen.

Tim's early years were spent in an orphanage. He described himself as emotionally handicapped and troubled. Though he enlisted in the army at seventeen, Tim's poor education doomed him for failure. In his words he was "rowdy and unruly, a nastiness seemed to develop in my nature."

In his late twenties Tim's life and marriage were in shambles, but a series of events and a radio message from Billy Graham caused Tim to bow his knee to Jesus to be born again. This was the beginning of Tim's walk of simple, childlike faith that resulted in miracles, a life that spoke to everyone he met.

God began to pave the way for him by his unusual acceptance into teachers' college. Then, in 1970, God called Tim from a technical teaching position to minister with an international fellowship of evangelists holding special meetings for revival in the churches. Tim's efforts in this fellowship were directed towards helping the underground churches behind the Iron Curtain. He also accompanied a ministry team to work in a suburban Presbyterian church for five weeks. God so moved by His Holy Spirit in that church that Tim was asked to stay. For the following fifteen months God continued to move in miraculous ways.

Later God directed Tim's ministry among people in the "street-scene." Again, God moved by His Spirit to perform endless miracles—miraculously providing for their daily needs as they lived together in community. This was when Tim learned to literally live by faith. This led to ministry in Indonesia, Australia, and New Guinea. Tim's faithful reliance on God and His Word paved the way for many miracles, especially among addicts. Tim wrote two books that contain testimonies from the community he shared with "street-scene" people ("Albany" and "A Man From Down Under").

Finally God directed Tim to go to America to strengthen the hands of the brethren, promising He would heal their land. Tim, his wife Marjorie, and four of their six children came to America from New Zealand in December of 1974.

Childlike faith, belief in the miraculous, and his quaint New Zealand accent made him a sought after speaker. However, the desire of Tim Ruthven's heart was to draw believers into an intimate, daily relationship with God and His Word.

America weighed heavily upon Tim's heart, and his years were spent on a rug with the map of America where he interceded. One conversation with God, which he recorded in his book, "A Man From Down Under," went like this:

"'Father, the American brethren are well taught . . . There seems to be a such a gap between what they know about Christian living, You, and the reality of the spiritual life.' And God answered me, 'Son, they are a people who know about Me but do not necessarily know Me. Their knowledge about Me has become a substitute for knowing Me. The things I have built into your life and which you have taken for granted are the very things they need. Son, the people of God are failing to meet with Me in the closet or have a daily quiet-time experience.'"

That's when the Holy Spirit inspired Tim to write the *Gems* devotionals and other books, to give practical application to those who desired a deeper walk with God.

Tim pastored a church in Colorado while traveling and speaking extensively throughout the United States to stir believers' hearts to expect a great spiritual awakening, ministering through television, radio, camps, and conventions.

Tim also understood God's heart and plans for Israel in the last days. He served on the original Board of Directors of the International Christian Embassy in Jerusalem and led many tours to the Holy Land.

Donald Thomas Timothy Ruthven went to be with His heavenly Father December 7, 2007. These *Gems From God's Word* are his legacy and ours as believers.

I served for thirteen years as managing editor of *Gems* with Tim, and I can personally attest to the value of the daily quiet-time— intimacy with God in His Word each day.

Sharon Spicka
Editor 2017

Made in United States
Orlando, FL
24 May 2023

33430549R00108